QUEER INK

This historical interdisciplinary book contextualises the Rorschach ink blot test and embeds it within feminist action and queer liberation.

What do you see when you look at an ink blot? The Rorschach ink blot test is one of the most famous psychological tests and it has a surprisingly queer history. In mapping this history, this book explores how this test, once used to detect and diagnose 'homosexuality', was later used by some psychologists and activists to fight for gay liberation. In this book the author uses the test in yet another way, as a lens through which we can reveal a queer feminist history of Psychology. By looking closely at the lives and work of some women psychologists and activists it becomes clear that their work was influenced by their own, often queer, lives. By tracing the lives and actions of women who used, were tested with, or influenced by, the Rorschach, a new kind of understanding of gay and lesbian history in Britain is revealed.

Pushing at the borders between Psychology, Sociology, and activism, the book utilises the Rorschach to show how influential the social world is on scientific practice. This is fascinating reading for anyone interested in the history of sexuality and Psychology.

Katherine A. Hubbard is a feminist academic at the University of Surrey. Her research focuses on gender, sexuality, and the history of Psychology. She can often be found running around campus between lectures in which she teaches about Sociology and Psychology.

Gender and Sexualities in Psychology
Series Editors: Elizabeth Peel and Elizabeth Stokoe

Gender and Sexualities in Psychology is a book series showcasing scholarly work over a wide range of areas within gender and sexualities in psychology, and the intersection of gender, feminism, sexualities and LGBTIQ psychology with other areas of the discipline.

The series includes theoretically and empirically informed scholarship including critical, feminist, queer, trans, social, and intersectional perspectives, and encourages creative and innovative methodological approaches. The series adopts an inclusive approach to the discipline of psychology, as well as its cross-cutting relationship to related disciplines, and recognizes diversity in research on genders and sexualities.

Titles in the series:

Emergent Identities
New Sexualities, Genders and Relationships in a Digital Era
Rob Cover

Queer Ink
A Blotted History Towards Liberation
Katherine A. Hubbard

For further information about this series please visit: https://www.routledge.com/ Gender-and-Sexualities-in-Psychology/book-series/GSP

QUEER INK

A Blotted History Towards Liberation

Katherine A. Hubbard

LONDON AND NEW YORK

First published 2020
by Routledge
2 Park Square, Milton Park, Abingdon, Oxon OX14 4RN

and by Routledge
52 Vanderbilt Avenue, New York, NY 10017

Routledge is an imprint of the Taylor & Francis Group, an informa business

British Library Cataloguing-in-Publication Data
A catalogue record for this book is available from the British Library

Library of Congress Cataloging-in-Publication Data
A catalog record for this book has been requested

ISBN: 978-1-138-36251-2 (hbk)
ISBN: 978-1-138-36252-9 (pbk)
ISBN: 978-0-429-43203-3 (ebk)

Typeset in Bembo
by Apex CoVantage LLC

Printed in the United Kingdom
by Henry Ling Limited

CONTENTS

ACKNOWLEDGMENTS

This book represents the research I conducted during the somewhat inky and messy time of my doctoral and post-doctoral work. During this period, I was lucky enough to have been supported by a range of funding opportunities and various people who gave me temporary and permanent jobs. Many thanks to the Science Museum for partial PhD funding, to the Funds for Women Graduates for their grant, and the British Federation for Women Graduates for the Mary Bradburn Scholarship. This work would similarly not have been possible if it were not for the dedicated work of the staff and archivists at the British Library, the Wellcome Library, and the London School of Economics Library. The London School of Economics Library also needs to be recognised for kindly giving permission for the use of some of the images contained in this book.

Those at the Science Museum have equally been incredibly helpful, namely Phil Loring during his time there and afterwards, Tim Boon, Justin Hobson, and Beata Bradford. Again, many thanks for providing two of the images in the book. I would also like to thank Cynthia Reid for her permission to print the *Arena Three* cover image as well. There was also a number of people who were very generous with their time in sharing their experiences of the Rorschach who I also sincerely thank, as well as those who long ago shared their feelings which have been retained by careful restorers and librarians.

Those at Routledge and beyond who were involved in the proposal, review and production processes have been incredibly supportive. Special thanks to Editor Eleanor Reedy, Alex Howard and Autumn Spalding. I am very grateful to the Routledge Gender and Sexualities in Psychology Series Editors Elizabeth Peel and Elizabeth Stokoe for accepting my proposal for this book and the anonymous reviewers for their comments. To the non-anonymous reviewer, Rose Capdevila, thank you for all your support with this project (as well as all the others). I have been further supported by a number of other wonderful feminist academics and further mention is much deserved by Alexandra Rutherford, Rebecca Jennings, and Ruth Pearce for their assistance and advice.

Various versions of some of the materials and chapters in this book are also available in the form of journal articles. Many thanks to the *Journal of the History of the Behavioural Sciences* Editor Ian Nicholson and *Psychology of Women and Equalities Review* Editor Lisa Lazard for allowing partial reproductions of:

> Hubbard, K. & Hegarty, P. (2016). Blots and all: A history of the Rorschach Ink Blot test in Britain. *Journal of the History of the Behavioral Sciences, 52*(2), 146–166.
>
> Hubbard, K. (2017). Queer Signs: The women of the British projective test movement. *Journal of the History of the Behavioural Sciences, 53*(3), 265–285.
>
> Hubbard, K. (2017). Treading on delicate ground: Comparing the Lesbian and Gay Affirmative Rorschach Research of June Hopkins and Evelyn Hooker. *Psychology of Women Section Review, 19 (1), 3–9.*

During the time of conducting the research unfolded within these pages I have had the pleasure of being involved with a range of networks of feminist gender and sexuality scholars. These networks have been both formal and informal and the friendships made along the way has made the journey here thoroughly enjoyable. I have been incredibly lucky to work alongside some wonderful colleagues at the University of Surrey. To those who were also supervised by Peter Hegarty at the same time as me, those in the Sociology department while I wrote the book, and those involved in the Surrey gender and sexuality research group – thank you. Special thanks goes out especially to those whose friendship, advice and the odd pint has made all the difference. Kirsty Lohman, David Griffiths, Fabio Fasoli, Alice Motes and Jon Garland, thank you. Special thanks is also extended to Tasha Bharj for her long-distance support and friendship.

There is one person whose continued guidance has meant this book, and my entire career, has been made possible. I am so very grateful to Peter Hegarty – the best mentor, supervisor and advisor imaginable.

Similarly, I have received ongoing encouragement and support from: Isobel Goddard, Brenda Efurhievwe, Hannah Kasprzok, and Sarah Holgate - who I especially thank for letting me steal her script for the sub-title. All my thanks and much love to my entire family for their care, and to Pig who sat beside me (or on me) for the majority of the writing of this book.

Finally, my greatest thanks to Clare Butler. Thank you for the image on the cover, for saying yes, for everything.

1

INTRODUCTION

On the 16th October 2015 I apprehensively travelled to the Tavistock clinic, 20 Belsize Lane, London, to meet a psychologist. Once there, I did a Rorschach ink blot test. As soon as I sat down I altered the chair to face the psychologist and was swiftly informed that the chairs should stay next to each other and not angled. I was warned that there would not be much talking throughout. She asked me only once "What does this remind you of? What could this be?" when she handed over the first ink blot. I saw a mask (that looked like a rabbit) and some crab pincers. She wrote down, almost word for word, what I said. After what felt like an age, I put the card down – or 'plate' as they are technically called – and said I could not see anything else. She handed me card number two. This process was repeated for all ten cards.

Quite regularly, I was asked to repeat certain bits. Perhaps I had said two answers in one sentence. The pressure to respond plentifully was greater than I had expected. But 'seeing' things in the blots got a little easier (though I still struggled to say lots of things). At one point when I put the plate down having 'seen' all I could, she simply picked it back up and handed it to me again, indicating that I should say more. After each response, I tried to outline where I saw it, or why, how it looked. I felt this incredible urge to explain myself, to have a conversation and to try to get the psychologist to 'see' it too. There were a few things I felt rather more embarrassed to say that I saw than others. But I decided to be honest and uttered 'vulva', 'fleshy legs' and 'bloody', and afterwards I was applauded for being so open-minded.

Following this initial stage each ink blot was repeated again, in what is called the 'inquiry'. Here, it seemed, was the place to elaborate and explain where and how I saw each thing in each ink blot. Once I explained where and how I saw the psychologist made a note on mini versions of the blots on the inquiry form. But still the psychologist gave no suggestion that she could also 'see' the things I reported; or even that she was going to attempt to 'see' them. Instead I was asked where I saw each thing, how, what reminded me of it. Open-ended questions meant I gave greater explanations for some things. Though, on other occasions it was hard to not just say simply 'because it *looks* like a bat'. Each small thing I referred to was questioned which created a slight sense of fear for me that I might say something highly suggestive and be under immediate analysis, even though I knew the analysis is usually quite lengthy and takes some time. The whole testing procedure took just over an hour. I was surprised how long it took considering the test is only made up of ten cards; or in my case, several animals, a few people, an underwater world, and two pink lizards climbing a Christmas tree.

I found myself considering what it would be like to be tested as someone in therapy, or in a psychiatric unit. How would this experience be different if I was in prison, or undergoing testing for psychiatrists and psychologists to decide if my sexuality was having a detrimental effect on my mental health? Throughout the whole procedure, I eventually relaxed a little. Initially I found the process rather frustrating. The lack of communication and discussion instilled the realisation it was a serious testing procedure. Yet, I knew I was only a participant in a study of British Rorschach norm responses. How might my experience have been different in the 1960s when my 'homosexuality' would have been considered a mental illness? It is impossible not to be reminded of those queer people who came before me, some of whom underwent such testing, some of whom *did* the testing and fought against the pathologisation of 'homosexuality'. I was not tested because of my sexuality, but because I volunteered to be tested as someone who was mentally healthy and British. I wonder how comfortable I would have felt explaining how plate number nine looked like a skull peering through some bushes, how the ink blot that looked like a rug reminded me of my mum and why the two women facing one another looked so serene, had I been tested a few decades earlier. After all, it was only after significant work both inside and outside of Psychology and the social sciences that 'homosexuality' was removed as a mental illness '*per se*' from the Diagnostic Statistical Manual (DSM) in 1973, and the use of the Rorschach and other projective tests in this history is what this book will focus on. I encourage you now, to familiarise yourself with each ink blot. What do you see? (See plate section)

The Rorschach ink blot test is one of the most famous psychological tests in the world. Swiss psychiatrist Hermann Rorschach (1884–1922) developed the test in the early 1920s. But he was not the first person to be fascinated by the intriguing ink blots. People like Leonardo da Vinci in the 15th century and Victor Hugo in the 19th century (Tulohin, 1940; Lemov, 2011) were said to utilise them for inspiration. Just as it is possible to buy ink-blot-based games nowadays, in 1857 Justinius Kerner published a parlour game called 'Blotto', which prompted players to make poetic associations to ink blots (Erdberg, 1990). Rorschach was aware of such games and was so fond of the specific ink blot game 'klexographie' and of drawing in general that he was known as 'Klex' (meaning 'blot') as a student (Ellenberger, 1954). In 1921, Rorschach published his only book, *Psychodiagnostik*, which described his experiment involving the ten symmetrical, now highly iconic, ink blots.[1]

The subject is given one plate after the other and asked, "What might this be"? He holds the plate in his hand and may turn it about as much as he likes. The subject is free to hold the plate near his eyes or far away as he chooses. . . . An attempt is made to get at least one answer to every plate, though suggestion in any form is, of course, avoided.

(Rorschach, 1921 p. 16)

Rorschach argued the test, including the ten ink blots he drew himself, was able to test personality by analysing what people had projected onto the ink blots. His analysis was very much about *how* his patients projected meaning on the blots; he paid less attention to *what* was 'seen' *per se* (Rorschach, 1921, p. 19). For example, looking at the responses I gave, these would likely have been coded according to whether I used: the whole blot 'A bat – it just looks so exactly like a bat' (plate V); or smaller details 'the shape here looks like the Eiffel tower' (plate X). My responses would also have been coded according to whether I saw movement 'two women, stirring a big cooking pot' (plate III), or were concerned with colour 'the middle of the orange just looks like rain' (plate IX). For Rorschach, many 'movement' responses indicated 'introversion', while many 'colour' responses indicated 'extratension' (Rorschach, 1921, p. 88). Infrequent responses were also illuminating (so things are not looking good for my test . . .). For example, a lack of movement responses would suggest a reduced number of positive qualities of introversion such as imagination (Rorschach, 1921, p. 86; see Akavia, 2013, for a full discussion). Rorschach died of appendicitis and peritonitis in 1922 just after the publication of *Psychodiagnostik*. His test received so little positive attention immediately after its publication in the German-speaking world that some speculated that Rorschach died of heartbreak due to the failure of his test (Lemov, 2011). For example, Carl Jung later described Hermann Rorschach's method as merely a 'klexographic method' and likened it to debunked sciences including graphology and phrenology (Akavia, 2013).

But of course the Rorschach test eventually became one of the best known psychological tests across the globe. Over the mid-20th century it was the most popular psychological test in the US – wielded by psychologists using a range of analytical techniques on a range of people who could be diagnosed with it. In fact, projective tests – that is, those which analyse some projection onto ambiguous stimuli – were increasingly popular as psychoanalysis emerged as an important school of thought in Psychology. The stimuli for such tests varied dramatically: there were drawings of houses, trees, and people; mosaics; paintings; illustrations of ambiguous circumstances; sand-worlds; the list goes on. A whole range of projective tests were available, but the Rorschach reigned supreme as the most popular despite its early rejection. There has been a number of histories written about the Rorschach in the US. Buchanan (1997) carefully narrated the rise and fall of faith in the Rorschach with respect to the American Psychological Association's (APA) attempt to define test validity in the decades after the Second World War. Other recent critical essays have focused on faith in the Rorschach test's ability to reveal the minds of 'othered' groups in post-war American society. Such groups include:

the defeated Nazi enemy (Brunner, 2001); colonised and decolonising societies (Lemov, 2011); and gay men (Hegarty, 2003a), but more on this later. There is also considerable overlap between history and critique; the test's harshest critics have also written histories of the test's usage in the US and the history of empirical criticism of the test's validity (see Wood, Nezworski, Lilienfeld, & Garb, 2003). In various ways, these histories flesh out Galison's (2004) conceptual point that the Rorschach is not just a passive object, made up of just ten ink blots, but a means of 'making up' people and power relationships between people.

There is also a selection of histories available about the test outside of the US. It became very popular in Japan (Sorai & Ohnuki, 2008), Finland (Mattlar & Fried, 1993), Turkey (İkiz, 2011), and India (Manickam & Dubey, 2006). Such histories internationalise the history of Rorschach testing, but such 'insider' histories, often written by Rorschach testers themselves, are often celebratory narratives attempting to explain the origin of Rorschach networks in particular locations. The use of the Rorschach test in this book is not such an account. Instead, I use the Rorschach as a starting point to look a little more closely at who was using projective tests in Britain and how this linked to queer liberation in the latter half of the 20th century.

There are various difficulties in doing such history (or 'herstory' as this book focuses on the workings of women) and its always worth thinking about who is telling the story and why. So why am I telling this history? I am telling this history because it is *my* history. As a queer woman studying psychological science, what has come before me for other queer women in the field is a part of my, and perhaps your, trajectory. In writing about it I now I become, rather reflectively, a part of that history too. This embedded nature of doing history is rather important and I will elaborate on this further. However, first, I shall explain why I focus on the projective test movement as an arena for queer feminist history.

Why feminist, why queer, why the projective test movement?

There is a continual need to 're-place' women back into the history of Psychology because of the historical erasure of women in the stories told about Psychology (among, of course, many other areas). Bohan (1990) rightly argues this is a 're'-placement as women have been there all along. Yet, historians have traditionally paid little attention to the wealth of contributions women made to the field, mainly due to the androcentric and sexist social frameworks of both History and Psychology as disciplines. The erasure of women – particularly the really unconventional ones – is felt within the projective test movement in particular as women were rather prominent within the scene. This feminist endeavour to account for the actions of women in the past is therefore ongoing, as is the sociological study of such erasures. After all, we not only need to re-place these women, but also analyse the contexts in which such eradication occurred.

At the turn of the 20th century, during the emergence of projective tests, many gendered ideals from the 19th century were still paramount. Medico-scientific conceptualisations of women as inferior, infantile, and emotional meant women scientists had their ability questioned both professionally and socially. 'True' women were said to have virtues such as piety, purity, submissiveness, and domesticity (Bohan, 1990). Scientific theory, influenced by evolutionary notions, proposed men were more variable in their abilities and intellect than women (Milar, 2000). In fact, it was thought an over-stimulation of education could detract from women's more natural abilities and cause them harm. Because of this, femininity and science were often viewed as incompatible and the 'women scientist' was considered a contradiction in terms (Bohan, 1990; Rossiter, 1982).

These sexist frameworks regulated the entry of women into Psychology in the early 20th century (Bohan, 1990). Significant challenges were faced by women working in Psychology and other medical and scientific disciplines at this time, as they were in the wider social world. In Britain, women were not as easily accepted into Psychology as in the US, and early British women psychologists did not question the sexist foundations of Psychology as early as those in the US (Shields, 2007). It is likely this was due to the higher reluctance of Oxford and Cambridge, the main and most prestigious Universities, to accept women students at all compared to selective US colleges.

Following from post-Darwinian ideas, the majority of gender differences were explained as having a 'natural basis' (Weeks, 1977). Shields (2007) argued that women's emotional traits were perceived as complimentary to men, justifying the social hierarchy, women's submissive nature, and consequential inferior status. Ideas of women as inferior, more susceptible to influence, and easily damaged by education continued to be prominent even among those highly influential upon early British Psychology. For example, Henry Maudsley, the main funder of the Maudsley hospital, said:

> the affective life is more developed in proportion to the intellect in the female than in the male, and the influence of the reproductive organs upon mind more powerful
>
> *(1879, as cited in Shields, 2007)*

In the US there has been a number of feminist scholars accounting for the history of women in Psychology. Furumoto and Scarborough (1986) studied the lives of the first 22 women psychologists in the US joining soon after the profession was formed in 1892, achieving doctorates around the turn of the century. All of those who attained assistant professor or higher were unmarried and each experienced discrimination. Milar (2000) found that in the first group of women psychologists, only 50 percent had a professional rank compared to 65 percent of psychologists who were men. All of those professional women were single and worked predominantly in women's colleges; many also had to work for free or for very little pay. Most women's colleges only employed unmarried women. Christine Ladd-Franklin, an unpaid lecturer at Columbia University wrote in 1917 that she had no other option but to lecture for nothing. She also said that women "ought to be taught that she cannot serve two masters, that if she chooses the higher path of learning and wants to do herself and her sex justice, she must forgo matrimony" (Milar, 2000, p. 618).

Similarly, in Britain, Valentine (2008b, 2010) considered the positions of women in early British Psychology, and in particular provided an account of Beatrice Engle (2006), one of the first women in the British Psychological Society (BPS). Despite the overarching sexist culture of early Psychology, women psychologists were major contributors to Psychology as soon as the profession was born in the late 19th century (Bernstein & Russo, 1974; Furumoto & Scarborough, 1986; Milar, 2000; Rutherford, Vaughn-Blount, & Ball, 2010). Valentine (2008b) explored this with particular emphasis on women in the early days of the BPS. Her analysis and comparative work with that of Perrone (1993) suggested that women found Psychology as a discipline more accessible than other sciences, especially Physiology, in Britain in the first half of the 20th century. This was perhaps, Valentine (2008b) suggests, because of the wish to 'swell the numbers' of the recently developed BPS, particularly after the First World War, or because Psychology was such a new science that men's dominance had yet to gain a foothold.

The proportion of women involved in the early BPS, which included Beatrice Engle, Alice Woods, Jessie Murray, Julia Turner and Susan Isaacs, also reflect the perhaps surprisingly high proportion of women involved in the British Projective test movement. The majority of the women involved in early Psychology were middle/upper-class, worked in teaching roles and two-thirds (11/16) were unmarried. This is despite the fact that the marriage ban only affected school teachers from the 1920s and therefore did not impact the college and University level teaching these women were doing. However, as Valentine (2008b) points out, Liverpool University did try very hard to enforce such a ban. The unmarried status of the early women involved in Psychology has also been explored by Furumoto and Scarborough (1986) and Milar (2000). The efforts of these women have often been untold within the *his*tory of Psychology (Bernstein & Russo, 1974; Furumoto, 2003). Because of the misogynistic positioning of women throughout the majority of the 20th century, and androcentric history-telling, the global effort to re-place the women in the history of Psychology has gained real support from feminist psychologists and historians, and I pay particular attention to those in the US, Canada, and Britain.[2]

The advent of psychoanalysis into Britain and the US provided fertile ground for projective testing. In 1913, Ernest Jones developed the London Psycho-Analytical Society. In the same year physician Jessie Murray and teacher Julia Turner opened the Medico-Psychological Clinic, the Maudsley Hospital (having received funding from Henry Maudsley) also opened in London. Social upheaval during the First World War meant that Psychology was desperate for new ways of thinking about madness, sanity, normality, and deviance (Richards, 2000). Due to the greater economic and social disorder caused by the war, those in Britain were especially susceptible to the appeal of psychoanalysis (see Bogacz, 1989). Psychological thinking was also not yet influenced by behaviourist approaches, which were becoming popular in the US. Psychiatrist W.H.R. Rivers began adopting Sigmund Freud's ideas to treat shell-shock whilst at Craiglockhart War hospital in Edinburgh. Those at the Medico-Psychological Clinic also rehabilitated soldiers but the clinic was disbanded in 1922 due to the death of Murray in 1920 and the subsequent debt of the clinic (Hayward, 2014; Hinshelwood, 1999). In 1920 the Tavistock clinic was opened by psychiatrist Hugh Crighton-Miller and here psychodynamic and 'applied psycho-analytic' approaches were adopted with vigour (Dicks, 1970; Hall, 2007a, 2007b). In 1925 the London Psycho-Analytical Society attracted more members including members from the Society for Psychical Research and others from Cambridge, those involved with military psychiatry, those who had been involved with the Medico-Psychological Clinic, general practitioners, and of course, members of the Bloomsbury group (Hayward, 2014; Hinshelwood, 1999).

Psychoanalytic ideas are still popular, especially at certain institutions such as the Tavistock and the Anna Freud Centre from which Anna Freud taught her version of child psychoanalysis (Sayers, 1991). In fact, Hermann Rorschach even sent Sigmund Freud a copy of *Psychodiagnosik,* writing inside: "Herrn Professor Freud in Verehrung u. Dankbarkeit zugeeignet H. Rorschach" which translates as "To Professor Freud in admiration and gratitude, with affection H. Rorschach." Indeed, there are even some reports of Rorschach tests at the Freud Museum archive. The psychologist who conducted them was Dorothy Burlingham, who lived and shared children with Anna Freud. Burlingham tested two young sisters, continuing the tradition of Rorschach testing children. Using the Rorschach in 1954, she said that for one sister the test was a painful experience, but the other was more relaxed and 'did not manifest any severe tension (unlike her sister)'.[3]

The themes of psychoanalysis and the relationships between women is relatively strong in this British history. The preceding example of Burlingham testing children with the Rorschach demonstrates that despite the small size of the projective movement in Britain, it still is an important and rich history that involves women. This history also appears ripe for a queer feminist analysis as evidenced by the relationship between Burlingham and Freud as does the relationship between Murray and Turner, who had met in 1898. They formed what some have called an 'attachment', though Valentine (2009) described it as an 'intimate friendship' and recognised the life-long commitment and marriage-like partnership they had.

Following the First World War many women were looking for education, training, and careers, and the specific context of feminist thinking and an emerging 'new psychology' meant more women were involved with Psychology. Indeed, there was also a particularly interesting time for lesbian women as the war had provided a wealth of working opportunities and exposure to queer scenes. I fully recommend the work of Rebecca Jennings (2007a), who explores in depth this history in regards to lesbian women and their careers after 1945. By the end of the 1930s psychoanalysis was somewhat embedded in Psychology in Britain but it did not develop to the same extent it did in the US where it gained greater popularity up until the 1950s (Richards, 2000). In contrast to the US, British psychoanalysts remained situated within smaller clinics and the offices of self-employed analysts and there was a reluctance to use psychoanalysis widely in practise (Hinshelwood, 1999), though the Tavistock did develop a psychoanalytically sympathetic approach which continues to this day (Hall, 2007a, 2007b). Befittingly, the Rorschach was adopted according to the differing levels of psychoanalytic acceptance in different institutions; for example, it was at the Tavistock where I was tested in 2015. It was from this context of 'new psychology' and a zeitgeist of concern about the unconscious in the US and in Britain that the Rorschach emerged, thus mapping onto social and psychological understandings of gender and sexuality in the early- to mid-20th century.

Despite social attitudes remaining about the status of women and of 'sexual deviants', a consensus did begin to emerge about the need for sexual reform especially around women's rights and sex education (Richards, 2000). The suffragette movement, which Murray and Turner were deeply involved with, evidences this (Hinshelwood, 1999), as does the influential work of British sexologist Havelock Ellis, who declined Jones' invitation to join the London Psycho-Analytical Society (Hinshelwood, 1999). Thought to be a legacy of Murray and Turner, 17 of 54 members (31%) of the London Psycho-Analytical Society were women in 1924 (Hinshelwood, 1999). This was in contrast to the *International Psycho-Analytical Society* where women only made up 12–15 percent of members (Hinshelwood, 1999). However, despite women's presence within psychoanalytic circles (Sayers, 1991), gender issues remained. Alice Woods, one of the founding members of the BPS described how in 1913 all of the women attending the very first reading of Sigmund Freud's work were asked to leave the room (Valentine, 2008a).

A number of women psychoanalysts began specifically working with children (Sayers, 1991). Child Psychology was deemed highly important after the war especially in Britain (Richards, 2000), and this emphasis only increased after the Second World War due to the child evacuations from major cities. Child Psychology was also considered more *appropriate* for women. Such attitudes were evident in Britain and in the US and in relation to women's apparent abilities and skills in in nurturing, nursing, and the caring professions (Furumoto & Scarborough, 1986; Rutherford, Vaughn-Johnson, & Rodkey, 2015; Scarborough & Furumoto, 1989). The way 'caring' professions were gendered therefore highlights the need for feminist history (also see Valentine, 2010). Because women were also less likely to be accepted within academic areas of Psychology, their work remained largely invisible and was less often cited (Stevens & Gardner, 1982). Even in death women psychologists are portrayed differently, as the image of Psychology continues to be represented by the 'male scientist' (Radtke, Hunter, & Stam, 2000).

In the post-war years Psychology began to grow at an unprecedented rate. Furumoto (2003) argues that these testing practises had a large impact on the overall development of Psychology. However, what is interesting about these testing practises is that it was usually women psychologists doing the work. Testing was viewed, despite its importance and impact upon Psychology, as lower status and was thought to require less technical knowledge. It was therefore deemed suitable for women and so provided them with opportunities in lower salaried jobs than their male counterparts (Bohan, 1990). Unsurprisingly then, testing boomed in areas such as employment, educational, and developmental Psychology where there were higher concentrations of women working as they were deemed better suited due to women's natural nurturing abilities (Bohan, 1990; Furumoto, 2003). Under the control of mainly women psychologists, applied psychology and testing practises greatly advanced the profession of Psychology.

Within more women-centred histories of Psychology, there have been elements of the projective test scene. For example, Bernstein and Russo (1974) used the projective Thematic Apperception Test (TAT) author Christiana Morgan as an example of a prominent woman author in their engaging quiz to introduce their paper *The History of Psychology Revisited: Or, Up with Our Foremothers* (Morgan & Murray, 1935). In their conclusion they state how far women have come in Psychology considering the bias and adverse circumstances they faced and question how much women could have done given equal chance. Additionally, both Weisstein, Blaisdell, and Lemisch (1975) and Rutherford et al. (2010) in their discussion of Weisstein drawn upon work with the Rorschach. Both examples illustrate how projective testing has been used within feminist histories, yet there has been little recognition of feminist history of the projective test movement itself.[4] Indeed, these examples are also US based and considering the presence of women in British projective Psychology a British focus is also timely.

More specifically, Rutherford and Pettit (2015) in their recent discussion of feminism and/in/as Psychology discuss how there is a need for a growth in recent moves to include lesbian, gay, bisexual, trans (LGBT), and intersex history within feminist histories of psychology. Indeed, Rutherford and Pettit (2015) also criticised the historians' conception that the middle of the 20th century was a 'silent' period of feminist action. Throughout this book I will retain a focus on queer history and on the middle of the 20th century in hopes to contribute to more intersectional feminist histories of Psychology and the social sciences. However, it should be noted that the book does focus mainly on middle (and in some cases upper) class white women with significant privileges from which they established their career in Psychology.

The queer perspective within this book particularly important because a) there seem to be some significant queer people in the history and b) because of how the Rorschach was used as a diagnostic tool in the homophobic practises of Psychology over the 20th century. As already demonstrated some queer women were pivotal in the development of Psychology, particularly within psychoanalysis – Jessie Murray and Julia Turner, for instance. The presence of (queer) women continued to have a particular relevance in the history of projective testing, then later became implicated in the movements for queer liberation from the 1960s onwards. As will be fully described in the next chapter, the Second World War acted as a catalyst for Rorschach testing in Britain and the US, though the British military engaged with projective testing much less. In the US specifically, one reason for this was that officer screening included Rorschach testing in order to identify those who were gay (and those who were malingering as gay, see Bérubé, 1989, 1990; Hegarty, 2003a). Specifically, Due and Wright (1945), Wheeler (1949), and Fein (1950) conducted research on what they believed were clear diagnostic signs of homosexuality.

These included seeing feminine clothing, ambiguously sexed figures, sexual content, and castration/phallic symbols in the ink blot (also see Lindner, 1946). Similarly, having an artistic interpretation or one which could be viewed as paranoid (e.g. seeing masks or eyes) was also indicative of homosexuality (Due & Wright, 1945).

Interest in homosexuality continued in Psychology and Psychiatry but with a rather more homophobic and pathologising tone from the middle of the 20th century (see Jennings, 2008). King and Bartlett (1999) reviewed British psychiatry and homosexuality paying particular attention to treatments offered for homosexuality. These included behavioural treatments first developed at the Maudsley such as electroshock treatments and aversion therapy. Oral histories from both the professionals involved in such treatment (King, Smith, & Bartlett, 2004) and the patients of such treatment (Smith, Bartlett, & King, 2004) in the 1950s revealed the shocking impact treatments had on patients and a worrying trend that some professionals continued to support homophobic and abusive treatments (see also Dickinson, 2015). Psychoanalytic thinking that largely positioned 'homosexuality' as something that should be prevented, avoided, and treated was common in Britain. As well as behavioural treatments, psychoanalysis also continued to have a presence in the treatment of homosexuality and psychoanalytic thinking continued to prevail as a theoretical understanding of the genesis of 'homosexuality'.

Therefore, there is a double need to re-place women back into the history of Psychology, but also begin to remove the queer erasure which has occurred. Such critique is able to raise questions about historical injustice around the normalising projects of Psychiatry and Psychology regarding gender and sexuality. Indeed, Duggan (2006) argued that the history of sexuality was not often considered a serious historical inquiry and discussed the need for greater conciliation between queer theory and lesbian and gay history. This endeavour was also supported by Minton (1997). Such a queer history has several benefits, and so to conclude on why this history is so important I quote King and Bartlett (1999):

> History is always written from a perspective, our perspective was as gay and lesbian psychiatrists. Mental health professionals in Britain should be aware of the mistakes of the past. Only in that way can we prevent future excesses and heal the gulf between gay and lesbian patients and their psychiatrists.
>
> *(p. 111)*

Perhaps ironically, the history of the Rorschach has potential to contribute to the healing of this gulf when looked at through a queer affirmative lens, especially when it reveals how such history is linked to queer liberation.

The problems of doing queer history

There are a number of difficulties in conducting feminist and/or queer histories which need to be addressed in order to begin. As briefly mentioned the histories of women have been recorded less reliably than those of men (Bohan, 1990). This is especially true for lesbian women. Cook (1979a) described this as the 'historical denial of lesbian women'. Such historical denial of lesbian women has been particularly true for those in Britain where the experiences of women, and those women who desire women especially, have been undervalued and unreported (Jennings, 2007b). This is perhaps because Britain, unlike several other European countries, from the medieval era and early modern times onwards avoided legal prohibitions of lesbian behaviour, unlike that of men's (Brown, 1989). A number of historians identify such a lack of legal documentation about lesbian behaviour as an obstacle to lesbian history (see e.g. Brown, 1989; Donoghue, 1993; Weeks, 1997). Of the documents that historians do have access to, criminal records are one of the best kept and so queer history is often about criminality. This is of course especially true for the history of gay men as sex between men was criminalised in the modern era under Sodomy Laws until 1967 (see Weeks, 1997, 2016). Of the reports in newspapers that *were* about women desiring women, there was a level of sensationalism. In the US, the trials of Alice Mitchell (who murdered her lesbian lover) in 1892 for example, became the benchmark by which other women who desired women were compared (Duggan, 1993). However, overall lesbian history has regularly been considered one of silence, invisibility, and denial (Jennings, 2007a, 2007b).

Conducting queer history in a disciplinary context where 'homosexuality' was considered a mental illness is difficult. Many queer psychologists would not have been safe to 'come out' at the time and without clear self-identification erasure is very possible due to prevailing heteronormativity. Historians must therefore 'read between the straight lines' of the archive to prevent historical erasure (Koaureas, 2014). In order to challenge the double invisibility of queer women a number of histories of the lives of women desiring women have been produced to great effect (see Donoghue, 1993; Duberman, Vicinus, & Chauncey, 1989; Giffney, Sauer, & Watt, 2011; Weeks, 1977).

Conducting queer history in the early 20th century is also particularly difficult as terms like 'lesbian', 'invert', and 'homosexual' became known, yet shrouded by medico-scientific pathologic meaning, few women directly identified with them and many rejected such labels. It is likely only middle- and upper-class women would have had access to medico-scientific texts and thus been able to identify themselves within the literature in order to reject (or perhaps accept) such labels. Radclyffe Hall is a particularly famous example of someone who self-identified as an 'invert' in the 1920s, as does her protagonist Stephen in *The Well of Loneliness* in which such identification was a direct association of reading medico-scientific texts about homosexuality. However as discussed by Duggan (1993), newspapers would have run sensationalist stories about women transgressing gender and sexual norms and many stories, terms, and ideas would still have been accessible through word of mouth meaning working class women who desired women would not have been unaware of the scientific/social understandings and connotations of their desires. For example, the 'female husband' is viewed by lesbian historians as a distinctly working class component of lesbian history (see Donoghue, 1993; Faderman, 1981; Jennings 2007a, 2007b).

Turn of the 20th century sexologists had a major impact upon understanding of sexuality, for example the work of Havelock Ellis including his introduction of the term 'sexual invert' (Ellis & Symonds, 1897; Crozier, 2008, for a history of earlier psychiatric writings about homosexuality in Britain prior to Ellis). The 1920s and 1930s, the time in which the projective test movement began, saw a pivotal change in the way sexuality was seen, as illustrated by the 1928 ban of the lesbian novel *The Well of Loneliness* by aforementioned Radclyffe Hall (Hall, 1928, see Jennings, 2007a, 2007b, 2007c). In fact, Ellis wrote the original preface of the book, giving it some form of psychological legitimacy. Psychology began to develop constructs of homosexuality around illness and sickness instead of it being framed as a problem of morality as it was in the previous century (Jennings, 2007a). Following from the work of Ellis, psychological theories suggested homosexuality was indicative of sexual 'inversion' – though Ellis argued that gay men were not necessarily effeminate, he did believe lesbian women were masculine (Weeks, 1977). Medico-scientific texts informed readers that lesbians were promiscuous, predatory, and psychopathic (Jennings, 2007a). The category of 'lesbian' and the presentation of 'inverts' gained greater cultural significance after the Second World War, but it was still treated as a neurotic sickness – a mental disorder. These cultural shifts in understanding about gender and sexuality mean the early 20th century is a challenging period for historians conducting queer history.

By the end of the Second World War fears of the middle- and upper-class 'New Woman' abounded – that is the more independent, masculine, and feminist woman (Jennings, 2007a). Women enjoyed more freedoms and political rights, they experienced employment in higher numbers than ever before. However, despite these changes marriage was still deemed to be in opposition to career and many believed that once the war effort was over women would return to their 'natural roles' as care-givers and homemakers. Weeks (1977) identified the post-Second World War era as a particularly hostile time for lesbian women in the US (also see Bérubé, 1989). Having experienced, in some cases, relative tolerance in the military, the enforcement to maintain pre-war social order meant many lesbian women were immediately discharged and trialled for having relationships with other women; whereas during the war only those 'addicted to the practise' were formally dealt with (Faderman, 1991; Weeks, 1977).

Attention to the early 20th century has been fruitful for historians interested in gender and sexuality. The associations with the women's movements and first wave feminism influenced shifting attitudes about women's social role as well as the slowly growing lesbian community (Jennings, 2006). Specifically, Jennings (2007b) identified middle- to upper-class women gaining careers (especially in education and the professions), choosing not to marry and living more independent lives, some of whom lived their lives with their lovers, as central to the telling of lesbian histories of this period. As explored previously this is applicable to some of the women in psychoanalytic circles.

Despite the fact that terms such as 'homosexual', 'invert' and even 'lesbian' were known in the early 20th century, issues of inappropriate presentism remain. Perhaps the most widespread issue in the history of sexuality is the essential/constructionist debate which corresponds onto presentism (see Stocking, 1965). The essentialist position is that queer people have been present in all historical time, and the constructionist position is that, because identities like 'lesbian' and 'gay' are recent constructions, it is improper to make this claim. As Foucault (1976) succinctly argued, sexuality is historical and the 'homosexual' has come into being only recently. Yet as historians and activists have highlighted, same-sex sexual behaviours, desires, relationships, and loves have occurred throughout history (Plummer, 1981; Weeks, 1981). Rupp (1989) explained:

> In the simplest terms, we are faced with a choice between labelling women lesbians who might have violently rejected the notion or glossing over the significance of women's relationships by considering them asexual and Victorian.
>
> *(p. 398)*

In conducting queer histories there is the continual problem of 'projecting' identities onto people of the past who would not have conceptualised their lives in such a way; this is particularly interesting when looking at history about projective testing. Donoghue (1993) was realistic about the essentialist/constructionist debate and argued most historians are somewhere in the middle. Jennings' (2007b) provides a short account of the historical changes in emphasis on both positions and clarifies the motives behind each position. Presentism is also challenging when conducting histories that are hidden, especially in Psychology where 'deviant' sexualities were symptomatic and considered evidence of mental illness.

Yet sexuality is not the only identity that historians should be wary of projecting onto individuals of the past. Women of the past are often identified as feminists in ways they may have ultimately rejected as the terminology and meanings of things change over time. The same can be true for all sorts of identities and descriptions, yet it often appears that it's the gender and sexuality labels which lead to particular concern.

There have been vastly different perspectives about the problems of lesbian history. Cook (1979a) for example states that:

> women who love women, who choose women to nurture and support and to form a living environment in which to work creatively and independently are lesbians. Genital "proofs" to confirm lesbianism are never required to confirm the heterosexuality of men and women who live together for 20, or 50, years. Such proofs are not demanded even when discussing ephemeral love relations between adult women and men.
>
> *(p. 64, see also Cook, 1979b)*

Similarly, Faderman (1981) investigated a range of relationships between women; all were passionate but not necessarily sexual. Focusing on Britain, Donoghue (1993) equally argues that sex is not necessary for a lesbian history, and how it is possible to broaden the meaning of lesbian history to include variety whilst avoiding reducing lesbian history to mere sisterly affection. Such historical perspectives echo Rich's (1980) assertion that women are coerced into heterosexuality via heteropatriarchy. Rich responded by creating a lesbian continuum upon which all women's relationships with other women sit. This continuum allowed all women, whether lesbian or not, to recognise their moving relationships with other woman. By recognising *lesbian existence* and *lesbian continuum* she argued it was possible to remove lesbian erasure from feminist scholarly work (Rich, 1993). Different ideas about relationships and intimacy, for example, 'romantic friendships' (Donoghue, 1993; Faderman, 1981, 1991; Jennings, 2007b) and school crushes (Jennings, 2007a, 2007b; Vicinus, 1989), initially suggest that such relationships were not necessarily sexual. Yet the diaries of Anne Lister revealed the occurrences of sexual relationships between women in the early 19th century and it appeared that lack of evidence of sexual activity was a symptom of documentation more than a lack of sex between women (Whitbread, 1988).

Other lesbian historians have developed different methods to confront these issues with presentism. Bennett (2000) uses the phrase 'lesbian-like' to describe the lives of those she views as lesbian prior to the sexual identity. Doan (2006) clearly argues that because understandings of sexuality, gender, and thus inversions of both were not understood as they are today such projections of the present onto the past cannot, and should not be done. Using the example of women dressing in a more masculine manner in the post-war years, she argues that masculine dress was not at the time indicative of lesbian identity/behaviour; such dress was viewed as a reaction to the war, not as a sign of sexual deviance. Doan (2006, 2013a) argues, following from the work of Foucault (1976), how sexuality should be considered historical and that there was not a panic over the increase of 'masculine' women *per se*; their appearance was more humorous and a novelty (Doan, 2006). Whether viewed as threatening or not, the increased independence of women and the shifting expectations means that navigating this period can be tricky. In contrast, a number of lesbian historians have identified such 'cross-dressing' as distinctly queer. For example, working class women 'passing' as men in to gain work, to marry their lovers, and to gain other privileges given only to men (Duberman et al., 1989; Jennings, 2007a, 2007b; Newton, 1989)

While the presence of homosexuality historically has been debated, little attention has been paid to the presence of 'heterosexuality' (see Katz, 1995). While some argue that sexuality as we understand it today does not map onto how it was understood in the early 20th century (Doan, 2013b), barely any attention has been paid to how heterosexuality may have been understood. Heterosexuality is regularly conceptualised as historically essential and this is often taken for granted (see Doan, 2013b). Lochrie (2011) called for a heterosexual history because of the perceptions that heterosexuality has been constant, which it has not. The emergence of heterosexuality came after that of 'homosexuality' due to the describing of deviance and illness in contrast to 'normal' which of course alludes to the presence of the powers at play in such distinctions (see Hegarty, 2007; Katz,1995). No other topic appears to have such fraught negotiations concerning anachronism. A fear of anachronism surrounds the history of sexuality as if there is something inherently offensive in misidentifying a person of the past as gay or lesbian. As Giffney et al. (2011) point out anachronism is present in all historicism, it is inevitable to some extent. Indeed, it can be used for good, for example, Giffney et al. (2011) describe their use of 'lesbian' in their edited text *The Lesbian Premodern* as deliberately provocative. Similarly, Donoghue (1993) too uses 'lesbian' as shorthand for all of the terms used to mean women loving women throughout centuries and accepts the connotations of each under this terminological umbrella. Faderman (1981) states how it is impossible to account for 'what really happened' and lesbian historians must move forward with the project to protect lesbian history from further erasure (see also, 1991, 2011). In some ways then, using what might be perceived as presentist language is in fact a conscious act of reflexivity about historical questions pertinent to the present. This effort is of course, political (Traub, 2011) and deliberate, as is all historicism.

A number of methods to deal with presentism around sexuality are available. As previously outlined one can use 'lesbian-like', or 'heterosexual-not' (Lochrie, 2011). From the 1990s increasingly historians and writers have used queer theory. Jennings (2007b) used the work of Judith Butler, stating one is not born queer but is named queer by the wider community. Hegarty (2013) applies this thinking specifically to Psychology and the history of testing in Lewis Terman's analysis of gifted boys and their apparent effeminacy, inversion, and possible queerness. In regards to the question of whether sex is necessary in lesbian history Jennings (2007b) argues that explicit sources are not necessary but instead historians can consider context and the ways mainstream society understood desire between women. Without such associations or recognition, as Vicinus describes it, women of the past and their desires are underestimated (Jennings, 2007b). Jennings (2007c) also argues that by adopting a queer approach lesbian historians are able to free themselves from the search for historical sources directly about lesbian experience and instead focus on the roles of lesbian sexuality in constructing 'normative' sexuality. Though historians should avoid searching the past for women who fulfil modern ideas of lesbianism, Vicinus (2011) argues that it is still possible to relate present and past understandings, even if those in the past would not have understood our conceptualisations – such relationships between the past and the present are still meaningful.

In many ways the idea that lesbian history is one of silence and invisibility, is not strictly true. Rather there is evidence of historical terms for 'lesbian' but these have been ignored, and misunderstandings of terms and confusions surrounding sexual acts and identities. Donoghue (1993) suggests 'Tribade' and 'Tommy' as potential words meaning 'lesbian' in past centuries. 'Tommy' associated with 'tom boy' alludes to masculine women. Similarly, 'Molly' was used in the 19th century to refer to men who frequented 'Molly houses' which were taverns and meeting places for men who desired men (see Sedgwick, 1985).

It is, of course, important to be careful as it can be inappropriate to apply labels in a presentist way onto the past. However, there is also the additional issue that it is precisely this fear of misapplying labels and queer sexualities onto the past that has contributed to the invisibility of queer history. This fear of being anachronistic when it comes to sexuality does occasionally have echoes of homophobia and biphobia as it suggests that there is something inherently offensive about calling someone gay, bisexual, lesbian or queer when they were not. We do not have the same fear assuming someone from the past is heterosexual – indeed this has happened repetitively, consistently, and without a second thought. Of course it would be a terrible shame to identify someone in such a way that they may have vehemently rejected, and indeed doing so would be bad historical practice. The descriptions of people's lives have to be nuanced, careful, and well considered. But perhaps we can be somewhat less fearful in our uses of queer labels in efforts to see history through an anti-heteronormative lens.

Approach and structure

The aim of this inter-disciplinary historical book is to explain how Rorschach ink blots initially pathologised queer people but later assisted in gay liberation in some specific circumstances. This bizarre history focuses on the borders between academic scientific research and queer activism. A border, which at first appears to be distinct, is found to be surprisingly porous. In fact, it is just as blurred and smeary as the edges of the ink blots themselves. I hope to respond to calls in the past decades for more women-focused histories of Psychology and sexuality studies. I therefore present a distinctly queer feminist history which places women and queer women at the centre.

Using tribady as a metaphor Donoghue (1993) suggests it as a method for doing lesbian history in a way which I think is particularly compelling:

> Tribady, an activity that is rarely discussed, provides a stimulating metaphor for the business of doing history. The researcher is not so much penetrating the past to find what she wants as making contact with it, touching the surface of her present interests to the details of the past; the more she touches, the more she will become sensitised to the nuances she is exploring.
>
> *(p. 24)*

I have explored this history, borrowing from multiple disciplines including Psychology, Sociology and Gender, and Sexuality Studies. In blending these I aim to demonstrate a way in which inter-disciplinary stories can be told that enrich our understandings of events. By adopting a social constructionist approach (such as those utilised by historians such as Danziger, 1994; Hacking, 1995) I firmly believe that all history must be understood within context. That, however, is not to say constructions are not meaningful; constructions can be highly significant. Constructions are meaningful, powerful, and enforced by powerful objects such as psychological tests. In providing a highly contextualised account of the Rorschach, the work and lives of women involved in the projective test moment and the queer liberation movements in Britain from the 1960s, I navigate some of the issues of presentism.

Both women's histories and queer histories have been hidden, denied, or not deemed important. They have been expunged, effaced, or eradiated. Therefore, the first thing for a queer feminist historian to do is to track down the archives which contain something of interest to them. For this project I am indebted to the collections at: The British Library (for the British Rorschach Forum publications, the Hall-Carpenter collection, and the Mental Health Testimony archive); the Wellcome Library (for numerous materials in the BPS collection, including those of Charlotte Wolff, plus those of Margaret Lowenfeld); and the British Library of Political and Economic Science (LSE, for the materials of Mary McIntosh, and the Gay Liberation Front).

I also draw to some extent on oral history interviews, four of which I conducted myself and others available in the aforementioned Mental Health Testimony archive. Oral histories have been said to be 'the first kind of history' (Thompson, 2000). Throughout millennia, history has been told through word-of-mouth, story-telling, and nostalgic conversations between people; and yet this form of history making had fallen out of favour. Many of the histories that have been recorded have been told by scholars who had little contact with their subject matter. However, in the 1970s oral history began to develop into a key area of social history. And, in contrast to previous notions of how to write, research, and discover history, oral histories told by individuals with unique understandings have become more prevalent. Not only have oral histories changed the way in which histories can be recorded, but they have also changed who it is telling the history. Instead of elitist historical story-tellers, oral histories have instead promoted the stories of those 'from below', that is the otherwise forgotten and untold story-tellers from the past. This technique has allowed histories to be told from rare and individual perspectives, thus revealing 'hidden histories' (Portelli, 1997; Thompson, 2000). For this reason, they have been especially useful in the telling of feminist histories (Gluck & Patai, 1991) and in queer histories (Boyd, 2008). For examples of the uses of queer- and woman-focused oral history see Summerskill (2013) and Traies (2018).

The approach I have taken in the use of oral history in my thesis has been one of acceptance. I have not queried or debated whether the oral history participants described what 'really' happened despite concerns that some researchers may have about long-term memories being unreliable. There are two main reasons for this. First, oral history participants have ownership of their own experiences and perceptions and I, as someone without such experiences, am in no position to question these. Second, all historical documents from which historians derive their narrative are written within context, with motives and objectives, and the narratives developed by oral history are no different. Just as an event might be misremembered or re-framed considering present understandings when using oral history, so too can historical documents be misinterpreted by historians and framed by present understandings. Dickinson (2015) in *Curing Queers* used the oral histories of both gay men and trans women who received aversion therapy, and nurses who administered such therapy, in Britain in the middle of the 20th century.[5] I use a similar approach to oral history as Dickinson (2015) as he is aware of potential motives behind participant's narratives yet allows these to construct the history. After all, who are we to inform those who experienced history, what 'actually' happened? Feminist scholars have been less concerned about the reliability of oral history but rather the appropriation that is possible when people's narratives come under analysis and are presented by others (Gluck & Patai, 1991). Therefore, I have used oral history to inform my understanding of the history, and taken these to be as equally 'true' as other forms of historical data (which have their own biases and potential inaccuracies).

In conducting my research on the women working in the British projective test movement I have considered biographical data, their publications, and where possible oral histories or other forms of character description such as obituaries. I discovered several features that indicate these women led feminist, and in some cases, queer lives. Broad examples of evidence of lesbianism include resisting social pressures to marry and have children, and developing supportive networks with other women. Many, if not all, of the women I identified could be argued to fulfil aspects of this definition. In fact, it could be argued that their mere presence within Psychology at this time provokes a strong sense of their feminist values; or at least that they can be reclaimed by feminist psychologists now. In a time of highly gendered expectations of women to be homemakers and mothers, all of these women fought against these societal beliefs about what women ought to do.

As explored throughout this chapter, the relationship between Psychology and feminism has been complex throughout the 20th century and as Rutherford et al. (2010) state, are bound with the concepts of gender, gendered roles, and gender relations. Despite ideas that feminist approaches opposed empirical Psychology, Morawski and other feminist thinkers, namely Harding (1986, 1987), argued feminist methods and reflexivity are necessary in scientific endeavours. Such feminist thinking has been instrumental to moves towards more bottom-up approaches in scientific methodology (Harding, 2008). Indeed, efforts to include the voices of those being studied has also been evidenced in Psychology more broadly (e.g. Wilkinson & Kitzinger, 1996). Attempts to gain the voices 'from below' go some way to dismantle the power relations involved in scientific research. Oral histories are a particularly useful method by which to gain such voices. Feminist Psychology has also shown the reflexive nature of Psychology in relation to feminism. It has also assisted in the removal of heteronormative approaches in Psychology. These are some reasons why I take a queer feminist approach, but also simply because I come from a queer women's perspective. No historian is able to fully detach from their own interests, lives, and perspectives to provide an objective or unbiased history. Archives are collected with an eye for what is considered important and those materials are both written and read through the lens of people's own perspectives encompassing intentions, agendas, aims, and beliefs. As rather succinctly described by someone I interviewed:

> How do you write a report on a projective test and write a report and say "well it could be this, it could be this, or if you take a feminist perspective it could be this, actually traditionally you might have said that . . ." Somebody has got to choose *the* lens that gets elevated.

While this was about interpretation of analysis of projective tests themselves, this also described the act of doing historical research. "Somebody has got to choose *the* lens that gets elevated" – and this is true for all historicism, but the choice of lens is not often made explicit. Morawski (1994) argued that more honest and reflexive accounts are needed for the history of Psychology and that such feminist lenses were especially important. In this book, I adopt a queer feminist lens. The questions we pose, the archives we seek, and the documents we find most interesting, as well as the interpretations we make, are all influenced by our own identities and privileges. In writing from a British queer feminist perspective, I write a no less 'biased' history than any of the histories of Psychology available about the (straight, cisgender, white) men of Psychology that are abundant.

In addition to the queer feminist perspective I also adopt Richards' (2010) distinction between 'Psychology' the discipline, and 'psychology' the subject matter. Throughout the book, when discussing psychology as a studied subject, or somebody's psychology, I deliberately use the 'little p' version, and when discussing the discipline that studies it, I use 'big P'. These distinctions are important for the clarification of the reflexive quality of p/Psychology, and becomes especially important when considering how psychology influences Psychology and vice versa. It is also useful when considering the relationship the public has with Psychology, through psychology.

In using the Rorschach as a way to springboard through a history of Psychology and queer liberation I am not intending to argue for or against projective testing. Whether it is 'valid' or not, for me, is not an answerable question. It is a matter of perspective. It hinges on what you believe to be 'reliable', 'valid' 'evidence'. It depends on the assumptions you have underlying your beliefs about psychological testing. The assumptions that a projection can tell you about personality is strikingly similar to the assumption that the image from an fMRI brain scan tells you what the brain is 'doing'. Using the same criteria it could be possible to dis/credit all manner of psychological tests, past and present. It is therefore not my aim to focus on this debate within this book, but rather think about the history of such testing and use it as an entry point through which to explore a queer feminist history in Britain. I'm also deliberately using 'a' history. There are all sorts of histories available and this is just one. It is not 'the' history (though I, unsurprisingly, think it's the most fascinating).

The structure of the book is mostly chronological and will stem from the 1920s when the Rorschach arrived in Britain, to the 1970s onwards following the start of gay liberation movements. It will also follow a structure which transgresses the academic/activist border across the chapters. Early chapters will be more focused on academia and Psychology 'proper' then move across the boundary to finally focusing on activism in the 1970s. This border is crossed throughout the book demonstrating how blurred and indistinct it is in practice.

Chapter 2 will first provide a brief history of the Rorschach in the US and in Britain and explore how the test came to be involved in military practises to detect gay men in the 1940s during the Second World War (Hegarty, 2003a). It also centrally provides accounts of the pathologisation of 'homosexuality' in Britain and in the US, and demonstrate how this is a key example where societal beliefs have structured and been embedded within scientific practise thus legitimising stigma, hatred, and prejudice. The 'gay signs' that were used to test queer people and used to diagnose 'homosexuality' will be outlined, thus leading to the explanation of how the Rorschach was implicated in the psychological treatment of queer people in the mid-20th century. This is accounted for by looking at not only the accounts of psychologists during this time, but also at the accounts of those lesbians and gay men who were tested.

Chapter 3 will introduce two key women working in projective testing – Evelyn Hooker and June Hopkins. June Hopkins, unlike some of the other women I explore, was an out lesbian, and is pivotal to my analysis of this history. She has also been almost completely ignored in histories of emancipatory Psychology. Most notably, she was reclaimed in the 2002 special issue of *Lesbian and Gay Psychology Review*. In introducing her I contribute to this effort and add to Minton's (2002) work on reclaiming some psychologists as those who were gay and lesbian themselves and whose research contributed to depathologisation efforts in the mid- to late-20th century. Hopkins' research in 1969 and 1970 used the Rorschach among other methods to show lesbian signs on the Rorschach were a) different to gay men's and b) that meant lesbian women were not neurotic or pathological. At the core of this chapter is my comparison with research conducted in the US by Evelyn Hooker (1957) who used the Rorschach to show instead there were no differences between gay men and heterosexual men's responses on the Rorschach.

Chapter 4 will introduce some of the individual psychologists themselves who can be identified as queer working within the projective test movement prior to June Hopkins. I pay particular attention to lives of three key women: Margaret Lowenfeld (1890–1973), Ann Kaldegg (1899–1995), and Effie Lilian Hutton (1904–1956). These women lived fascinating queer feminist lives in a period of the early 20th century when the institutionalised homophobia in the field they were working in pathologised their lives, how they dressed, and their relationships. This chapter will therefore switch the lens somewhat and instead of studying queer people from a psychological perspective, it will study the psychologists themselves, most notably the psychologists who were using the Rorschach and other similar projective tests. Alongside their psychological research, this chapter will also explore their personal lives and consider how their work and experiences were shaped by the contexts in which they lived and how they rebelled against gendered expectations.

Chapter 5 represents the broadening of scope in the book. It focuses less on Psychology as a discipline and more on the activists who became involved either from within, or outside of academia. In this chapter I will outline the important role the Minorities Research Group had on the blurred boundary between activism and research. As a lesbian group they maintained they would actively take part in research in order to quash the notion in scientific literature that lesbian women were neurotic and pathological. Importantly, it was the Minorities Research Group who volunteered as the lesbian sample for June Hopkins' research. They also contributed to the research of Charlotte Wolff who is also described in this chapter as another out queer woman working in Psychology at this time.

Based on the breadth of the previous chapter, Chapter 6 will go beyond Psychology and expand its analysis to Sociology and other social sciences. In this chapter I explore the work and life of Mary McIntosh, examining her academic work which distinctly aligned with her activism. As an active member of the Gay Liberation Front, McIntosh was an out queer woman whose political beliefs in relation to Marxism and feminism were at the centre of her research on sexuality. In this chapter I outline her own membership to the Minorities Research Group and the subsequent splinter lesbian group Kenric, which still runs today. This chapter will particularly explore how the context of the 1970s was of a very different flavour to the earlier decades explored in the previous chapters. Yet, despite such shifts, there remain many important similarities.

In the Conclusion I describe how in telling this British history, I question the apparently strict boundary between academia and activism and suggest that this border is blurrier and more like the edges of an ink blot than they might first appear. This chapter will draw on the history over the 20th century and extrapolate it to the 21st century. It will do so by arguing that the positioning of academia as separate and distinct from the social world continues to eradicate the actions of academic activists. By looking historically with a queer feminist lens, we are able to re-position the actions of women from both the past and present, as deliberate, intentional, and empowered.

Throughout the book I tell a contextualised and more social narrative, demonstrating the ways in which Psychology is influenced by society and influential on people's lives. In using the Rorschach and projective methods as a lens through which to interrogate this history, I utilise these tests to do something good for the queer people they once so eagerly hurt when in the hands of some psychologists in the past. But doing so is certainly not 'straight' forward, if you'll forgive the pun. The history is inky, messy, and blurred. The ink which made up the printed Rorschach ink blots is basically the same as the ink which printed the typewritten pamphlets, and posters of queer liberation movements in Britain. And *this* ink you are reading now tells a very queer story of both.

Notes

1 Rorschach used the terms 'experiment' or the German 'Versuch' for the most part, especially when discussing the underlying theoretical ideas of the procedure. He referred to it as a 'test' only when referring to the technical aspects and the ink blot plates themselves (Akavia, 2013). Considering the popularity and subsequent understandings of the term 'Rorschach test', I will continue to use this terminology.

2 See Psychology's Feminist Voices, www.feministvoices.com. Also for web-based feminist resources in Britain, see the Open University Conceptual and Historical Issues in Psychology resource at www2.open.ac.uk/openlearn/CHIPs/index.html.

3 These two records of Burlingham using the Rorschach are available from the Freud Museum archive, London (specifically in the 'Documents' part of the archive under 'Dorothy Burlingham' and can be obtained by contacting the curator directly).

4 In Psychology's Feminist Voices (www.feministvoices.com) there are nine women in total included within the biographies who directly relate to Rorschach research. They are: Theodora Mead Abel, Louise Bates Ames, Eugenia Hanfmann, Molly Harrower, Evelyn Gentry Hooker, Lois Barclay Murphy, Maria Rickers-Ovsiankina, and Marion MacDonald Wright.

5 In Dickinson's book he interviewed two trans women who were referred for aversion therapy by medical professionals. The experiences of these two women demonstrate how aversion therapies were thought to be broadly suitable to a range of people who were thought to be outside of cisgender and heterosexual norms.

2

QUEER SIGNS ON THE RORSCHACH

. . . so I trotted off to start that, or to look into starting that. And part of the assessment for that was, they put you through a battery of, I think they were all projective tests. There was an interview, there was a Rorschach, there was a house tree person [test] . . .

The above passage begins to describe the experience of a psychotherapist I interviewed who was tested with a range of projective methods in the 1980s in the US. He had heard that in order to be a therapist you must have experience of being in therapy, so in order to begin his career in psychotherapy, and psychoanalysis he 'trotted off' to begin. The testing itself, although not especially traumatic ". . . it wasn't the kind of thing as a therapist that [he] would want [his] clients to experience now." Overall, he felt there was a mismatch of expectations of what the testing procedure and results would be like. A simultaneous nervousness of providing inappropriate responses conflicted with a pressure to produce responses, something I similarly felt in my own testing experience.

> I mean the person wasn't particularly vocal in either of them I don't think. I seem to remember a bit of confusion with the Rorschach because, I'd say something and either there wouldn't be a response, or kind of or, they seemed to want more than I could see, and I guess that's what a projective test is about, you put some effort into it and you project and something comes out of it. But, I don't think I understood it full . . . I think I said something about clouds a lot, and I don't think they wanted the clouds all the time. I think there was "what else?" question that came up a lot.

It was the interpretation, and the decisive nature of the results of the testing, which especially upset him. He was described as being 'paranoid' and being obsessed with death. This he attributes to seeing a squashed rabbit in one of the ink blots, which for him was a regular sight living out in the countryside on the outskirts of a major city in the US. He rejected the results of the projective tests and described his feeling of shock at the definiteness of the written report and the way it was verbally presented to him. Perhaps one of the most shocking elements to the results was that he was accurately identified as gay by the projective tests (the House Tree Person test in particular), despite not being out at the time.

> So . . . so, um, so I'm just laughing because if I had taken some of it on board sooner I would have been a lot happier a lot earlier. So I was still defended at this time, and it wasn't that I was gay and I was anti-being gay, I was just, hadn't embraced *me* as a sexual being, so the house tree person came back and, I can't remember the wording used but basically I experienced it as: "well you're a rav- you're a raving homosexual." And I was kind of like "ah how dare you!" . . . But it was done with some kind of authority that, as we're now talking, I quite liked at work, "oh we know something the poor patient doesn't know" I quite liked that but when it was done to me I really objected to it . . . I was quite defensive, well you know just because I've drawn people in this way or this, that and the other. You know that could mean all kinds of things . . . I might just be highly attuned to beauty or – I came up with all kinds of stuff.

The reflexivity in the preceding passage is particularly compelling. As a therapist himself now, he was aware of the powerful nature of knowledge, and how being the person with knowledge and power is a much more comfortable experience than being without. He also recognised the irony that if he had accepted the 'homosexual diagnosis' he would have been happier with his sexuality sooner. The wish to explain away and make sense of the results is also interesting and is perhaps one of the most intriguing elements to the Rorschach. It is not just what you *see*, but what it *means* which is most captivating.

While this description is of a testing procedure in the 1980s, a time with substantial societal homophobia issues particularly in light of the HIV/AIDS outbreak, it still provides an insight into how the Rorschach may have been experienced for others prior to the depathologisation of homosexuality *per se* in 1973. This is of course true for people who were 'diagnosed' as queer regardless of how they identified themselves. For the person I interviewed, it was the lack of transparency and unexpected prognosis which created the most discomfort. In fact, the participant described it as a 'seduce and reject' tactic:

> That was part of why I didn't like the result. It seemed like I was seduced, or it was made to be kind of . . . there was an encouragement and a kind of . . . "oh don't worry about it, just doing it, just a bit of fun, just do this, that and the other, this that and the other, boom! – you *are* this!"

So it seems, in this instance, a projective test was able to 'detect homosexuality', though some of course would argue this was a lucky guess, or a fluke (Wood, Nezworski, Lilienfeld, & Garb, 2003). Yet the history of projective methods and the detection of 'homosexuality' is a particularly important one, regardless of whether the Rorschach or other tests can 'detect' sexuality. It is not an aim of this chapter, nor of this book, to argue for or against the Rorschach's ability, reliability, or validity to *do* such things. Instead, this chapter draws together the history of the Rorschach, comparing the US and Britain and the use of the test on queer people, indicating the apparent 'gay signs' psychologists were looking for. I argue that, regardless of whether the Rorschach can 'detect', it was certainly able to diagnose. No matter your position on the Rorschach's actual ability, it has been (and in some places continues to be) a powerful object which ironically projected back onto people labels, symptoms, and stigmas.

The Rorschach in Britain and the US

Following the publication of Herman Rorschach's *Psychodiagnostik*, in which he introduced the world to his ink blot test, his test received little attention. However, it was first publicly recognised in Britain four years later in 1925 by psychiatrist Mary Rushton Barkas, from the Maudsley Hospital. The detailed review of *Psychodiagnostik* in the *British Journal of Psychiatry* described Rorschach's data, the test's use in Swiss Psychology, and offered the prediction that the test "may well prove worth introduction into those of this country" (p. 330). Barkas thought that Rorschach's test, like Jung's Word Association Test, was "most useful if applied in a more general way, less for the object of rigid diagnosis than as a means of approach to the patient's complexes" (Barkas, 1925, p. 330). Barkas also expressed disbelief in Rorschach's powers of insight that foreshadowed the idea that the test had to be used by experts to be effective, which became increasingly common in both Britain and the US from the 1930s:

> Yet in reading the data on which Rorschach's conclusions were based one cannot but feel that he either made lucky guesses, rather in the mode of the fortune-teller, or else that his extensive experience of the test combined with great intuition gave him a skill in interpreting the data which few could attain.
>
> *(Barkas, 1925, p. 331)*

A year later in the *British Journal of Psychiatry*, W.D. Chambers published his psychiatric notes from a trip to Zurich that described Rorschach's test as a "novel method of testing apperception" (Chambers, 1926, p. 277). By the early 1930s, reports of clinical practice with the Rorschach were evident in British journals. In 1931, Gordon and Norman reported using the Rorschach to test different types of 'mental defectives' in the *British Medical Journal*. In 1933 and 1934, *The British Journal of Psychiatry* published summaries of research which included Rorschach publications.

In 1932, Oscar Oeser (1932a, 1932b) of the Cambridge Psychological Laboratory published two research studies on form and colour in the Rorschach. Oeser described the Rorschach as an item that had "so often been found useful in experiments on perceiving and imaging, for here the subject is absolutely free to react in whatever way suits him most" (1932a, p. 19). His Rorschach work was cited by his mentor Frederic Bartlett in his magnum opus *Remembering* (1932).[1] Oeser was not alone among Cambridge students in taking an interest in the Rorschach. In 1933, Philip E. Vernon, a recent Cambridge graduate, published four papers on the Rorschach (Vernon, 1933a, 1933b, 1933c, 1933d, also see Vernon, 1935a, 1935b). Vernon described how to use the test, expressed enthusiasm for its use, and considered the development of new blots. While aware of criticisms, Vernon remained optimistic about the development of the Rorschach test:

> the deficiencies of the Rorschach ink-blot method as a psychometric test have been amply demonstrated, in particular the uncertainties and subjectivity of its scoring, the lack of adequate norms, poor reliability, and almost complete lack of scientifically controlled validation. Yet I cannot agree that these deficiencies should lead to its rejection by investigators in the field of personality . . . I am unable to call to mind any other test of personality . . . which tells me as much about my subjects in so short a time as does the Rorschach test.
>
> *(Vernon, 1933c, p. 291, also see Hearnshaw, 1964)*

These papers appeared after Vernon spent a year at Harvard collaborating with Gordon Allport on the measurement of personality-related values (Vernon & Allport, 1931). In the same year, Vernon joined the Maudsley Hospital and he soon became more critical of the Rorschach which was to be a key theme in the Maudsley's approach to projective testing.[2] For example, Audrey Lewis, who was Chair of Psychiatry at the Maudsley, described the Rorschach as of 'limited or doubtful value' in 1934, although other Cambridge Psychological Laboratory alum continued to be more supportive of the Rorschach, for example, Oliver Zangwill (Zangwill, 1945). In 1932, the *British Journal of Psychology* received a review of Samuel Beck's *The Rorschach Test and Personality Diagnosis* (1930), exposing British psychologists to further US influence and recent developments.

As suggested in Chapter 1, women were especially important for the development of the projective test movement in Britain. Magdalen Vernon, whose brother was the aforementioned Phillip Vernon, also later published projective work while studying under Bartlett at Cambridge (see Vernon, 1940). Her work however, while projective, was more concerned with phantasy, play, and projection through cognitive processes. She was also influenced by the work of Margaret Lowenfeld, who began developing her own projective tests at this time in Britain. The two later had regular correspondence, and Lowenfeld became a major player in the projective psychotherapeutic scene in Britain. Lowenfeld also presumably exerted some influence onto Theodora Alcock who worked at Lowenfeld's Institute of Child Psychology (ICP) in the early 1930s (see Chapter 4).

Alcock is said to have discovered the Rorschach in 1933 (see McCarthy Woods, 2008), and soon introduced it to C. J. Earl, a psychiatrist who tried to popularise the Rorschach within medical circles, and Eric Trist, a clinical psychologist. Under Alcock's leadership the three of them established a network of Rorschach users in Britain and continued to discuss the Rorschach throughout the Second World War, eventually establishing the British Rorschach Forum in 1942. At the point at which the group was formed, all the founding members were working at the Tavistock, which acted as the institutional centre for the Rorschach, in its decades of relative popularity in Britain.

The Second World War acted as a catalyst for the development of Psychology in both the US and Britain, but it has to be said the engagement of Psychiatry and Psychology with the military effort in the US outstripped that in any other country at war. Psychologically healthy recruits were required, and so mental testing was not only used to test the 'feeble-minded' but also to screen all recruits (Capshew, 1999; Rose, 1999). From 1920 to 1946, the American Psychological Association (APA) membership grew from 393 to 4,427 (Herman, 1995). Key psychologists became involved; for example, B.F. Skinner of behaviourism fame helped train missile guiding pigeons. Henry Murray, who helped develop the projective Thematic Apperception Test (TAT) test with Christina Morgan, began work for the Office of Strategic Services at Station 'S'. Here military screening for officers involved three and a half days of assessment including the newly developed time-effective group Rorschach, where the Rorschach could be administered to groups, not just individuals, at one time (Harrower-Erickson & Steiner, 1941; Herman, 1995). By 1948, Murray was a Captain and had helped publish the *Assessment of men*, which outlined how Station 'S' ranked each individual recruit on a 1–6 aptitude scale for their application (Rose, 1999).

In total, 12 percent of men who enlisted were deemed unfit for service for psychiatric reasons, a higher rate than any other country (Herman, 1995). Such 'psychiatric reasons' could include 'homosexuality' as detected by the psychiatrists and their tests during this process (Bérubé, 1990; Hegarty, 2003a). David Levy, who was also pivotal in the development of Rorschach analysis in the US, organised a 'personality screening center' during the war (Herman, 1995; Rose, 1999), and William C. Menninger organised most of the general military recruit screening as Chief Psychiatric Consultant to the Surgeon General of the Army (Menninger, 2004).

Hegarty (2003a) outlined how in screening procedures in the US military, potential servicemen were screened for homosexuality amongst other things. Recruits were encouraged to be honest with psychiatrists about any concerns about homosexuality, yet such concerns were then directly reported to military officials. Psychiatrists therefore acted as both therapist for a supposed mental disorder and also as informants. Hegarty (2003a) noted how some psychiatrists deliberately misdiagnosed some men as to avoid then being dishonourably discharged, whereas others specifically developed the Rorschach in order to distinguish between those men who were true 'sexual psychopaths' and those were malingering as such to avoid service.

In total, 3,000 psychologists in the US assisted in the war effort compared to 700 in the First World War (Herman, 1995) and Rorschach workers were no exception. In 1936, Bruno Klopfer had begun editing the *Rorschach Research Exchange*, having left Germany in 1933 like many Jewish intellectuals (Ellenberger, 1954; Million, Grossman, & Meagher, 2004; Lemov, 2011). On his way to the US he spent a year in Switzerland with Carl Jung and on his travels was introduced to the Rorschach. In 1939, he established the *Society for Projective Techniques and the Rorschach Institute*.[3] In addition, David Rapaport and Roy Shafer, who both worked at the Menninger Clinic with Klopfer, developed the Rapaport-Schafer Rorschach scoring system in the early 1940s (Rapaport, 1942, see Buchanan, 1997). Klopfer also organised a 'Volunteer Rorschach Unit' in 1942 for those who worked with the Rorschach and were in active service (Hegarty, 2003a). The Rorschach was therefore deeply integrated in military efforts during and after the War and continued to be extremely popular in American Psychology until the 1960s.

The British military were more wary of testing in general and projective testing in particular than their American counterparts. Although the Rorschach was not used for initial screening in either country, it was not used for assessment after battle or officer selection in Britain as it was in the US (Hegarty, 2003a). When the Rorschach was initially suggested for officer selection it was swiftly rejected in part because it was believed to be 'middle European absurdity on par with Kindergartens, Rudolf Steiner, Herbal tea and foreign plumbing' (Shephard, 2002, p. 193). Psychiatrists J.R. Rees and Ronald Hargreaves became consultants to the Army in 1939 and Rees initially unsuccessfully attempted to show the military the benefits of intelligence testing recruits (Shephard, 1999, 2002). In 1941, Rees was formally appointed as a Consultant Psychiatrist to the British Army and he assembled a group of psychologists and psychiatrists to deal with such military issues as the screening of recruits, the selection of officers and the rehabilitation of soldiers after battle (Bourke, 2001). War Officer Selection Boards (WOSBs) were set up in 1942 that combined the work of both psychologists conducting testing and psychiatrists conducting interviews to serve these ends. Those psychologists involved in the war effort included John Raven and Eric Trist from the Maudsley (though Trist joined the WOSBs in order get involved with the Tavistock group), as well as Tavistock psychiatrists such as John Bowlby, Rees, and Hargreaves (Shephard, 1999; Murphy, 2008).[4]

Projective tests were adapted as group tests for officer selection in Britain as in the US. From 1942 onward, potential officers were tested with self-description questionnaires, intelligence tests, the Word Association Test, the TAT, and physical military tests (Shephard, 2002; Murphy, 2008). Simeon Gillman's (1947) *Methods of Officer Selection in the Army* described the methods used for officer selection in Britain in the Second World War. These included failed tests of a modified Rorschach in Edinburgh for use in WOSBs. The intelligence tests and the modified group versions of the TAT and Word Association Test in contrast were deemed useful in providing 'personality pointers', which psychiatrists on WOSBs could expand upon in interviews with each officer (Gillman, 1947). In fact, Murphy (2008) recalled that it was his dislike of the Rorschach that lead him to be invited to become a sergeant tester/psychological assistant.

> I joined the Royal Armoured Corps in 1941 and after two years as a regimental instructor with armoured vehicles and a short period in hospital, where it was noted that I had argued with a visiting psychologist on the merits of her Rorschach test, it was decided that I might be better employed with WOSBs where there was a shortage of psychologists to carry out testing, and the category of sergeant tester/psychological assistant was invented.
>
> *(Murphy, 2008, p. 20)*

In sum, although there was some experimentation with projective testing for military ends in Britain, attitudes to the Rorschach were far more negative than those in the US.

The civilian experience of the Second World War also differed between the two countries, shaping the forms of psychological distress that would come to psychologists' attention. The war was not fought overseas for the British and the heavy bombing of London, often referred to as 'the Blitz', deeply impacted the lives of British people. The same wartime context that occasioned Bowbly's theory of attachment – the evacuation of children from London – also sparked the interest of Alcock. Alcock's first published paper, *The bombed child and the Rorschach test*, was a brief note published in the *British Medical Journal* in 1941. Alcock reported that 70 percent of her evacuee sample had 'fire or explosive K responses' to the ink blots, but cautioned that these children's responses might not necessarily be due to a 'bomb-induced neurosis'. The history of the Rorschach in Britain was therefore less about military strength as in the US, but more about the effects of war-related trauma, especially on children.

The Rorschach quickly became the most popular test in clinical practice in the US after the Second World War (Sundberg, 1961). After the war, the field of Clinical Psychology expanded exponentially in training and practice (Leveille, 2002; Scull, 2015). Post-war American psychologists aimed to maintain a scientific discipline that was increasingly statistical and to prove the utility of scientist-practitioners who would apply Psychology to an expanding range of contexts. New schemes of Rorschach interpretation that had become popular through military and forensic work included 'content analysis', which allowed for direct Freudian interpretations of responses to the ink blots, in a marked deviation from Rorschach's original focus (Phillips & Smith, 1953). These dubious schemes raised concerns among statistically minded psychologists who developed the language of 'test validity' and 'construct validity' to manage the investment of trust in psychological tests in clinical contexts (Cronbach, 1949; Meehl, 1954; see Buchanan, 1997; Wood et al., 2003). Research output on the Rorschach peaked, and the tests were taken up enthusiastically by heavily funded social scientists, who often carried them to remote locations to make sense of unfamiliar societies (Lemov, 2011), but tensions between pro- and anti-projective methods began to emerge.

Such tensions were also very evident across the Atlantic in Britain. The scientist-practitioner model also took hold in Britain in the 1950s as it did in the US and so trainee clinical psychologists completed training in therapy as well as research (Pilgrim & Treacher, 1992). This balance between science and practice played out very differently in different institutions in London. At the Maudsley, under Hans Eysenck's influence, psychotherapy and psychoanalysis were critiqued (see Pilgrim & Treacher, 1992; Derksen, 2001a; Buchanan, 2003), while the Tavistock remained an institutional base for psychodynamic thinking (Derksen, 2001a). The tension between the two institutions shaped the uptake of the Rorschach test in the practice and in the training of British practitioners.

The first programme in Clinical Psychology in Britain was taught at the Institute of Psychiatry, which was positioned at the Maudsley in 1946. Lewis, who had been critical of the Rorschach as early as 1934, was Chair of Psychiatry at the Institute from 1946 until his retirement in 1966. In 1942, Lewis employed Eysenck, following a recommendation from Philip Vernon (Jensen, 1989; Hall, 2007b; Buchanan, 2010). Eysenck took over the role of Senior Research Officer previously held by Eric Trist who had by then gone to work at the Tavistock to continue his interest in projective methods (Trist, 1993; Buchanan, 2010). Eysenck oversaw the training of the first British clinical psychologists at the Institute of Psychiatry from 1947 onward, but the training itself was mainly the responsibility of psychologist Monte Shapiro (Buchanan, 2010). Shapiro, however, did not wish to teach the Rorschach himself and instead employed Swiss expert Maryse Israel to provide Rorschach training in the late 1940s (Buchanan, 2010). By 1955, those at the Maudsley had decided to discontinue using the Rorschach.

In fact, a 'critical discussion' meeting was held on Saturday May 21, 1955 and all members of the Committee of Professional Psychologists were invited to give their comments on this decision. The discussion appears to have done nothing but confirm the anti-Rorschach position of many at the Maudsley. The Maudsley training programme dominated clinical teaching in Britain producing twice as many graduates as the Tavistock, whose courses declined further in the 1970s (Buchanan, 2010). Eysenck's 1959 scathing review in Buros' influential *Mental Measurements Yearbook* described no less than ten damning criticisms of the Rorschach's validity, likened the test to phrenology, and concluded that "the Rorschach has failed to establish its scientific or practical value" (Buros, 1959, p. 277).

The British Rorschach Forum

In contrast, to the anti-Rorschach position at the Maudsley, a small Rorschach group formed and persisted at the more psychoanalytic Tavistock Institute. Having discussed the Rorschach via letters throughout the war, psychologists Theodora Alcock, Eric Trist, and Psychiatrist C.J.C. Earl formed the *British Rorschach Forum* at the Tavistock Institute in 1942, ten years before the founding of the International Rorschach Society. Earl was one of the first in Britain to use the Rorschach, and his work at Caterham Hospital in South London had influenced Theodora Alcock's paper on evacuated children. Dr. W.E.R Mons – a Swiss Psychiatrist who had had also informed Alcock's early work – was Honorary Chairman of the Forum. Alcock was its first Honorary Vice Chairman. Herbert Phillipson, who had worked on WOSBs and began to work at the Tavistock from 1945, was Honorary Secretary. All of the society's technical meetings, summer conferences, workshops, seminars, and courses took place at the Tavistock from the late 1940s to the late 1990s.

Alcock was considered the main driving force of interest in the Rorschach in Britain (McCarthy Woods, 2008). Her presence in this history reiterates my point in Chapter 1 that the history of the Rorschach is ripe for feminist investigation. Here I will briefly outline her life in relation to the Rorschach before returning back to the history of the Rorschach Forum more generally.

'Miss' (Augusta) Theodora Alcock, or 'Theo' as she was known to friends, was born in 1888. Very little is known about her childhood and early life. In 1933 she joined the Tavistock where she discovered the Rorschach. She worked as a playgroup leader and as a Child Guidance Officer during the Second World War (Phillipson, 1981). After the war she became one of the clinic's first child psychotherapists. Presumably she did not gain a doctorate as she is continually referred to as 'Miss' throughout *The Rorschach Newsletter* and its subsequent publications. This indicated not only her lack of doctorate level qualification but also her unmarried status. Having discovered the Rorschach Alcock effectively established Rorschach interest in Britain and led the way for a formalised projective testing movement. Alcock was often thought of as the mother of the Rorschach in Britain. One oral history participant reported that:

> She was a lovely lady. I think that I probably do not remember much of her apart from meeting her because I was full of awe.

In 1954 Alcock's commitment to teaching continued when the Tavistock appointed her to teach the Rorschach summer schools, which carried on until her semi-retirement in 1968. Those who were taught by her reported that:

> This was one of the most enjoyable and fruitful training occasions of my life. We met weekly and she ruled us quietly, but with a rod of iron, and woe betide any of us who had not completed this week's programme
>
> *– Dr Geoffrey Barker*

> I learnt an awful lot in the seminars apart from the use of the Rorschach. Her basic psychoanalytic understanding, and her even more basic attitudes of respect – and indeed, love – for her subjects was of inestimable value . . . she always had a light and unassuming touch in talking about her work and ideas. She gave much time, and gave unstinting thought, to help her students understand the records that they took, and the subjects from whom they had taken them
>
> *– Mrs Celia Williams*
> *(In Phillipson, 1981)*

Alcock was not only involved in the British scene; she visited the US in 1961 upon the invitation of Bruno Klopfer, and France in 1964. In 1963 she published her book *The Rorschach in Practice* which was highly celebrated in Britain (Kaldegg, 1964). She also went to Dublin to teach the Rorschach and become more involved with religious groups. She became Roman Catholic and in 1967 moved to Dublin permanently from her home in Yorkshire. Her Rorschach work continued and in 1971 she established the Irish Rorschach Forum.

Returning now to the Society itself, in 1952, the associated biannual publication *The Rorschach Newsletter* was published. It ran until 1997, perhaps somewhat later than many Rorschach critics would have expected. In the first issue, it was announced that Earl had resigned as Chairman due to ill-health, but would remain the Honorary Vice-President of the Forum. The society was initially exclusive in its membership, its object being to "safe-guard professional standards in the use of the Rorschach and restrict membership to society selection" (Editorial, Williams, 1952). Membership was to be decided by a subcommittee and required the candidate to be 'experienced and proficient'.[5] However, the society also expressed an aim to widen its interests to other projective tests early on. Methodologically, the group was focused on case studies, and the aim of *The Rorschach Newsletter* was to "enable all members of the Rorschach Forum to keep in touch with work that is being done" (Editorial, Williams, 1952).

To understand why Rorschach testing might have remained confined to this small Tavistock-based group, it is necessary not only to consider the lack of national investment in the projective hypothesis during wartime and the influence of the Maudsely on training, but also to consider other major institutional changes in Britain after the war. In 1948, the National Health Service (NHS) was founded on socialist principles that health care should be free and available to all irrespective of the ability to pay, altering the ways in which mental health services were provided in Britain (Hall, 2007a; Hayward, 2014). General practitioners were expected to have greater psychiatric knowledge than before (Hayward, 2014) and the role of clinical psychologists became more clearly defined (Derksen, 2001a).[6] The Rorschach was therefore in clinical use in Britain in some sites beyond the Tavistock, such as Tooting Bec Hospital in London (e.g., Scott, 1965; Barker, 1970), and in Child Guidance Clinics (e.g., O'Kelly, 1972). Many vocational centres also adopted projective methods for assessment in the following decades (see Orford, 1965; Kaldegg, 1966).

The majority of Rorschach testers in Britain were psychologists. Earl had attempted to popularise the test among psychiatrists but with little success, mirroring the military's earlier rejection of it. Relatedly, the British scene was far more concentrated on psychotherapeutic uses of projective tests, unlike the US where the Rorschach was a frequent object of academic research. Few members of the Forum achieved academic posts – a notable exception being Boris Semeonoff, who taught Rorschach techniques from his position on the faculty at the University of Edinburgh. The use of projective tests in Scotland was also supported by Ralph and Ruth Pickford at the University of Glasgow, and John Raven described the three-year clinical psychologist training course provided by the Crichton Royal in

Scotland in 1956, which required experience of a whole range of tests, including the Rorschach. Due to the growing interest in the Rorschach, and the lack of uptake in universities, Alcock successfully ran training courses at the Tavistock in response to high demand from 1954 until her retirement in 1968 (McCully, 1981; McCarthy Woods, 2008). In sum, the Rorschach found a network in Britain, but one that was marginalised from academic Psychology and much less firmly embedded in clinical practice than in the US.

Despite the rejection of the use of projective tests in the 1960s in Britain, namely at the Maudsley, most Clinical Psychology training did include some use of projective techniques. The following is an excerpt from an oral history of someone who did their undergraduate degree in Psychology in Britain then went on to be trained as a clinical psychologist in the late 1960s:

> I do remember us going to . . . hospital in [Northern city in England] so thirty of us students sat in this room and a patient was bought in and quote "demonstrated" to us. I mean, we weren't even trainee psychologists, when I look back at it I mean it was a grossly humiliating and demeaning experience but that was standard. So when I started my clinical training course in 1966, I had no real understanding of the range of assessment methods that – so when I started I didn't have doubt about it, I didn't know anything about psychological assessments at all anyway. . . . So as a trainee we would routinely give patients projective tests in particular, the Rorschach and the TAT, um, I hesitate to say whether they needed to be assessed but actually to give us clinical practise using that. . . . So I can remember the first few times using the Rorschach and I have to say being somewhat sceptical about but it but then becoming fascinated by the fact that essentially you're showing people these random series of, of meaningless ink blots and how then the ten narratives of the patients hung together. And you could see that certain themes were emerging from them.

Testing was clearly viewed as important for clinical psychologists. All trainees on this particular course were expected to be knowledgeable of intelligence scales, cognitive abilities, attainment tests and personality tests, including projective ones. In all, there were 31 psychological tests they were required to learn. One of the exam questions that was posed to this oral history participant whilst training in the late 1960s was: "Describe briefly any diagnostic problem where one might use a projective technique and why."

Trainee Psychologists (outside of the Maudsley) saw psychological testing, and that included projective testing, as an essential part of the tool kit for a psychologist. The person I interviewed went on to say:

> So behaviour therapy was really just still a twinkle in people's eyes and so the core role of the psychologists was very seen as an assessor and a researcher. And if you were going to be an assessor then you were seen to need to know

> something about projective tests, not least because a psychiatrist whose own training in Psychology would have been lamentable, would have expected it. You know it was entirely on the cards that when you were on a ward rounds that a psychiatrists would say "Should we try a projective test?" and so we, as a young psychologists said "Oh yes yes let's try that."

Despite an overwhelming sense that projective tests were becoming much less popular compared to other more cognitive tests, some Rorschach users maintained their support. Another oral history participant who used the Rorschach reported:

> Well I'm of course a defender of the Rorschach but having also worked with the MMPI and the WAIS and things like that . . . they all function on cortex level, conscious, the Rorschach does not function on that level, so it tells you many things that you don't even find out when you do a psychoanalytic interview. Because it depends on what the person wants to tell you. Consciously or unconsciously.

On August 4, 1968, the work amassed using the Rorschach in Britain climaxed at the seventh International Rorschach Congress held in London under the title 'The Projective Approach to the Study of Personality'. The six-day congress was opened by Bowlby, and has become viewed by Rorschach users as the high point of British Rorschach history (Campo, 1993; McCarthy Woods, 2008). It was criticised by some international visitors who reported that it was 'very British' and had lost the 'international element' (McCully & Palmquist, 1968). Despite this, the conference was deemed very successful and drew in a large crowd of projective workers.

However, by this time, scientific criticisms of the Rorschach's validity became increasingly inescapable (see also Meehl, 1954; Suinn & Oskamp, 1969; see Buchanan, 1997; Wood et al., 2003). By 1961, the Minnesota Multiphastic Personality Inventory (MMPI) had become more popular than the Rorschach as a diagnostic test in the US for the first time (Buchanan, 1997). The anti-psychiatry movement also gave vocal critique to the power of testing and diagnosis without consent or transparency (Crossley, 1998). This movement, which was tied to gay liberation movements in some ways, is explored in more detail in Chapter 6. Critique about the Rorschach had progressed beyond demonstrations of projective tests' lack of validity, but also included cognitive explanations of the illusory diagnostic power of the Rorschach test (Chapman & Chapman, 1969). That is to say, Rorschach testers reported seeing 'signs' in a person's responses that correlated with their diagnosis, even when such signs were not actually present.

In this context, John Exner breathed new life into the Rorschach by reviewing the US history in terms of the five major systems of Rorschach interpretation that had developed, and acknowledging that those systems all fell short of psychologists' standards of test validity (Exner, 1969). Exner proposed a new 'comprehensive' system of interpretation, which held out the promise of addressing those criticisms (Exner, 1969, 1993, 2003). In the US, Exner's work was taken up enthusiastically despite ongoing criticism of the Rorschach test (Wood et al., 2003). While some participants in the British Rorschach Forum recall the global influence of Exner's work at this time, his work did not revive the test's reputation in Britain.

The British Rorschach Forum adopted the strategy of broadening the group's focus from the Rorschach to a wider range of projective techniques. In June 1968, the title of the journal was changed to the *British Journal of Projective Psychology and Personality Study*. Simultaneously, the *British Rorschach Forum* changed its name to the *British Rorschach Forum and Society for Projective Techniques*. These changes were made to "reflect development in the scope of the society's interests, which now include a range of projective techniques in addition to the Rorschach" (Editorial, Williams, 1968). In 1970, the name of the society was changed again to the *British Society for Projective Psychology and Personality Study* omitting the word 'Rorschach' altogether. Other attempts to widen membership led the society away from its earlier strategy of making membership exclusive to experts. Mirroring the uptake of Exner's system in the US, more attempts were made to include psychotherapists in the group by loosening membership restrictions (Mahmood, 1986). Appropriately, this was also a moment for historical review. In June 1968, Alfred Friedemann, then Secretary General of the International Rorschach Society, published the first history of Rorschach testing in Britain (Friedemann, 1968), which celebrated the developments of the Rorschach in Europe, its associations with psychoanalysis, and the achievements of the British society led by the teaching of Alcock. These changes were not successful in offsetting criticism of the test's validity. Writing in the *British Medical Journal*, Rollin (1970) predicted that the Rorschach would soon be no more in British Psychology, and posited in the event of a "psychologist of the year (or decade) award" then it "must go to Professor H. J. Eysenck, the most famed and English, perhaps the world, stage. . . . And if a toast were to be drunk to absent friends then it would be to poor Dr. Rorschach and his ink blots." (p. 543).

Several changes in the journal's contents are evident in the 1970s. Reflecting the broader focus, fewer Rorschach papers appeared and more journal space was devoted to studies using the TAT and the Object Relations Test (ORT). Speaking to the inescapable concerns about the validity of projective tests, studies with an experimental design became more common, quite in contrast to the society's original commitment to case studies. From 1968, a greater proportion of articles were contributed from overseas countries including India, the US, Canada, and Spain. This pattern continued for decades and in his 1989 editorial Mahmood, who edited the *British Journal of Projective Techniques* after 1985, suggested the British readers should try to match the interest shown by their international colleagues.

By the 1980s, surveys began to show psychologists had firmly moved away from projective techniques in Britain, as they had begun to do in the US. In 1987, Dr L.F. Lowenstein published a literature review under the title 'Are Projective Techniques Dead?' in the *British Journal of Projective Psychology*. Referencing the survey of US psychologists reported by Pruitt, Smith, Thelen, and Lubin (1985), Lowenstein argued that projective techniques were far from dead, but undeniably used much less frequently than in previous decades. Similarly, Mahmood (1984) described the

Rorschach as more popular in several other countries – including the US – than in Britain. Also in the *British Journal of Projective Psychology*, Elias (1989) published a paper reviewing the projective scene in the US. Elias (1989) certainly referenced a "lessening of fervent interest in projective techniques" (p. 33) in the US but maintained that projective tests remained very much in use in psychodynamic psychiatric and psychological centres.

An oral history participant explained how, in 1980 when they became a Head Clinical Psychologist, they also became responsible for:

> a number of shelves full of beautiful psychological tests, all made out of hard wood lithography and one thing or another. But I also became the guardian of *the* set of Rorschach cards for the adult mental health department. I remained in that post for 22 years, I remained guardian of the Rorschach cards and I don't think that in those 22 years I was ever asked by anyone to use the Rorschach cards.

This scene in Britain is in contrast to several other countries. For example, the Rorschach is still taught to every clinical psychologist in France and the spread of psychoanalysis has continued. The removal of projective tests from the training of clinical psychologists in the 1970s and 1980s was therefore distinctly strict in Britain.

More 'objective' standardised tests (named according to the *Mental Measurements Yearbook* projective/objective dichotomy), such as cognitive and IQ tests increased in use as the use of projective test decreased (Buchanan, 1997). This switch of testing preference can be somewhat attributed to increasing concerns surrounding validity, reliability, and the statistical nature of tests from the 1950s (e.g. Cronbach & Meehl, 1955). The development of the Diagnostic Statistical Manual from 1952 (DSM, Grob, 1991) and North American attempts in 1954 to standardise tests such as the Rorschach (APA, *Technical Recommendations for Psychological Tests and Diagnostic Techniques*) indicate the increased emphasis on validity and statistical approaches. Also from the 1950s, there was an additional concern regarding the ethics of testing and the appropriateness of psychologists' reliance on psychological tests (Hetherington, 1981).

In 1980, the Standing Committee on Test Standards was established by the British Psychological Society (BPS, Tyler & Miller, 1986). This group instigated a survey of BPS members regarding their attitudes towards tests, how frequently they were used, and which ones were utilised. According to Poortinga et al. (1982), this was done in reaction to the anti-test attitudes from the 1950s and "societal discontent about psychological assessment." An initial questionnaire was circulated with the BPS Bulletin in May 1980. The first questionnaire was returned by 1425 psychologists and 567 respondents returned the second questionnaire. Most respondents were clinical and educational psychologists. Sixty percent of respondents said the purposes of test use were 'selecting assessment' or diagnosis for more than half the time, or for 'selecting treatment goals'. Cognitive/intelligence tests were the most commonly used, followed by achievement/attainment tests (unsurprisingly most popular among educational psychologists). In third place were personality tests (which were more popular among clinical psychologists) and finally developmental tests. For personality tests, questionnaires were the most popular measure, with attitudes measures and personal construct measures following a close second. Projective tests came in third place. For those clinical psychologists who did use projective methods, the Bene-Anthony Family Relations Test, the Rorschach, and the TAT were the most commonly used. However, the Rorschach was criticised more often by respondents than they were supported.

In 1988, Mahmood published research on the attitudes and opinions of the British projective society members (of which there were 48 in total). Of the 33 members who replied to his survey, only about one-quarter of members frequently used projective tests and half used projective tests 'occasionally'. Ninety percent of members surveyed agreed that the use of projective tests had declined, and only 56 percent believed the tests had a future. Mahmood echoed this belief, describing one participant who believed that the use of projective tests had not declined as 'an incurable optimist'. Of the reasons for this decline, 83 percent reported that it was because of the changes in Clinical Psychology practice and in the roles of psychologists. They cited a focus away from assessment toward a focus on therapy, especially behavioural therapies with outpatient populations meaning that "the types of patients and problems referred to them . . . do not require a traditional diagnostic assessment" (Mahmood, 1988). Only 23 percent of respondents reported that the decline of the use of projective tests was due to their non-scientific status.

In the same year, the title of the journal was changed to *British Journal of Projective Psychology* under which it continued until 1997, with Mahmood as editor until 1995. Mahmood (1988) stated that contributors needed to demonstrate projective tests' usefulness in modern Psychology so that projective techniques did not become "nothing but a blot on the landscape of Psychology." However, there were few successes in convincing others of the utility of the Rorschach test in Britain after 1988. Again, this situation contrasts with the boost to projective testing that occurred in Forensic Psychology in the late 1980s and early 1990s in the US (Wood et al., 2003). In contrast to the US, there was little revival of the Rorschach after this point in Britain; however, a small amount of Rorschach work continued at the Tavistock into the 21st century (McCarthy Woods, 2008).

Detecting women, detecting homosexuality

Embedded within the history of the Rorschach outlined in the previously section are some substantial queer and feminist themes. In this section I will explore some of the 'gay signs' that psychologists were looking for on the Rorschach and also outline some of the cures and experiences of queer people taking projective tests. But to begin I want to emphasise how different the British projective scene was in terms of gender representation.

As outlined in the introduction, the acceptance of women into British Psychology was generally slow. Both Oxford and Cambridge universities were reluctant to accept women students (Shields, 2007), many military positions for psychologists were closed to women (Bohan, 1990), and the pressure to choose *either* a career or marriage was common (Milar, 2000; also see Buchanan, 2003; Myers, 2012). Yet, women were well-represented among British clinical psychologists until the 1950s. The original Committee of Professional Psychologists established in 1943 within the British Psychological Society was overwhelmingly made up of women and early meetings of this group included no men at all. The representation of women was tied to the focus on working with children, which was considered more suited to women in the middle of the 20th century. Women were often persuaded into such areas as they were more receptive and offered more opportunity (Rutherford et al., 2015). The evacuation of children from London during the Second World War heightened a concern for research and therapy with children in Britain (Richards, 2000).

However, from the 1950s onward new members of the Committee of Professional Psychologists were increasingly likely to be men (Hall, 2007b), and the original emphasis on educational and child psychology was subsumed by the growth of adult clinical psychology (Hall, 2007b). In both Britain and in the US, the influx of men into Clinical Psychology in the 1950s was precipitated by deliberate attempts to articulate a vision of a mentally healthy relationship between family and work around male breadwinners and female homemakers – effectively pushing women back into the home (Morawski & Agronick, 1991; Herman, 1995; Jennings, 2007a).[7]

Yet, in the marginal British projective community, women remained surprisingly well-represented even in the 1950s and 1960s despite the growing dominance of men in Psychology generally. Bohan (1990) has suggested that women psychologists often found work in testing because it was sometimes believed to require less technical knowledge than other forms of Psychology, and was viewed as lower status. This argument applies to the British Rorschach Forum. In 1958, there were eight women and five men on the committee, and women occupied 62–71 percent of committee positions until 1969. In December 1966, a register showed that 48 percent of all society fellows, members, and associates were women. Among the first authors of publications in *The Rorschach Newsletter* from 1952 to 1968, 41 percent were women, 58 percent were men, and 1 percent could not be identified. In contrast, there were few women among notable US Rorschach researchers, excluding Marguerite Hertz, Molly Harrower-Erickson, and Evelyn Hooker (who features heavily in Chapter 3).

However, at the December 1968 Annual General Meeting, following the 1968 international congress in London, one woman and seven men were elected onto the committee of the new *British Rorschach Forum and Society for Projective Techniques*. Women never again made up a majority of the committee. But individual women did occupy important roles after this point. Notably, psychologist Liz Gleed was Chair of the forum 1982 and Editor of the journal from 1995. Plus, women remained highly represented in the membership, for example in 1971, 48 percent of the published list of members were women and this did not include Theodora Alcock as Honorary Vice-President as she had retired in 1968 (McCarthy Woods, 2008).

Not only did the World Wars impact who was considered to be appropriate to do projective testing, it also impacted who was thought to be appropriate to be tested. For example, following the Second World War, the Rorschach was used on the Nazis trialled at Nuremburg (Dimsdale, 2015). Brunner (2001) recorded this history of psychologists attempting to assess if the Nazis were mad or bad, and quotes Hermann Göring stating in 1946:

> Oh those crazy cards again . . . *you know one of the old gents said you showed him a lot of vulgar pictures.*
>
> *(emphasis original, Brunner, 2001, p. 233)*

Dimsdale (2015) also accounts for the use of the Rorschach with Nazis. He described the Rorschach as being a 'musty . . . relic'; nonetheless, he describes the responses of those being trialled and considered the Rorschach testing as "an enormous and unusual effort in the history of medicine. Never before have we studied so closely leaders who had steered a country into such an abyss" (p. 4).

In the US military the Rorschach was used to diagnose and detect homosexuality, though there was less emphasis on detecting sexuality in Britain. The Second World War was the first occurrence of psychiatric exclusion based on homosexuality (Bérubé, 1990) and the Rorschach was used to detect 'homosexuals' as well as straight men malingering as gay as to avoid active service (Hegarty, 2003a). In America, there was a wealth of research on the topic, which was somewhat emphasised by the Cold War (Lemov, 2011), and the concerns surrounding masculinity (Nicholson, 2011). British psychologists, however, did not conduct research to the same extent on the detection of homosexuality during or after the war.

In fact, in 1922 there was a, perhaps surprising, suggestion in Britain that 'tougher' soldiers coped better by 'resorting openly to perverted practises' (aka having sex with one another, p. 109 as cited in Bourke, 2001). These ideas that in some way same-sex attraction would benefit soldiers was repeated in 1937 by R.E. Money-Kyrle who argued that 'unconscious inverts' were likely to turn their aggressive natures towards the enemy and defend their fellow soldiers (Bourke, 2001). In 1942 Berg further distinguished the kinds of men who could be potentially desirable and those who were not. He separated 'homosexuals' into two types: the 'active invert' and the 'passive invert'. The 'active invert' is the type which, presumably, Money-Kyrle was describing. These 'active inverts' were said to be aggressive in battle and good soldiers, their only 'danger' being long periods of inactivity. The 'passive invert' however was continually dangerous, and was said to be liable to psychological collapse, likely to panic and surrender and to lack aggression. Berg also describes how he felt that unfortunately such men are incurable as the 'inverts' argued that it was in their nature to be 'homosexual' (Anderson, 1956 as cited in Bourke, 2001).

Such suggestions, though affirmative in part, are steeped in ideas of queerness being equated to femininity and thus passivity and the late 19th-century conceptualisation of the 'homosexual invert' clearly remained.

In the Second World War, Hegarty (2003a) argued that according to these Rorschach researchers, the 'homosexual personality' appeared in those with particularly colourful descriptions, who utilised the brightest ink on the cards. The response of "huge repulsive breasts covered with the most exquisite delicate brown silk" was considered evidence of 'genuine' homosexuality, as it revealed an unconscious disgust with the feminine body and a simultaneous attempt to disguise the fact (p. 409). Any response that alluded to both a desire for, and fear of, penetration, was also said to be indicative of a 'homosexual personality'. Specific responses regarding this were often objects which moved between or within other objects, for example, "a ship cleaving through water" (Hegarty, 2003a).

In the US, Due and Wright (1945) and Fein (1950) conducted research on what they believed were clear diagnostic signs of homosexuality. These included seeing feminine clothing; ambiguously sexed figures, sexual content, and castration/phallic symbols in the ink blot (Due & Wright, 1945; Lindner, 1946). Similarly, having an artistic interpretation or one which could be viewed as paranoid (e.g. seeing masks or eyes) was also indicative of homosexuality (Due & Wright, 1945). Wheeler (1949) disagreed with the methods of Linder and the interpretations of Due and Wright and so developed his 20 signs of homosexuality using the Rorschach. His conclusions were that a gay man could be identified when he presented as a somewhat paranoid person with derogatory attitudes towards women despite a feminine identification (Wheeler, 1949). He also reported that gay men had sexual fixations, especially anal ones, and paid attention to relationships between 'similar beings' (i.e. those of the same gender). To see a mask, eyes or faces in a Rorschach ink blot considered a particular sign of paranoia in the psychological literature indicating homosexuality (Dubrin, 1962).

Schafer (1954) also disagreed with Lindner (1946) and moved towards more thematic analysis of Rorschach responses, whilst maintaining reliance on Due and Wright (1945) and Wheeler (1949). Under the theme of 'Fear of and Rejecting Attitude Toward Masculine Identity; Feminine Identification in Men' Schafer (1954) included responses which were ambiguous or 'mixed' about gender representation; responses with a 'feminine emphasis'; or those with reference to 'perversions' such as 'lesbians embracing' (p. 136). Though considered less often, Schafer (1954) also recognised women's responses that were considered evidence of 'Fear of and Rejecting Attitude Toward Feminine Identity; Masculine Identification in Women' and referred to the first piece of projective research on 'female homosexuality' by Fromm and Elonen (1951). Themes for these women included the same 'signs' of gender reversal, 'masculine emphasis', and 'perversions' but also included rejecting women's 'conventional feminine role and status' (p. 137).

Lowenstein and Lowenstein (1984) in their review of research on homosexuality after 1978 indicated a mixed bag of research. Some researchers still promoted the use of treatments including 'exceptional methods' such as exorcism, religious conversion, and castration; whereas others began to allude to social prejudice impacting the lives of gay men rather than their sexuality directly. In all, they argued, since the early 1980s there had been a move away from attempting to 'cure' homosexuality.

The Rorschach was therefore used as a tool to detect, diagnose, and define the 'homosexual personality'. The history of the test in Britain and the US is one which includes military intervention, therapeutic practices, and academic research; but what was it like being tested at this point in time?

Being tested with the Rorschach

In drawing on archived oral histories from both the Mental Health Testimony Archive and the Hall-Carpenter Archive at the British Library, it is easy to draw parallels with the interview I discussed at the beginning of this chapter and my own experience of being tested with the Rorschach. One of the notable features of the four oral histories referring to the Rorschach and/or psychiatric treatment of homosexuality from the British Library is that they were all from women. Indeed, the gendered social roles of the mid-20th century and the expectations of women remained a feature in some of the interviews. For example, one woman appeared to have a difficult relationship with a psychiatric nurse whilst she was in hospital and explained their animosity via the expectations of women:

> I don't know what was the matter with her. She was . . . [laughs] well you say oh yes, she was a frigid spinster, I don't know . . . you do get people like that, women don't like younger women, you know, especially married and got a family, all the rest of it.

An older unmarried woman is therefore presented within a 'spinster' framework and this is undoubtedly considered both amusing and derogatory. Similarly, queer women tested with the Rorschach similarly felt these pressures around enforced femininity and representing 'proper' (heteronormative) womanhood.

Several queer women whose interviews are in the Hall-Carpenter archive explained some of the difficulties they had fighting against their 'tomboy' personas and described a severe dislike of the social heterosexual expectations that were applied to them. Jennings (2007a) also draws upon these oral histories in her exploration of British lesbian women's lives from 1945–1971. In her more recent work on Sandra Willson, Jennings (2013) explored how Wilson's lesbianism was viewed as symptomatic by psychiatrists during her psychiatric treatment and imprisonment for murder in Australia. She received electro-convulsion therapy amongst other interventions in attempt to 'cure' her.

Within the oral history records, one queer woman described being almost forced by a youth group worker to seek psychiatric help at fourteen for her being a lesbian:

> You don't have to be [a lesbian], you can be cured . . . and he produced this little card in a little envelope, with the name of a doctor on it. Dr . . . at the Stepney Jewish Hospital and it was this . . . the, anyway the point I'm trying

> to make is the appointment had already been made for me with this Doctor
> at the Stepney Jewish Hospital. And Peter said: will you go? And I said yes, I
> will go and see this Doctor . . . and he gave me this card

The card was then accidently intercepted by her mother who begged her not to go.
Her mother still had memories of Nazi Germany and told her that once 'they' got
hold of her name she would be in the records.

For those who did see a psychiatrist projective tests appear to have been especially memorable.

> Well they were called . . . some of them . . . they were world tests and synonym
> tests. Some of them were ink blobs. Somebody had made special kinds of blobs
> onto a piece of paper . . . I think they were called the Rorschach . . . R O R S C
> H A C H . . . I think it was, test . . . and you had to . . . usually they say "What
> springs to your mind when you look at this?", and what people say is very
> indicative of their state of mind, although they don't realise that at the time.

Another queer woman also remembered the different forms of tests that she was
subjected to:

> I just remember sort of being in the locked ward, and . . . I did see a Psychia-
> trist I think once a week, a male one, who, most of the time just asked how
> I was, and . . . showed me blotting paper . . . had all these tests of . . . shapes
> on blotting paper, and what they reminded me of
>   And most of the time they have you the blotting paper to look at, and ask
> you questions that you didn't want to answer, like about your childhood or
> your parents . . . and . . . those like square block things you had to put in the
> right shape, you know.

The preceding passages not only indicate how the Rorschach was used within psychiatric settings but also allude to the suggestion that psychologists and psychiatrists
were perceived as mere testers. There is also some suggestion that the Lowenfeld
tests were used; for example, the 'square block things you had to put in the right
shape' may refer to the Mosaic Test and the 'world test' could be Lowenfeld's World
Technique.

The deception used in testing practices experienced by the person I interviewed
and evidence in the preceding passages is also noted by Derksen (2001b) in his
exploration of the manual of four psychological tests. In relation to the projective
test called the 'Four Picture Test' those being tested are deliberately told there are
four unrelated cards which are spread out and whilst pointing to each one in an
arbitrary order testers state "You can choose the order in which they are to appear,
you can start here, here or here." The second edition of the manual also stated testers
should say: "you are completely free to choose" (Derksen, 2001b, p. 37). However,
the order that is chosen is in fact the first aspect of the test that is analysed. The

feelings that the oral history participants felt, especially in relation to projective tests is certainly one which in some cases is embedded within the procedure of testing, and deception can be rather deliberate.

Such skepticism of the tactics used and the usefulness of the Rorschach was not only felt in psychological circles at this time, but also by some of those being tested. The following shows how the same queer woman who had been previously given the Rorschach when diagnosed with depression was especially amused once again to be provided with an ink blot test during a later prison sentence:

> I remember sitting in front of this psychiatrist and . . . and I couldn't believe it when more blotting paper come out . . . [laughs]. I thought blotting paper days had gone and I just started taking the mick out of . . . mickey out of him, you know, but . . . I was making things up. He was saying, "what does this one . . ." and I was saying "Donald Duck". You know, told him he looked like Alfred Hitchcock, and he wasn't impressed and he said "I don't think I need to see you again", you know and I didn't need to see him either, you know, so that was my psychiatric treatment in the whole of the . . . sentence.

A mismatch between expectation and reality appears to be a common thread throughout the testimonies of those who were tested with the Rorschach. In fact, all of the people I conducted oral histories with reported that clients tended not to expect tests, yet it does remain a common misconception that psychologists are mind-readers, and that the tests act like 'X-rays' of the mind. One of my oral history participants described how, at the time of being tested, he felt psychologists had this ability.

> I still had, I picked up the notion you had some ability to read people's minds and kind of empathise, it think it was a bit enthralled by, I don't think I was particularly critical

Yet later, having been trained, this participant expressed the annoyance of others making this assumption:

> But the moment you go "I'm a psychologist" you get the "Oh, I don't want sit next to you then" or "hahaha can you tell what I'm thinking?" and that happens at parties but it happens with clients as well.

The assumptions that psychologists have mind-reading abilities, or super powers, has many connotations given the power psychologists can hold. By extension, the tests also exercise power on their own, but especially in the hands of psychologists. One of the central ways psychological tests had power was in the ways this power was enacted upon queer people and framed 'homosexuality' as something to be prevented, avoided, and treated. Queer people were considered to be pathological perverts with neurosis and psychopathic tendencies. They were distinctly not normal.

What a test does

The ways in which psychologists have deduced if people are 'normal' or not have changed dramatically throughout the last century, as demonstrated by the preceding history of the Rorschach. And tests are developed with one basic idea in mind – to tell if you can be categorised as 'normal' or not. Foucault in his thinking about medical and psychiatric sciences reminds us:

> if you are not like everybody else, then you are abnormal, if you are abnormal, then you are sick. These three categories, not being like everybody else, not being normal and being sick are in fact very different but have been reduced to the same thing
>
> *Michel Foucault in interview, 1975*[8]

The changes in test preference and use illustrate the socio-historical shifts and cultural understandings of psychological tests throughout Psychology's past. The tests themselves are therefore constructed and historically situated. As demonstrated by the influences on and from the Rorschach, psychological testing is not intrinsically objective and value free. Tests are evidently constructed in the sense that they are developed and created by psychologists, by real people. They do not grow on trees, nor do they emerge from the psychological laboratory fully formed. Just like the games that the Rorschach was based on, such as 'Blotto' and 'Klexographie', the test itself is made. In fact, there were really supposed to be 15 ink blots but Hermann Rorschach was only allowed ten by the publisher. Therefore, arguing tests have a socially constructed nature may appear obvious. However, it is important to be aware of the effect of such testing. Tests are developed and, in turn, often also contribute to the construction of mental disorder. For example, intelligence is often defined by a person's score on series of IQ tests. The test, therefore, constructs what it means to have intelligence, despite the test's own constructed nature and aim to test a real thing. And these tests, and what we consider to be intelligence, has changed dramatically. One reason tests are so convincing in this manner are the statistics used to demonstrate that they can validly *do* what they claim to do.

Rose (1999) considered the precise British military context in which many psychological tests arose. Drawing heavily on the work of Foucault he described the developments of institutions and the documentation of information for classifications, which Hacking (1986, 2000) later echoed in several of the points he raised: that is, the creation categorisation of humans begins with the measurement and scaling of something (or someone) upon which 'normal' is ascribed to some components and non-normal is applied to others. By counting, generalising, and potentially pathologising, a 'human kind', or category of being, is created. What becomes specially judged, controlled, and accountable is not what a person *does* but rather what a person *is*.

Being queer is just one of the many ways of being categorised as a person that we understand today. As described in Chapter 1, the ways of being queer, for example, an 'invert', a 'lesbian', a 'pervert' for example – have changed historically. Indeed, today we might recognise ourselves and others as being left handed but this does not have the same consequences as being left handed did in the medieval period. This way of being is still a category but it holds much less social meaning and consequence nowadays. Those who are constructed into human kinds are, more often than not, the marginalised, the non-normal, the effect to be explained (Hegarty & Pratto, 2001). They are the 'other'. Adopting Foucauldian thinking, they are controlled, observed, and powerless (Foucault, 1975, see Downing, 2008). This can be somewhat evidenced in how the term 'invert' or 'homosexual' came around before the ideas of 'heterosexual' or 'straight', because before the conceptualisation of 'heterosexual' queer people were compared to 'normal'. The same is true for trans people, indicating the need for terms like 'cisgender' to identify the alternative group and prevent pathologisation of gender and sexuality minorities.[9]

The Rorschach can be seen as a means for both good and evil. This chapter has outlined how the Rorschach was used in actions we now recognise as homophobic and deeply problematic. It was used to pathologise and diagnose men as gay in the Second World War and was used as a tool for the 'treatment' of homosexuality for queer people throughout the 20th century. Yet, it has also been utilised to remove such pathologisation as we shall see in the next chapter. It is incredibly important to identify the scientific practices of racism (e.g. Gould, 1996), sexism (Bohan, 1990; Morawski & Agronick, 1991; Furumoto & Scarborough, 1986; Shields, 2007), and homophobia (e.g. Hegarty, 2003a; King & Bartlett, 1999) in Psychology. In addition, by conducting analysis on the 'goodies' and 'baddies' of history, with the motivation of doing anti-racist, anti-sexist, and anti-homophobic work, it is sometimes possible to complicate who the 'goodies' and 'baddies' were.

Indeed, it remains crucial to consider historical events in the context of their own time. As explored in Chapter 1 it is important to be mindful of presentism when thinking about the past. That is not to say, however, that we cannot look back on the actions of Psychology and describe its diagnoses and treatment of queer people as horrifically homophobic and transphobic (see Dickinson, 2015; King & Bartlett, 1999; Tosh, 2016; Stryker, 2008). Context is all important, but so is the recognition of the disciplinary systematic violence enacted upon queer people in Britain and the US in the 20th century. The Rorschach, like all psychological tests, is not a mere passive object. It *does* things (whether you think it is reliable or not). It diagnoses, projects, and creates the boundaries of 'normal'. But it also has power and action in terms of changing Psychology too. After all, the Rorschach was also central in the depathologisation of 'homosexuality' as a mental illness.

Notes

1 Both Oeser and Bartlett influenced Eric Trist who was later one of the founding members of the British Rorschach Forum. For more information on this group at Cambridge, see Kennedy (2014) for his autobiographical biography of Oeser and Trist's own autobiography Trist (1993).
2 The Rorschach Forum made Philip Vernon an Honorary Fellow in 1966 and later published a complimentary obituary (Semeonoff, 1987) despite his later distance from projective methods.

3 Prominent figures in this group included: Marguerite Hertz, David Rapaport, Zygmunt Piotrowski, Margaret Mead, and Mortimer Myers (Hertz, 1992).

4 At the beginning of the Second World War, the Maudsley was relocated further out of London, to Mill Hill School and Belmont Hospital due to threat of bombing in central London (Hall, 2007b). The Maudsley Hospital staff worked in Emergency Medical Services (Hall, 2007b). At Mill Hill, specialist neuropsychiatric units were developed, which provided aptitude tests, occupational therapy, and vocational training (Jones, Fear, & Wessely, 2007).

5 The exact qualification was not specified in the early issues of the journal but later attendance to Alcock's training courses was presumably sufficient. In addition to summer schools, there was also a three-year postgraduate course provided by the Tavistock Institute of Human Relations (Alcock, 1963).

6 Lowenfeld shared a common view among clinical practitioners that a national service would increase uniformity and interfere with personal contacts between patient and doctor (Urwin & Hood-Wiliams, 2013). Her Institute of Child Psychotherapy became a non-profit limited company in reaction to the founding of the NHS, but through an arrangement with the North West Regional Health Authority it continued to work with poorer children (Traill & Hood-Williams, 1973; Urwin & Hood-Wiliams, 2013).

7 In the US, the 'Servicemen's Readjustment Act' of 1944 and the 'Vocational Rehabilitation Act', commonly known as the 'G.I. Bill' prioritised veterans who wished to train in Psychology making the influx of men into Clinical Psychology even greater.

8 In Roger-Pol Droit (Ed.) (2004) *Michel Foucault, Entretiens.* 'Je suis un artificier'.

9 See Ansara and Hegarty (2012, 2014) for a discussion of cisgenderism in Psychology. I also recognise how the development of another binary (cis and trans gender) does not necessarily assist in the breakdown of the gender binary more broadly (that, is the belief that there is women and men only, to the exclusion of other genders such as non-binary and gender queer). However, I have used it here as a useful term to name the often invisible position. Like Pearce (2018) I consider cisgender to be "a broad, unstable, social category with fluid boundaries, denoting a range of social experiences" as opposed to a fixed discrete identity (p. 43).

3
QUEER APPROACHES TO DEPATHOLOGISATION

"An old Victorian oil lamp. The shape of the lamp. Two girls – at each side going to kiss each other. Big breasts, very slim, high heads, only one leg. Red lipstick." These are the responses to Rorschach ink blot Card number 3 by a woman 'who was deeply involved in a homosexual relationship' while at her stay in a psychiatric hospital in London in the late 1960s (Barker, 1970). Similarly, in my own testing experience in 2015, as another woman 'deeply involved in a homosexual relationship' I reported:

> Two figures, two women, stirring a big cooking pot, they're wearing tiny high heeled shoes, like old Victorian boots that are pointed. Their boobs and bums are sticking out. The red bit in the middle looks like lungs, with the bit joining them in the middle.

I also claimed to see two women in Card number 7 who both looked rather 'serene'. What strikes me now as I look at these cards is that not only do I still see these two women, much like the woman in the 1960s, but I can name the women I see. Now when I look at this card, I 'see' Evelyn Hooker and June Hopkins. Hooker's research was absolutely pivotal in the depathologisation of 'homosexuality' as a mental illness in the US and Hopkins' work, comparatively, was the only Rorschach research used for queer affirmative ends in Britain.

In focusing on the work of these women I concentrate not only on their academic work but also the context and lived experiences that influenced them. Sangster (1995) argued that despite the shift from women's history to gender history both are required and that more inclusive approaches that involve sexuality, amongst other factors, should be used. Scarborough called for a greater, more inclusive, and detailed women's history of Psychology and for more scholarship about the less well-known women in the history of Psychology, as well as a more analytical approach to such histories.

> I submit that if we are to construct a fully-fledged women's history of psychology, we need more than a record of women's life experiences. . . . So, more than just a "for-the-record" reporting, we now need interpretation and analysis.
>
> *(Scarborough, 2005, p. 6)*

What is and what is not investigated by historians reveals social power, hierarchies, and what is considered marginal and what is considered important. This is especially true in the history of Psychology which includes additional intersections of the power of psychologists and psychological testing.

Power relations between the studiers and the studied need to be taken into account. This is one reason why, thinking historically, psychologists using the Rorschach is so fascinating; because it complicates the idea of the apparently objective and separate psychologist (of course, a misnomer). It turns the lens and the focus away from those they studied onto those who did the studying. In this chapter I therefore switch the lens onto those who did the testing and pay particular attention to the work of Hooker and Hopkins (see Hubbard, 2017a). Specifically, I uncover exactly how they used the Rorschach to argue that there was nothing pathological, neurotic, or psychopathic about being queer, albeit in rather different ways.

Evelyn Hooker

Evelyn Hooker was born Evelyn Gentry in her grandmother's one-room farm house in North Platte, Nebraska (US) on 2nd September 1907. The sixth of nine children to Edward Gentry, a tenant farmer and Jessie (née Bethel) Gentry, who was a nurse during the 1918 flu epidemic. Her mother had only a third-grade education but deeply encouraged Evelyn, or as she pronounced it 'Eva-leen', to get an education because that was one thing that could never be taken away. To this end, the family moved to Sterling, Colorado in a covered prairie schooner wagon when Evelyn was 13 years old to further her education.

Coming from a relatively poor family on the wrong side of the track meant Evelyn described growing up as a painful process. She was particularly conspicuous as a nearly 6-foot-tall teenager, and her feeling of never being 'becoming' continued into adulthood. Having moved to study she attended Sterling High School which was relatively progressive and she was encouraged by her teachers to continue her education. She enrolled in an honours programme with a course in Psychology and graduated in 1924. At 17 she joined the University of Colorado in Boulder and worked cleaning houses in order to bolster her scholarship. Having been awarded her undergraduate degree in 1928 she stayed on to work with psychologist Karl Muenzinger for her master's degree which she received in 1930.

As she made her decision as to what to do next, the US was in the firm grip of the Great Depression. This undoubtedly had an impact on her own career options but she also faced other challenges, being a young woman embarking on a career in a predominantly sexist field. Despite being offered a place in the PhD programme at Colorado, her supervisor Muenzinger was keen for her to go to an eastern university, so she chose Yale. However, the chair of her department (a Yale man himself) refused to provide a woman with a letter of recommendation. Instead, Evelyn became one of only 11 women studying at John Hopkins University, where she was supervised by Knight Dunlap who agreed to take her on despite not approving of women doctorates. She completed her PhD in 1932 and later recollected that John Hopkins had been the right kind of place for her.

Following her PhD, she managed to secure a job by 'sheer luck' at Maryland College for Women. Such colleges were often the only places women academics could work. After a period of teaching and recovering from tuberculosis she spent some time in Europe studying at the Institute for Psychotherapy in Berlin. Here, she stayed with a Jewish family who she later found out died in the concentration camps (see, Minton, 2002). Upon her return, she applied for a job at the University of California, Los Angeles (UCLA) but she was told she could not be employed because there were already three women, who were largely disliked, in the department. Sexist barriers continued to plague her career as they did for many early women psychologists. However, she was accepted by the Extension Division at UCLA as a research associate and continued teaching experimental and physiological Psychology there, with the exception of one year at Bryn Mawr women's college, for the next 31 years. In 1941 Hooker married Donn Caldwell, a freelance writer. Their relationship lasted until 1947 and ended in divorce.

Throughout her life Evelyn was well known amongst circles of famous psychologists and artists. From her work at UCLA she knew Bruno Klopfer, the famous Rorschach psychologist. Her friendship with Klopfer and his expertise on the Rorschach was later essential in her famous studies of gay men. He was the one who most encouraged her while they shared an office in the Psychology department. Hooker also knew famous sexologist Alfred Kinsey (who she believed was queer, Bucknell, 1997, p. 979) and other famous queer people, e.g. Stephen Spencer, the poet. Throughout her life the connections she made with others highly impacted in her own research interests and beliefs about marginalised groups. She had experienced the Great Depression, been in Germany during the Nazi regime, and in 1944 she met a gay student who would change the trajectory of her life.

Sam ('Sammy') From, was initially a student of Evelyn's and she is said to have recognised he was the brightest student in the Introductory Psychology class. Once he had finished the night course their friendship was established. When Evelyn first introduced Sam to her husband, Donn Caldwell, he later asked: "Well, you told me everything else about him, why didn't you tell me he was queer?" (Minton, 2002). It was because of this friendship with an openly gay man, and at Sam's direct request, that she began to consider conducting research on non-pathological gay men. This research, initially ethnographical, enveloped her into gay communities and sparked her ongoing work to remove the pathologisation of homosexuality in Psychology. Prior to meeting Sam, Evelyn had accepted the pathologising perspective towards queerness that she had been taught, and she herself taught, in Psychology. However, her acceptance into these communities convinced her this uncritical perspective was false. Her newfound view and her ethnographic research into gay communities and sub-culture allowed her to make further gay friends. For example, in August 1949 Hooker met Christopher Isherwood at one of Sam From's all-night parties (Bucknell, 1997).

Evelyn married her second husband Edward Niles Hooker, a Professor of English at UCLA, in 1951. The two had met at UCLA despite graduating from John Hopkins the same year. In fact, Edward had allowed Evelyn to stay in his guest house when she needed new accommodation following her return from Bryn Mawr. This guest house, as it was to turn out, was a very important building in the removal of 'homosexuality' as a mental illness. It became the home of Christopher Isherwood in 1952 and the exact location of her research into the Rorschach responses of gay men compared to heterosexual men. In fact, in September 1953 Evelyn insisted Christopher Isherwood, then aged 49, move out because her husband felt that his relationship with Don Bachardy, who was 19, would cause a scandal.[1] After this short difficult period however, their friendship continued for years to come (see Bucknell, 1997).

Hooker's research on homosexuality began in 1953 when she applied for a six-month grant from the National Institute of Mental Health (NIMH). In a period of intense McCarthyism and homophobia, Hooker said she had to be as 'pure as the driven snow' (read heterosexual) in ordered to be authorised to conduct such research. She later claimed that this was part of the reason why she did not research lesbian women – if she had she would have been considered to have ulterior motives. At the time, 'homosexuality' was considered a severe and pervasive emotional mental disorder and gay men and lesbians were being investigated for being 'sexual perverts' with potential communist ties. The NIMH eventually agreed to grant the funding, even though it was warned it could be halted. Initially, the University insisted the research be conducted on campus, but Hooker rejected the proposal, arguing gay men would not volunteer to take part if they were so easily identified. Instead they agreed that the guest house could be used for testing the participants (see Minton, 2002).

With the funding Hooker conducted her research on 30 gay non-pathological men, a sample that had never been collected for psychological research before. These men were recruited through her own friendships and via the Mattachine Society, an early gay rights activist group. Unsurprisingly, confidentiality was absolutely vital to protect the gay men who took part in Hooker's research and she even was said to carry a letter explaining she was on the faculty at UCLA in the event she was caught up in a raid while at a gay bar recruiting participants (which occurred one time and she was held in Los Angles jail). However, while she managed to recruit gay men easily given her connections to the gay community of California and the Mattachine Society, she found it much more difficult to recruit heterosexual men willing to take part, despite her reassurances it was not a 'Kinsey Study'. Eventually she resorted to 'enticing men' who showed up at her home for inspections or repairs. Her husband commented "No man is safe on Saltair Avenue" (see Minton, 2002, p. 227). Her participants all completed three projective tests: a Rorschach test, a Make a Picture Story Test, and a Thematic Apperception Test (TAT). The 60 individuals were matched according to age, IQ, and education, so the only meaningful difference between them was their sexuality.

Both groups responses to the Rorschach were then provided to two experienced clinicians, one of whom was Bruno Klopfer. The Rorschach experts then were asked to separate out the two groups based on whether they thought they were gay or straight. They were unable to determine any better than chance which responses were from 30 heterosexual men and which were from 30 gay men. Hooker concluded '*very tentatively*' (emphasis original, p. 30) that "homosexuality as a clinical entity does not exist" (1957, see Hegarty, 2003b; Hooker, 1958, 1960, 1992).

The mid-1950s were a highly intense time for Hooker. In 1955 Sam From died in a car accident before seeing the impact Hooker's work was soon to have. In 1956 Hooker presented her research to the American Psychological Association. Just before she travelled to Chicago she and her husband visited Christopher Isherwood and Don Baccardy. Isherwood wrote in his diary about her paper and noted the potential historical significance of her work:

> We saw Evelyn Hooker on Saturday – just about to leave for the High Sierras with Edward. Then she's going to read a starting paper to a congress in Chicago which will state (1) that there are exactly as many well-adjusted homosexuals (percentually) as heterosexuals (2) that homosexuality may, in certain cases, be regarded as psychologically as well as biologically "normal." All this was arrived at by getting a great expert to examine a large batch of ink-blot tests. The expert arrived at these conclusions very unwillingly and against his own theories. Maybe this will be celebrated one day as a great historic event – Hooker reading the Declaration of Adjustment.
>
> *(Isherwood Diary, August 6th 1956, see Bucknell, 1997, p. 637.*
> *Footnote included that Isherwood specified 'Rorschach'*
> *in the margin and Bruno Klopfer was the expert)*

Following supper with Evelyn in December 1956, Isherwood again noted in his diary where she was with her research. The Chicago paper was to be published and her "future investigations into the social life of homosexuals, which will oblige her to go to parties, dance and get drunk." Isherwood reflected that "there is really something very noble and admirable about Evelyn. I love to think of her getting drunk and living it up in the interests of science – the good thing about her is she'll really enjoy doing this" (Bucknell, 1997, p. 669). The surprise at Hooker's findings in her Rorschach research was felt not only in the academic community of Psychology, but also in the gay community. Isherwood commented how:

> Evelyn told me how Klopfer, the great Rorschach expert, can actually tell from Rorschachs which patients have slow-growing cancers and which fast-growing ones – because patients who have made a good adjustment to life are able to put up a much greater resistance to them. *And yet*, Klopfer wasn't able from Rorschachs to tell a homosexual from a heterosexual.
>
> *(emphasis original, December 8th 1956, Bucknell, 1997, p. 669)*

In 1957 'The Adjustment of the Overt Male Homosexual' was published by both *The Journal of Projective Techniques* and in the *Mattachine Review*. Tragedy struck again in 1957 when Hooker's second husband unexpectedly died; the two had been married only six years. While Hooker's work was later called upon by activists and academics alike in the fight against the pathologisation of 'homosexuality', her work at this point continued but proved difficult given the tough context in which she worked. Following her husband's death, Isherwood commented she looked 'mortally tired' despite being about to embark on further research. He elaborated:

> her new project – the investigation of social patterns of homosexuality. As she says herself, the only way she can do this is to follow up every clue and see and talk to anybody who is willing.
>
> *(Isherwood diary, September 29th 1957, Bucknell, 1997, p. 730)*

It seemed, according to Isherwood at least, that Hooker's work was central to her during this tough time and she seemed a very lonely figure, working in solitude with her data collected from gay men.

> one always feels drawn to Evelyn, because she is indeed doing so much good in the world. And how lonely she must be! One sees her all alone in that garden house, surrounded by her tapes of statements – by the gay bar owner, the wealthy male prostitute, et etc.
>
> *(June 26th 1960, Bucknell, 1997)*

Later that summer in July Don Baccardy drew Hooker and she had found the experience very strange, "like having one's own Rorschach test made" (Bucknell, 1997, p. 888).

In 1967 Hooker was invited to be the head of the Task Force on Homosexuality. Their report issued in 1969 suggested that the medical model which labelled all 'homosexuals' as pathological was false. But they did still suggest that prevention was important for children and adolescents, and that treatment was also recommended for those who had some heterosexual leanings. Echoing the Wolfenden Report (1957) in Britain the general tone of the report was liberal and it was opposed to discrimination based on sexuality. The report's publication was delayed until 1972 but activist homophile groups in the US found out about the report prior to this. Groups such as the Mattachine Society, the Daughters of Bilitis, and ONE, first established in the 1950s, drew upon the work of Hooker in their arguments against the pathologisation of homosexuality – it is the blending of science and society, of activism and academia which fuelled the wave to change (see Minton, 2002).

In 1970 Hooker opened her own private clinical psychology practice in Santa Monica. Three years later American Psychology removed homosexuality 'per se' from their diagnostic manual of mental disorders and Hooker's work was cited as pivotal in the change, along with the work of people like Frank Kameny (see Minton, 2002). Previously, in 1959 Hooker had commented in conversation with Christopher Isherwood that she "wished the young would get excited about issues the way they did in the thirties" (Bucknell, 1997, p. 813), and they certainly did. From the 1960s–1970s political movements, student protests, and gay liberation were well underway, especially in the US. Within this history, Hooker continues to be recognised as a key figure in the movement to depathologise homosexuality: Hooker's place in the history of Psychology and gay liberation has been cemented (see Minton, 2002). She died in Santa Monica, California on 18th November 1996, having seen her work help in the depathologisation of homosexuality in 1973 in the DSM and later, the International Classification of Diseases also removed its classification in 1990.

June Hopkins

June Hopkins was originally from Texas where she gained both her degree in Psychology (University of Texas) and her master's in Psychology (from Baylor University). In the 1950s she joined the US Air Force as a Personnel Officer where she met "lots of lesbians who were absolutely smashing" (Clarke & Hopkins, 2002, p. 44). Despite the connections she made with other queer women, Hopkins married the chief Methodist Padre of the US Royal Air Force though they both knew she was lesbian.[2] In the 1960s the couple moved to Britain when her husband got a role in Scarborough, where Hopkins still lived in 2002, though she was still described as a 'proud Texan' (Clarke & Hopkins, 2002). At the point of getting this role, Hopkins' husband warned the church that "My wife will not be a second minister. She wants to work and she will." Her first role upon landing in Britain was a Probationer Psychologist at United Cambridge and Fulbourn Hospitals; a year later she qualified as a Clinical Psychologist.

In the mid-1960s Hopkins began her research into lesbians, directly because of her beliefs against the pathologisation of homosexuality at the time. In an interview with Victoria Clarke (Clarke & Hopkins, 2002), she said:

> When I was working at Cambridge Hospital, they kept calling certain patients, as a diagnosis, "lesbian" or "gay" and I thought that was very strange. What they were doing too was using a test that they had devised for male

homosexuals – the Rorschach ink blot test – for lesbians as well. I thought, "This can't be – I'm sure this isn't right".

Not only was she unconvinced that lesbians and gay men were pathological because of their sexualities, she had also been influenced by people she knew and social injustice. Specifically, she had been outraged by the dismissals of lesbian women she knew from the Air Force and wanted to prove there was nothing neurotic or pathological about lesbians.

> When I was in the Air Force, I had a great feeling of injustice: if you were found out to be a lesbian you would be discharged and it wouldn't be an honorable discharge. I was a Squadron Commander for a while and there were women in my organization whom I knew were lesbians. I *knew* it and I thought they were super. No way would I have ever had them investigated. But the minute I left there, there was a big investigation and some of my very favourite people were out. I was so appalled by this. This was another reason why I wanted to do something. I wanted to say, "Hey these are wonderful gals. Why are we getting rid of them?". That really bugged me and stayed with me. The Air Force had a lot to do with why I wanted to do the research and make some kind of contribution.
>
> *(Clarke & Hopkins interview, 2002, p. 46, emphasis original)*

Hopkins was the first person to publish original Rorschach research on lesbian women in Britain. Importantly, she used the word 'lesbian' in her 1969 and 1970 papers instead of 'female homosexual' as was more common given the pathological understanding of 'homosexuality' in Psychology at the time. For example, Barker (1970) – who conducted the study already mentioned at the very beginning of this chapter – also published Rorschach work on lesbians, but identified his participants as 'female homosexuals' in the same issue of the *British Journal of Projective Psychology and Personality Study* as Hopkins (1970) was published.

Hopkins published two central papers on lesbian women. In both she drew on data she collected using the Minority Research Group, a group of lesbian women volunteering for research in order to discredit the idea that lesbian women were pathological. She tested all her recruited participants with seven psychological tests, one of which was the Rorschach. The first paper compared the 24 lesbian women to heterosexual women on two personality tests, including Cattell's 16 Personality Factor test. However, instead of concluding there was no significant difference between the two groups as Hooker had done previously with gay men, Hopkins concluded that lesbian women *were* different, though she had not quite expected to find that result.

> I didn't think there would be differences, I didn't think lesbians would be any stronger, any weaker, than the heterosexual women but, as it turned out, there *were* differences and all of the differences, I felt, were very healthy and

were good ones – self-sufficient, that sort of thing. I also felt that my paper might change the opinion of people who thought lesbians were all neurotic. By definition, if you were lesbian or were gay, you were neurotic and I just didn't think that was true.

(Clarke & Hopkins, 2002, p. 44, emphasis original)

Published in 1969 in *The Lesbian Personality*, she argued that lesbian women have a distinct personality. But rather importantly, unlike the rest of the majority of psychological literature, she described lesbian women's personalities more positively compared to heterosexual women. She argued that her findings showed lesbian women were more independent, resilient, reserved, dominant, bohemian, self-sufficient, and composed compared to their 'heterosexual female counterpart'. Hopkins therefore represents one of the earliest 'signs' of progressive and affirmative queer thinking in British Psychology.

This 1969 paper, published the same year as the Stonewall riot in New York City, was according to Hopkins rather easy to publish. Serendipitously, John Bancroft had also written a paper about 'homosexuality' for the *British Journal of Psychiatry* and so both papers were published together. Hopkins was also rather deliberate in her choice of journal: "I Choose the BJP to publish in because it was the most prestigious journal at that time and because I wanted to open the minds of psychiatrists who viewed lesbians as neurotic" (Clarke & Hopkins, 2002, p. 46). Bancroft's paper, in stark contrast to Hopkins, is a much longer paper detailing the use of electric aversion therapy on ten gay men in attempt to cure them of their homosexuality. Only one 'case', or 'subject', was deemed completely successful, though seven were said to have a change in 'sexual attitude' after 'treatment' but only three men sustained this change short-term. Despite the subsequent anxiety in several men and depression detailed in all the descriptions of the participants, Bancroft was encouraged to continue his research to see if he could continually justify the use of what he called 'an inherently unpleasant method'. The use of aversion therapy is briefly discussed again in Chapters 5 and 6. For further detail on the use of aversion therapy in Britain I strongly recommend Tommy Dickinson's (2015) book *Curing Queers: Mental Nurses and Their Patients 1935–1974*.

The history of aversion therapy and its use in 'curing' gay men especially, illustrates the homophobic and highly medicalised contexts in which Hopkins was working. As a queer woman herself she was embedded within a discipline which pathologised her. She may not have been out at the time, but she knew 'in her own mind' she was a lesbian and despite the challenge and the stigmatisation she continued on with her affirming and pioneering research. In fact, she turned down an invitation for a job at a girls' school because of her research. She felt that it was too important to stop and she was dedicated to finishing it. She was also aware of the social stigma and implications if the head of a girls' school was interested in lesbians, or indeed, was one herself. This was not an easy time to conduct such work and Hopkins remembered the difficulties she faced when doing research on sex and sexuality:

> I was terribly isolated, just terribly. I did other research in the area of sex before I began the lesbian study. To read the literature on sex in the Cambridge University Library, I actually had to go into a separate room and be supervised by somebody. You had to be observed reading this salacious literature. . . . The literature was all under lock and key. I couldn't just go and get the books. Those were the days when, you didn't write about sex and you didn't talk about sex and anything aberrant like homosexuality, you were under suspicion [if you were interested in it]. Even in the hospital, everybody knew what I was doing but they didn't want to discuss it with me. I felt that was very apparent. They made snide comments about my research: I think they thought it was a bit of a bore and not at all important. So it wasn't a very happy time. Also, I didn't feel that I could discuss it with anybody on the outside at all.
>
> *(Clarke & Hopkins, 2002, p. 45)*

Hopkins' dedication to her research seemed to know no bounds. The data for both the 1969 and 1970 papers were collected single-handedly over a one-year period. In this year she individually administered seven separate personality tests, including the Rorschach, to over a hundred lesbians. Travelling to London every weekend for one year to test lesbian women, usually recruited via the Minorities Research Group (MRG, see Chapter 5), she remembered how she would return to Cambridge with a swollen wrist from 'just writing, writing, writing'. She had also visited the Gateways, a famous lesbian night club, to also recruit lesbian women for her research. However, she had to rely on personal contacts and wives associated with her husband's work to recruit the 24 heterosexual women she needed for her sample – a much more difficult task.

In 1970 she published her Rorschach research with these women. In her 1970 paper *Lesbian Signs on the Rorschach* she used the same data, and the Rorschach specifically, to show that there were particular 'signs' on the Rorschach for lesbian women, some of which matched the personality traits she had already found. Here she argued once again for lesbian difference. Quite unlike Hooker (1957) she argued there *were* lesbian signs on the Rorschach. The lesbian signs that lesbian women showed were: a) 'deprecated' female responses (meaning they were demeaning responses about women), b) lesbian women often provided less than three responses per plate, and 3) that Card 7 was often the least liked card.

These lesbians 'signs' are fascinating on their own because they contrast rather dramatically with the kinds of 'gay signs' that were uncovered in the US in mid-20th century. Hopkins did initially structure her work around the gay signs Wheeler (1949) identified but also argued that there was an androcentric aspect to this work and that specific lesbian signs were not available in the literature. In fact, in her article she noted how she considered all suggestions so far on what the signs were for male 'homosexuality' which included 'Hooker's male homosexual indicators'. However unlike Wheeler (1949) and Barker (1970) who suggested these signs were pathological and rather stereotypically sexual, Hopkins' (1970) signs were not attributing overly sexualised meanings to signs. Her findings contrasted with Shafer and Holt (1954) who seemed to apply gay signs for men onto women but in a reversed way. So 'masculine emphasis' and 'perversions', as well as the rejections of women's 'conventional feminine role and status' (p. 137) were considered signs for queer women.

What Hopkins did was rather more feminist, not to mention affirmative, in approach as she sought lesbian signs on the Rorschach from participants who were not experiencing psychological distress, nor did she deduce lesbian signs from that of gay men's. Indeed, the Psychology of Women as a subject grew out of this exact issue that women were often seen as defunct versions of men and so in Psychology, the findings of studies of men were liberally applied to women, and such Rorschach work on gay signs is just one example of this.

In reflection of this work in later interviews with Victoria Clarke, Hopkins highlights the distinctly difficult context of the late 1960s in doing this kind of work.

> I was a little worried because at the time it wasn't acceptable at all. We're talking about 1969 when the paper [The Lesbian Personality in the British Journal of Psychiatry] was published. I felt I was treading on very delicate ground.

It is also exceptionally important to recognise Hopkins' own sexuality and experiences within this context. She stated that:

> I didn't know whether I wanted to be a lesbian or not, whether I wanted to be identified as a lesbian. I decided later that I didn't care. After all the literature came out, it felt quite respectful. I was married and my husband knew I was a lesbian but I wasn't an active lesbian – I was one in my own mind. I had known for years in my own mind. I hadn't "come out".
>
> *(Clarke & Hopkins, 2002)*

Despite Hopkins' good intentions her research was perceived as homophobic by researchers in the US. The distinctions Hopkins made between lesbian and heterosexual women was concerning for many, as talk of difference signified pathology in the US context. Morin (1977) described her research as homophobic due to her search for 'lesbian signs' on the Rorschach. He presumed that by finding lesbian signs Hopkins was attempting to diagnose homosexuality, which she was not. Rather, all of her self-identified lesbian participants were engaged in research in order to prevent such diagnosis and pathologisation of homosexuality.

Similarly, in Britain, Hopkins' work was initially received rather negatively. She herself remembers a critique that she was working within the medical model, which she found strange as that had been the opposite to her intention (Clarke & Hopkins, 2002). Similarly, in 1987 Celia Kitzinger criticised Hopkins' 1969 study as one which removed the political aspects of lesbian experience, separating it out from the social world. This, Kitzinger, argued, was related to the veneer of objectivity used in such studies to remove the active nature of the researcher and imply passivity. It also meant that in the effort to reject lesbian pathology, researchers who tested such a theory still "take seriously the possibility that we [lesbians] might be less mentally healthy than heterosexuals" (Kitzinger, 2002, p. 50). However, later with Sue Wilkinson, they instead used Hopkins' research in a rather tongue-in-cheek way to demonstrate how perhaps lesbians were in fact *more* healthy than hetero-sexual women (Kitzinger & Wilkinson, 1993) – an interpretation which seems to be highly congruent with Hopkins' own interpretation of her findings.

Following decades of growth in Lesbian and Gay Psychology, Hopkins' work was remembered as pioneering and brave in a special issue of *Lesbian and Gay Psychology Review* (2002, Volume 3, part 2). Kitzinger, in reflection of Hopkins' work, concluded with a thank you to June Hopkins "for a brave, early, scholarly article which continues to contribute to both the science and to the politics of lesbian and gay psychology" (p. 51). Similarly, Julie Fish recognised the feminist perspective of Hopkins, highlighting specifically her explicit 'thank you' to her research participants in her research acknowledgments. In doing so, "Hopkins demonstrated both her respect for lesbians and her commitment to feminist principles" (p. 57). Hopkins continued with this feminist work into the 1980s when she focused on topics such as rape and sexual assault, once again having been influenced by the experiences of a friend (see Hopkins, 1984). In 1988 Hopkins retired but in 2002 she was interviewed by Victoria Clarke for the special issue and reflected on her own experiences researching lesbians, as a lesbian, in the 1960s. In looking back, she commented that:

> I find it extraordinarily amazing, having watched the changes. When you think about it, it's hard to believe. Anything that is pioneering is going to be hard but when you're doing it, you don't think about it as pioneering. I didn't think about what I was doing. I just did it because I wanted to.
>
> *(p. 47)*

While Hopkins herself has not been able to recognise her own bravery in her work, Halla Beloff echoes the thoughts of many when she described Hopkins as 'fearless and clear-eyed' (Beloff, 2002, p. 48; see also, Fish, 2002).

Reclaiming psychologists

Hopkins' and Hooker's work are distinctly comparable. However, while Hooker has been viewed as central to the depathologisation of homosexuality in the US because of her research on gay men, little attention, except the special issue mentioned above, has been paid to the work of Hopkins. Hooker's demonstration that there was no distinction between gay men and heterosexual men on the Rorschach appeared far more useful to efforts of depathologisation (1957; see Minton, 2002). In contrast Hopkins' work argued that lesbian women were different, and this type of progressive work was not reclaimed as distinctly affirmative until the turn of the

21st century. Despite the differences between the results of Hopkins' and Hooker's work, both are now recognised as being a part of the complex history of the removal of homosexuality as a mental illness *per se* in 1973. In the following I untangle the similarities and differences between these two researchers in an effort to contextualise the meanings of their results and explain how such different approaches can have the same overall objective.

Importantly, both Hopkins and Hooker aimed to stop queer people from being considered pathological based on their sexuality. Their work needs to be considered in light of their particular contexts. For example, Hopkins argued lesbian women were different, and used more positive language to describe them; these positives removed the idea that lesbian women were vulnerable and neurotic. However, it did echo some stereotyped ideas about lesbian women being particularly dominating and more masculine than straight women (Jennings, 2007a). Similarly, it is also worth taking into consideration Hooker's (1957) conclusion in which she suggested '*very tentatively*' (emphasis original, p. 30) that "homosexuality as a clinical entity does not exist" (1957; see Hegarty, 2003b; Hooker, 1960, 1992). Perhaps not quite the forceful pro-queer stance we might be looking for in the past, but within context this was certainly a significantly positive statement to make about gay men.

The differences between Hopkins' and Hooker's work are clear but they also have some striking similarities. It is worthy of note that while Hopkins was working in Britain and published her work in British journals, they are actually both American women working within a discipline largely dominated by men (Clarke, Ellis, Peel, & Riggs, 2010; Hooker, 1992). Though of course projective testing was seen as an area more suited to women, as we have explored in Chapter 1.

Both Hooker and Hopkins were studying homosexuality using the Rorschach and the tests' perceived reliability and validity were central to their findings. Without belief in the Rorschach's potential to discern people's psychology, Hooker's finding that psychologists could not successfully distinguish between 'homosexual' and heterosexual participants and Hopkins' findings that there were lesbian signs on the Rorschach would have been meaningless. For these studies to work and act against pathologisation, belief and trust in the Rorschach's validity was vital.

A distinction between the two women is that Hooker studied men and Hopkins studied women. Given the absolute focus on men within the US Rorschach literature, it is surprising to see a relative focus on lesbian women in the British literature (Barker, 1970; Hopkins, 1970). In fact, Hopkins distinctly highlighted androcentrism within the Rorschach research literature and argued against the application of gay men's 'signs' on the Rorschach being uncritically applied to women (Hopkins, 1970).

Both Hopkins and Hooker were said to have been influenced by their friends and it was their direct experiences of lesbian and gay people that led them to conduct such research. Hooker famously became interested in gay men because of Sam From, with whom she became friends (Minton, 2002). Hopkins similarly became interested from her experiences in the US Air Force where lesbian women were being discharged due to their sexuality (Clarke et al., 2010). Their work can in some ways be seen as efforts for social justice as they engrained their studies within the social context of the world. While Hopkins (1969) was later criticised for removing the political and attempting to overly objectify lesbians (Kitzinger, 1987), both Hopkins and Hooker were inspired by social injustices and used the psychological tools they had to try and demonstrate lesbians and gay men were not pathological based on their sexualities. Hopkins also highlighted how her focus on objectivity was deliberate, as was her publication in a prestigious journal as these would mean her work was more likely to have a greater impact on the psychological community and be more convincing to an audience of pathologising and homophobic psychologists and psychiatrists (see Peel, 2002).

The differences in the participants of these two studies are telling. Hooker has said that she had been asked later why she did not research lesbian women and do the same for them as she did for gay men (Hegarty, 2003a). However, she argues that to have asked the National Institute of Mental Health at the time would have meant she would be under investigation of being a lesbian herself. Hooker (1992) describes some of the ordeals she went through in order to investigate gay men, including suspicions of her own sexuality and dealing with the police in regards to both the confidentiality and illegality (at the time) of her participants' sexual behaviours. McCarthyism was also rife and so Hooker was continuously reinforcing her own heterosexuality, or as she described it, she had to be as 'pure as the driven snow' (Hegarty, 2003a). In contrast, however, Hopkins studied women and did so despite the fact she too may have been considered a lesbian herself – which of course, she was. "Back then, if you were associating yourself with lesbians, then you were a lesbian" (Clarke & Hopkins, 2002, p. 46). She also chose to publish her papers under her own name, whereas other people published anonymously: "they didn't want to be named but I was prepared to be tarred with the brush" (p. 46). It most likely helped reinforce the impression of Hopkins' heterosexuality however, in her acknowledgments where she thanks her husband for his assistance. However, she certainly did defy convention in her approach to her work and her perspective and she also demonstrated a level of bravery during a potentially difficult time when she was not out, but studying lesbians in a highly pathologising field.

In both matched paired studies, Hooker and Hopkins both needed heterosexual people to take part and to be similar in age and education to their queer participants. Hooker had to become fully submersed in the gay community and build trust in order to recruit the gay men for her study (1957). Her work was heavily supported by the gay community (e.g. *The Mattachine Review*, Hegarty, 2003a; Minton, 2002). However, she described difficulty in recruiting heterosexual counterparts because of the nature of her research (Hegarty, 2003a). Hopkins similarly found it much easier to gain lesbian participants because of the Minorities Research Group (MRG) and the Gateways club. She tested over 100 lesbian women but only reported findings of 24 because she found it so difficult to recruit heterosexual women because she had only recently moved to Britain (Clarke & Hopkins, 2002). It seems that being in a new place – a new country or a new community – and the stigmas of such research had profound effects specifically for potential heterosexual participants.

The key comparative feature between the work of Hopkins and Hooker is the idea of *difference*. Hooker in effect argued that gay men and heterosexual men are the same, whereas Hopkins argued lesbian women and heterosexual women are different. Hopkins arguably provided positive aspects of the lesbian personality to counter the pathology surrounding the psychology of lesbian women at the time (see Peel, 2002), whereas Hooker used a lack of difference as evidence of lack of pathology. These approaches also had different consequences in each national context. In America where difference suggested pathology, discourses of sameness were affirmative. In contrast, in Britain where there was little military involvement and a lesser concern of homosexuality in the post-war era, discourses of difference had more potential to be positive.

Hegarty (2003b) specifically discussed Hooker's use of significance testing; he described how Hooker's conclusion that there was no difference between the gay men's and straight men's Rorschach responses might hinge on what specific type of statistical test Hooker implemented. Hooker argued, quite rightly, that in a clinical setting psychologists would not receive two matched Rorschach responses. She therefore did unmatched analysis. Had she have chosen otherwise, it might have been possible for her to argue that there were distinguishable differences between the Rorschach responses of gay men and straight men. Statistics therefore require interpretation just as ink blots do. To quote Hegarty (2003b):

> significance testing is an inexact process, and that the means by which marginally significant results are determined to be "significant" or "non-significant" forms part of the historical process by which scientific "facts" about sexuality are constructed.
>
> *(p, 31, see re-print 2018)*

Overall there seems to be a major difference in attitudes in Britain compared to the US. Hopkins had a more affirmative approach and struggled less with the specific suspicious Cold-War context that was rife in the US at the time (Lemov, 2011; Lutz, 1997). However, it should be noted that Hopkins and Hooker were both studying homosexuality at different points in time, as mentioned. The British papers were not published until 1969/1970 whereas Hooker published her initial work in 1957. Separated by over a decade within very different cultural contexts of each time, these socio-historical differences should be taken into account when considering the differences between approaches. Hooker (1992) described her ordeals with studying homosexuality during the Cold-War era, whereas in contrast Hopkins was able to conduct her research in the late 1960s when gay liberation was underway. Yet she did still come across prejudice and substantial difficulties in conducting affirmative research. For example, both Hooker and Hopkins experienced isolation working in absolute solitude on their research projects. Isherwood described Hooker as working 'all alone' and theorised about her loneliness in her big garden house surrounded by the tapes of gay men she interviewed. Hopkins too, reflected on the loneliness in her work as she felt she could not talk to anyone and her colleagues were distinctly disparaging of her research.

Another key difference in these two studies is the sexuality of the researcher themselves. Hopkins identified (albeit only in her own mind at the time of publication) as a lesbian. This was in contrast to Hooker in the US who reinforced her own heterosexuality to avoid accusations of her being queer (Hooker, 1992). Such identification (or non-identification) with one's participants can be viewed in some ways as either bias or as beneficial. In the early days of Psychology, women researchers were treated as suspicious in regards to their study of women (Morawski & Agronick, 1991). Hookers' experiences somewhat mirrored this; she argued that people would have thought she had some kind of ulterior motive to wish to research lesbians. However, upon reflection of Hopkins' work, she can be viewed as having brave authority to have discussed possible lesbian signs on the Rorschach and lesbian personality traits. Within the comparison of Hooker and Hopkins it is possible to see how the shift of authority has developed. Hooker had to reinforce her own heterosexuality in order to be considered legitimate enough to be able to study homosexuality. The distancing of her own identity from her subjects meant her research was viewed as less biased and more objective. In contrast, however, Hopkins' later open identification with her participants has shown an understanding of her subjects' experiences and perspectives which also suggests her work is reliable.

Despite the directly comparable studies and the similar aims, Hooker has been remembered and claimed as an affirmative researcher to a much greater extent than Hopkins. Malley (2002), in recognising that Hopkins' work was like Hooker's, suggested they both had "blown the gaff on the fact that clinical judgements of lesbian or gay male populations were not derived solely from a scientifically objective stance" (2002, p. 55). Peel (2002) also suggested that Hopkin's work was ahead of its time due to a) its explicit focus on lesbians, b) its positivist-empiricist approach, and c) its emphasis on unpathological difference between lesbians and heterosexual women. It has been suggested as well that it might be that Hopkins' work was paid less attention precisely *because* of her focus on lesbians, rather than gay men, and because of it being conducted and published in Britain (Malley, 2002).

The Rorschach as a tool for good

As demonstrated in the research of Hooker and Hopkins, just as Psychology legitimised homophobic practices and the pathologisation of queer people via tests like the Rorschach, Psychologists used the Rorschach to try to depathologise 'homosexuality' and develop affirmative approaches. For this work to be successful it is worth noting that for this to work, psychologists had to be invested in the Rorschach as valid, reliable, and good scientific practice. Belief in the Rorschach has therefore not just had a history of homophobic practice but it was precisely belief *in* the Rorschach which meant that more affirmative work could happen. The Rorschach itself is therefore not inherently good, or bad, but works in the hands of those who use it. Our intentions influence the science we produce.

These studies, however, also needed to be considered within context and the actions of participants also need to be recognised. It was the specific social, medicalised, and historical context of the 1950s–1960s which meant this work could happen and by whom. For example, in both of these examples it is the people these psychologists knew who inspired them and the social injustices being acted against them which created the affirmative perspectives of both Hooker and Hopkins. Without Sam From's direct request and the Minorities Research Group actively inviting researchers to use them as participants, these studies would not have happened. The studies therefore represent an early integration of activist–academic work. Queer people at this time did a great deal for these researchers – volunteers to take part in Hooker and Hopkins' research vastly outnumbered the heterosexual people willing to take part. It is the work of these activist groups which I explore in greater detail in Chapter 5.

When looking back at Card 3 now, it is possible to reflect upon the young woman's interpretation of the ink blot at the beginning of this chapter. On the one hand her response can be interpreted as 'deprecating' indicating Hopkins' (1970) lesbian sign, or that such an interpretation would not be significantly different of that of a heterosexual women, in keeping with Hooker's (1957) conclusion. I argue that in Card 3, it is possible to see the outlines of two women, side by side, working tirelessly together, perhaps differently but with one common goal. Card 3 therefore represents to me Evelyn Hooker and June Hopkins. And just like the edges of an ink blot, the history of Psychology does not have a distinct and clear edge. It blurs into other areas, like gay liberation and activist groups.

Notes

1 In 1954 Don Bachardy was classified by the US military as '4-F' after revealing he was homosexual. Such categorisations of men were developed in order to distinguish groups of men available for the draft. Class 1 indicated men available and suitable for training. Class 4 was considered a deferral from military action for various reasons and the subcategory F was specifically for those who were considered to be physically, mentally, or morally unfit for military service. As well as ill-health, these included crimes such as murder and treason, plus sodomy and 'sexual perversion' (Bucknell, 1997). See Chapter 2 for further details on such military exclusion and the use of the Rorschach in detecting 'homosexuality' in potential officers in the US military.
2 For more information, see Amy Tooth Murphy (2013): "I confirmed; I got married. It seemed like a good idea at the time': domesticity in postwar lesbian oral history."

4

QUEER SIGNS IN THE PROJECTIVE PSYCHOLOGISTS

Have a look at some of the Rorschach ink blots and consider all the things you can 'see'. It is possible to 'see' lots of different things. In Card 1 for example, you might be able to discern a mask (like I did when I was tested) or a person's torso. If you can see one of these, take a moment to reflect that these are the kinds of signs which were believed to indicate 'homosexuality' in the mid- to late-20th century (see Due & Wright, 1945; Linder, 1945; Wheeler, 1949; and Chapter 2). In the same way it is possible to see queer 'signs' in ambiguous ink blots, it is also possible to see signs of queerness in the ambiguous history of projective tests.

By paying close attention to the history of the projective test movement in which the Rorschach work was situated, it is equally possible for other types of queer signs to emerge. In the previous chapter I went into more depth about two women using the Rorschach. Both Hooker and Hopkins were explicit about their own sexualities and aims. However, not all women working in the projective test movement were (able to be) as open. In this chapter specifically, I demonstrate that when you look at some other individual psychologists working with the Rorschach, it is possible to see signs that they too were queer, though this was not made explicit by them in their lifetimes.

However (and it's a big however), as explored in the introduction, there are key issues with projecting labels and identities onto individuals of the past. There are also substantial difficulties in conducting queer feminist histories. To review some of these issues briefly here:

First, there remains the need to 're-place' women's histories, but they have been recorded less reliably than those of men (Bohan, 1990), and this is especially true for lesbian women. Cook (1979a, 1979b) described this as the 'historical denial of lesbian women'. Second, conducting queer and lesbian history for the 20th century is particularly difficult due to the growth of the pathologisation of 'deviant' sexualities. Terms like 'lesbian', 'invert', and 'homosexual' became known, but were shrouded by medico-scientific pathological discourse. This meant few women directly identified with them and many rejected such labels. Third, this led to significant stigmatisation; medico-scientific texts informed readers that lesbians were promiscuous, predatory, and psychopathic (Jennings, 2007a). The category lesbian and the presentation of 'inverts' gained greater cultural significance after the Second World War, but it was still treated as a neurotic sickness (Hopkins, 1969, 1970; Jennings, 2007c).

Finally, there were substantial restrictions and barriers to women working in Psychology, whether they be marriage bans, no or little pay, sexism, or the social belief that women were weaker and less capable. It is therefore a careful procedure considering queer women working *within* the pathologising field of Psychology. They are not likely to have identified with terms which would have categorised them as mentally ill according to their own profession. Some identities are also more modern and have become understood as an identity in more recent years, ('queer' being the most obvious example) so it can also be argued that to label people of the past is inappropriate as they would not have even understood that word in that context. 'Gay' for example, in the mid-20th century, had the meaning of gaiety, happiness, and care-free joy and so would not have been understood as a sexual identity. Women in Psychology are also likely to have been pressured to conform and act in as a professionally acceptable way as possible to legitimise their own positions they had worked so very hard for. But that is not to say queer women did not operate within Psychology or that we should avoid all kinds of identity projection onto the past: without it we would have almost no queer history.

So how might it be possible to do queer history about potentially queer women working in Psychology in the early to mid-20th century? I propose to use the work of June Hopkins and her conceptualisation of the 'lesbian personality' (1969). Using this alongside other queer historical practices provides a potential new insight into methods of conducting queer history.

Projecting onto psychologists

In order to accomplish a 'herstory' without projecting today's assumptions onto the past I propose to use June Hopkins' *The Lesbian Personality* (1969) and *Lesbian Signs on the Rorschach* (1970) to frame the lives of three women (see also, Hubbard, 2017b). As explored in depth in Chapter 3, Hopkins used psychological tests to propose that a) men's 'homosexual signs' on the Rorschach do *not* apply to women, b) that the neurotic picture painted about the lesbian in Psychology was wrong, and that c) lesbians in fact have distinctive and positive features of their personalities.

In using this framework, I am not only using one of the central women of the projective test movement to frame both herself and the other women I have selected, but I am using relevant projective psychology. There is little historical research to date on lesbian women in British psychology, despite Morawski's (1994) suggestion that those on the margins are worthy of historical inquiry and reflexive study. Of course a number of biographies of women are available, (e.g. Valentine, 2006,

2009) and the project to re-place women in the history of psychology is ongoing. Naturally, there is extensive research on lesbian and gay Psychology, the formation of LGBT Psychology and prejudice research (see Hegarty, 2018). However, there is little literature to provide a framework of doing lesbian history in Psychology directly and so I have developed an analysis from which this ongoing project can begin. Borrowing from lesbian history, as well as psychological literature, I propose an original approach to the history of Psychology. Hopkins is one of the very few reclaimed lesbians in the history of Psychology (Clarke & Hopkins, 2002) and in adopting her papers as a form of analysis I provide evidence that there are other women who have the potential also to be reclaimed. There are a number of possible critiques of such an approach. For example, some may argue that it is an inappropriate application of a psychological study, and for others it may be too 'queer' an approach. However, my proposed analysis is not a complete and final solution to the problem of historical lesbian erasure in Psychology. In presenting these women I expose lesbian erasure in the history of Psychology and make moves forward in this broader project of including queer women in the re-placing of women in the history of Psychology (Rutherford & Pettit, 2015).

By using this research which in itself sits more comfortably within the past understandings of sexuality I aim to avoid some concerns of presentism by not explicitly describing these women as lesbian, when the majority of which would likely never have described themselves in such terms. Queer psychologists from the 1930s might have been unaware of the term 'lesbian', and more likely they would have understood 'invert', and I would argue it is unlikely they would describe themselves as such because of the pathologised way Psychology treated 'sexual deviance'. Hopkins is therefore positioned in a unique place among these prominent women in the projective test movement, as she is the only one who has identified herself publically as a lesbian who worked with the Rorschach. In addition, in using her work to frame my queer feminist reading I manage other historical problems and use an internal queer subject to frame my own queer external perspective.

This chapter focuses on the lives of three women involved in the British projective test movement in which the Rorschach was dominant. By foregrounding the life and work of June Hopkins, who conducted research about lesbian women using projective methods, I shift the gaze once again from those who were studied onto those who were doing the studying. Hegarty (2003a) and Hubbard and Hegarty (2016) outlined queer history in the US and in Britain in relation to what kinds of projective studies were conducted on queer people. Here I focus on the lives of British women psychologists themselves (see Hubbard, 2018). In order to accomplish a queer history without projecting today's assumptions onto the past I use June Hopkins' *The Lesbian Personality* (1969, also see 1970). Let us recap exactly what Hopkins argued the lesbian personality looked like. Using psychological tests, she argued lesbians were the following compared to their 'heterosexual counterparts':

- Independent
- Resilient

- Reserved
- Dominant
- Bohemian
- Self-sufficient
- Composed

By using Hopkins' findings of the 'lesbian personality' to frame the lives of some of the central women of the projective test movement, it is possible to thereby negotiate some issues around doing lesbian history. Hopkins' own perspective is vital in the use of her work as she is herself a lesbian, meaning her own viewpoint is one of a queer person working in projective Psychology reasonably close to the time the women I am considering worked. She also used the Minorities Research Group as a pool of participants (see Chapter 5) and had a lot in common with her participants despite the fact she was not 'out' at the time of the research.

In many ways Hopkins can be described in the same ways as her lesbian participants: independent, resilient, reserved, dominant, bohemian, self-sufficient, and composed. Despite this her work was only recognised for its affirmative approach and progressiveness in 2002. It is also possible, I argue, to identify Hopkins' work as distinctly emancipatory just as Minton (2002) identifies similar work in the US. Although the Rorschach has had a generally homophobic history as told so far (see Hegarty, 2003a), by adopting Hopkins as a theorist in framing the lives of women in the projective test movement it is possible to make the Rorschach (and psychological tests in general) *do* something affirmative for lesbian and gay history.

With Hopkins as a catalyst, in conducting my research on the British projective test movement I began looking for and indeed discovered several signs that indicate the women involved led feminist, and in some cases, potentially queer lives. Broad examples of evidence of lesbianism include resisting social pressures to marry and have children, and developing supportive networks with other women (Jennings, 2007b; Wittig, 1981). All the women I identify in this chapter fulfil these criteria. Their mere presence within Psychology at this time provokes a strong sense of their feminist values and their suitability to be reclaimed by feminist psychologists now.

The three women I pay particular attention are: Margaret Lowenfeld (1890–1973); Ann Kaldegg (1899–1995), and Effie Lilian Hutton (1904–1956). In the following section I present these women as independent, resilient, reserved, dominant, bohemian, self-sufficient, and composed. All of these traits are in line with Hopkins' (1969; see 1970) research on the lesbian personality. Hopkins also argued that the lesbian signs on the Rorschach were a) 'deprecated' female responses (meaning they were demeaning responses about women), b) lesbian women often provided fewer than three responses per plate, and c) that Card 7 was often the least liked card. Unfortunately, we don't have access to the Rorschach responses of Margaret Lowenfeld, Ann Kaldegg, and Effie Lilian Hutton, though it is likely they underwent some (likely projective) psychological testing themselves in their respective trainings for their career in Psychology.

In characterising these women's lives I use 'queer' rather than lesbian. Although 'queer' has a number of negative connotations and has only recently been reclaimed by the LGBTQ community, its use is apt in this case because of its multiple meanings. 'Queer' allows for a spectrum of sexual and/or gendered identities to be included and therefore does not prescribe lesbianism onto an individual who might have identified otherwise. These women could have been queer in the sexual sense, they may have even identified themselves privately as lesbians, 'inverts', or as bisexual, however this is debatable. An illustrative case in point is the life of psychotherapist Charlotte Wolff (1897–1986). Though Wolff did not identify herself as lesbian in her youth, she did so later in life, and described herself as having always known she was attracted to women (see Chapter 5).

In addition, 'queer' can be used to mean odd, or peculiar, in a wider sense. These women were certainly different, and so by using 'queer' I highlight their peculiarity considering the social contexts of their lifetimes and indicate potential for sexual/ gendered queerness as well. In using Hopkins' personality framework to explore the biographies of these women I use appropriate projective psychology, their own field, and do not reduce their lives to identities or experiences (see Scott, 1991). Instead, my analysis uses Rorschach history to open up queer possibility.

Margaret Lowenfeld

Margaret Lowenfeld (1890–1973), or 'Madge' to her family, was born 4th February in Lowndes Square, London. She was born to Henry (originally Heinz) Lowenfeld and Alice Evens. Both she and her sister eventually became internationally known in their own circles, Margaret as a child psychotherapist, and Helena as a gynaecologist and advocate for birth control (Evans, 1984). At the age of six Helena declared she wanted to be a doctor and Margaret soon followed suit. In contrast to Helena however, Margaret was frail, found everything rather difficult and although had 'ingenious' ideas struggled to carry them out (Evans, 1984). One shared interest was that of religious spirituality that they had received from their mother (who would regularly hold séances at the house).[1]

Both daughters attended Cheltenham Ladies' College and growing up regularly travelled around Europe, returning to their father's Polish home near Kraków (Urwin, 2004). In the biography of Helena, Evans (1984)[2] described their childhood as a rather unhappy one, with frequent travels and a complex parental divorce in 1902. The two sisters fought for independence and their father was said to have been disgusted that they wanted to gain careers in medicine exclaiming: "what has fate done to give me two intelligent daughters?" (Evans, 1984). He had intended for them to both be conventional women who would marry rich men. The parents' divorce and their subsequent relationships had a profound effect on Margaret; she was regularly ill and as a teenager suffered great emotional strain resulting in several breakdowns.

In 1912, defying her father and following in the footsteps of Helena, Lowenfeld entered the London School of Medicine for Women. Just before the First World War

ended in 1918 she finished and was allowed to practice medicine. She began working 19-hour days at the South London Women's Hospital as a house surgeon but
less than a year later was called for in Poland to manage the staff who were at the
family home. In 1919 she visited Poland and was heavily involved in the Chris-
tian Student Movement (see Urwin & Hood-Williams, 2013). Her experiences
of Poland and the poverty she witnessed and the number of orphaned children
inspired her to forge her career in child psychotherapy, in spite of the perceptions of
such work in upper-class circles. An oral history participant said:

> Well yes she belongs to that ah, the same as Marie Stopes and Helena Wright
> her sister, she comes from the milieu where she was presented to court, so if
> you're a debutante its world I know nothing about. But she was very much in
> touch with the poorer neighbourhoods and the children in the poorer neigh-
> bourhoods in Kensington . . . to sit there and understand children of the poor
> that you know, that's dross, as far as that era was concerned they were dross.
>
> I mean she talks about the deprivations of the rich as well, well you know
> you have no idea of the deprivations that the rich would suffer, that she suf-
> fered. There's no good saying she didn't have any toys because she probably
> did, it wasn't that you see it was the deprivation of the, other sorts you see
> which is not, you can't buy. With money or position. You see it's the contrast
> of what she found during after the First World War, in the aftermath of it,
> when she was going round with the mission, when she was rounding up all
> the children who were fending for themselves and she was impressed, she
> said "it's ridiculous, these children are surviving by themselves" if Freud was
> correct, they would be so damaged having lost both their parents that you
> know, when they were so tiny that they wouldn't survived. But there they
> are surviving.

As mentioned, throughout her life Margaret suffered from bouts of mental illness,
she was fragile, and often sought the help of professionals. On returning to London
in 1921 she experienced another collapse and was hospitalised at Bowden House
Nursing Home in London, under the care of Wilfred Trotter who was interested
in both neurosurgery and psychoanalysis (Urwin, 2004). Lowenfeld underwent
analysis several times in order to try and understand the route of her problems.

In 1922 she underwent a year of personal analysis, during which time she wrote a
note containing some insight into her understanding of herself. She wrote: "When
I look inside myself I find I am some kind of sham – that inside the outer shell there
is chaos, I don't know really what I want, & don't know what I think – I only seem
to know that I am miserable." She continually discussed fear and bewilderment, at
some kind of 'proposal' and appeared to be writing to someone. She stated:

> I think I wanted to establish a kind of semi unromantic slightly emotional
> relationship with you that would put a kind of glamour over these hours &
> take the edge off the humiliation. Because of that I find I have come to want

to gain your friendship which must necessarily be a hard thing to win & felt a crude stark kind of exposure of oneself can only be revolting.

The note concludes with the title 'Ultimates' of which the final one reads: "If I am going to be able to do anything for women I've got to go their common way."[3] It is tantalisingly unclear as to what was meant by this note, though it is possible to deduce Lowenfeld was clearly struggling with a kind of turmoil and was having difficulty with certain feelings which led to additional feelings of shame and disgust. However, in many regards Lowenfeld did not go the traditional 'common way'.

On 25th October 1928 Lowenfeld opened her Children's Clinic that later became known as the Institute of Child Psychology (ICP) in the ground-floor rooms of the North Kensington Women's Welfare Centre (Traill, & Hood-Williams, 1973). However, it was moved on the 4th March 1929 as

> it appeared that a certain amount of suspicion has been aroused in the minds of the authorities owing to the position of the clinic in a Birth Control building. A certain amount of fear existed in some quarters that there might be some connections between the two and the clinic is an obscure form of birth control propaganda. For this reason also, a move to another address became important.[4]

Interestingly then, despite Margaret's removed interests from those of her sister, the connotations of the birth control movement still affected her work.

The ICP was staffed by many women at this point in the early 1930s, including a 'Miss AT Alcock' as Psychological Superintendent. Theodora Alcock later became one of the central pioneers in the use of the Rorschach in Britain and was responsible for the establishment of the British Rorschach Forum. While Alcock and others, such as Anna Freud and Melanie Klein, focused on children in their psychological work in first half of the 20th century, Lowenfeld's focus on children was unlike much of the psychoanalytic literature popular at the time (Hutton, 2004).

In her 1935 book *Play in Childhood* Lowenfeld adopted the thinking of historian Robin Collingwood, from whom she had developed an interest in philosophy having known him in the 1920s and 1930s (and with whom she was rumoured to have had a relationship of some kind). Lowenfeld adopted Collingwood's controversial relativism and allowed children the freedom of expression. The ICP was moved once again to Hertfordshire due to the outbreak of the Second World War, and after the war upon returning to London the ICP had to be reorganised as a Limited Company as Lowenfeld was greatly concerned about the consequences of the introduction of the NHS in 1948. As reported by Margaret Mead in Lowenfeld's obituary, although the "ICP was officially recognized as part of the training program in clinical psychology, it remained a rather special institution" (Mead, 1974).

Quite rightly, Mead (1974) described the ICP as "somewhat outside the more conventional types of child guidance clinics – stimulated and illuminated by Margaret Lowenfeld's special diagnostic insights, techniques." These included her varied tests, including the Lowenfeld World Technique and the Mosaic Test (see, Hutton, 2004; Lowenfeld, 1954, 1979). These projective methods were imaginative and creative and the ICP allowed children to play, explore, and express themselves freely. This approach is evident in Lowenfeld's tests; for example the World Technique consists of a sand tray, lots and lots of miniature toys, and water in which children create their own little world. Aspects of Lowenfeld's character and her establishment of the ICP goes someway to demonstrate her independent, resilient, and self-sufficient nature. Certainly Lowenfeld resisted marriage, rejected the expected norms of her class and gender, and continued to surround herself with hard-working and supportive women, including Alcock. But there were two other women who were particularly influential on Lowenfeld.

Urwin and Hood-Williams (2013) described the meeting of two women in the late 1940s as particularly important in the life of Lowenfeld. The first was the famous anthropologist Margaret Mead, whom Lowenfeld met in 1948 in London at the World Federation of Mental Health Conference. They became friends and regularly corresponded. Mead herself is also known for her relationships with other women, most notably Ruth Benedict (Banner, 2010), and for her anthropological work on understandings of sex and gender in *Coming of Age in Samoa* (1928). Mead would later use Lowenfeld's Mosaic test as a part of her research in cross-cultural anthropology and this inspired the use of such tests by other anthropologists such as Rhoda Metraux.

The second woman who was to have a profound effect of Lowenfeld's life was Ville Anderson. Having met in Denmark (where Anderson was from), Anderson moved to London to be with Lowenfeld and train at the ICP in the 1950s. Upon completion she stayed at the ICP "as a psychotherapist, research worker and assistant to Margaret Lowenfeld, remaining with her as a colleague, living companion and confidante until the time of Margaret Lowenfeld's death" (Urwin & Hood-Williams, 2013, p. 14). The two of them lived together and split their time between their Harley Street flat and 'Cherry Orchards', a house in Cholesbury, Buckinghamshire, which Lowenfeld had bought when her mother died.

Despite Lowenfeld's enduring contributions to child psychology and psychotherapy she was not a major figure in Psychology at the time (Bowyer, 1970; Hutton, 2004). Nonetheless, Lowenfeld contributed two famous projective tests (the Lowenfeld World test and the Mosaic test), Poleidoblocs, the theory of 'e', and her thinking on the protosystem (see Lowenfeld, 1954, 1979). However, unlike Melanie Klein, Anna Freud, and Dora Kalff (who visited and took inspiration from the ICP) she did not disseminate her ideas with as much force (Evans, 1984). Great rivalries began between the different schools of thinking and although Lowenfeld had met Jung and Adler in the 1940s she did not consider herself psychoanalytic. Klein, who was also at odds with the psychoanalytic establishment, took a great dislike to Lowenfeld and disputes appeared quite common between students of the different schools (see Sayers, 1991). Considering Klein's attitudes towards homosexuality (O'Connor & Ryan, 1993) one cannot help but wonder whether the dislike of Lowenfeld was personal, as well as professional. Lowenfeld however did enjoy popularity among anthropologists and educational psychologists. These effects were felt internationally thanks to Mead who adopted some of Lowenfeld's methods (also see Lemov, 2011 for a history of projective methods in anthropology).

Magdalen Vernon, an educational psychologist, and Lowenfeld began a regular correspondence from the mid-1960s and had a shared interest in child psychology (also see Chapter 2). Vernon, like many of the women considered by Valentine (2008b), Furumoto and Scarborough (1986), and myself, remained single, had no children, and had a highly interesting career. Vernon remained at Reading for her whole post-doctoral career and became Chair of Psychology in 1956. She was president of the BPS from 1958–1959 (her brother Philip had been president in 1954–1955). Yet she too remains conspicuously absent from histories of Psychology, conspicuously in contrast to how her brother has been recognised in some histories.

Lowenfeld and Vernon's correspondence became affectionate; in letters throughout October and November 1965 Vernon was referred to as 'My Dear Magdalen' and she herself signed off 'Your ever, Magdalen'. They discussed premature rumours of Vernon's retirement, visits to 'The Guidance Unit' at Reading and sought each other's advice on their work. Having arranged to meet on the 26th November 1965, Lowenfeld wrote the following day:

> My dear Magdalen, It was refreshing to see you yesterday, like a wind off the moors.[5]

The prevalence of single (according to the law) and career-focused women at this time in Psychology is interesting, but what is most fascinating here are the clear links and friendships between these women. The networks of such women – particularly ones which include notable queer women such as Margaret Mead – therefore suggest support and care towards one other in a somewhat hostile professional environment.

By 1970 Lowenfeld and Anderson spent most of their time at their home in Buckinghamshire, with Lowenfeld only visiting London once a week to lecture (Evans, 1984). By this point, Lowenfeld and Anderson had been together for over 20 years. Towards the end of her life Lowenfeld suffered from confusion and alteration of mood (Evans, 1984). She was moved to a nursing home near her sister's house in 1972 and died a few months later on 2nd February 1973.

Lowenfeld's death is believed to have been particularly hard for Anderson. An oral history participant reported:

> This is why Ville, it was terrible, she had a very lonely life after that because she devoted herself to Margaret and after Margaret died then you know she was in Denmark and it was terrible to her. And you know she didn't die until much later because she was much younger. And then of course *she* held on, she said "*I'm* the torchbearer, *I* think that's correct."

After her death Anderson started to archive Lowenfeld's papers, letters, and work, including childhood letters that Lowenfeld had given her. The archive now resides at the Wellcome Library. However, the ICP was disbanded only six years after Lowenfeld's death, having received a lack of support from the psychological community. Anderson is often referred to publicly as a close friend, colleague, or carer of some kind, due to Lowenfeld's fragility. For example, Urwin (2004) stated Lowenfeld "was supported by her close friend and living companion, Ville Andersen, a Danish citizen who had trained at the ICP in the 1950s." Yet the fact that Anderson made major moves to continue Lowenfeld's legacy following decades of relationship certainly suggests she was more than a mere colleague, close friend, or carer. Their relationship spanned decades and included intimate knowledge of each other through care and living with one another. I am certain that had Ville Anderson been a man few historians would lose sleep describing this relationship as romantic, sexual, and heterosexual. It appears to me that only by compulsory heterosexuality (Rich, 1980) and through the actions of lesbian erasure is it possible to draw heterosexual and normative conclusions about Lowenfeld.

Overall, Lowenfeld has been described as intuitive, humble, and innovative yet she continually experienced "struggle between the unstinting attention she gave her patients, her urge to expand her work in every possible direction, an imagination that far exceeded her bodily strength, a shortage of funds and a terrific sense that time was running out" (Mead, 1974). In addition to this description I also argue Lowenfeld embodies an uncanny resemblance to the description by Hopkins (1969) of the lesbian personality and appears to have led a feminist and queer life – she is at the very least 'lesbian like' (Bennett, 2000).

Ann Kaldegg

Ann Kaldegg was an active member of the British Rorschach Forum and regular contributor to their journal *The Rorschach Newsletter*. Kaldegg, originally Kohn, was born in 1899 to Jewish parents Max Kaldegg and Rosalia Czises. Her father had changed their surname to avoid anti-Semitic prejudice in his professional life as a financer in the French stock exchange. Though born in Vienna, Kaldegg spent much of her childhood in the Austrio-Hungarian Embassy in Paris but the family returned to Austria at the beginning of the First World War (Francis-Williams, 1996). Kaldegg then insisted on attending university against societal expectations for a woman of her standing. Defying convention, she studied history and business in Berlin until the rising of the Third Reich. Due to the increasing danger she fled to Switzerland with her nearly expired passport and then forged another one to get to Britain. Her brother Erwin, however was captured by the Nazis and spent four years in the North-Italian concentration camp of Fossoli from which he was transported to Auschwitz where he died.

During the Second World War Ann Kaldegg was interned on the Isle of Man as an enemy alien, and then picked fruit in Gloucestershire. Here she was billeted with Ann Ridding and her daughter Joyce Ridding. After the war she completed a degree in Psychology in 1947 and went on to do a PhD which she finished in 1952 (Francis-Williams, 1996). She then moved to London with Joyce Ridding, 'setting up house together' as it was described in her obituary in *British Journal of Projective Psychology and Personality Study* (Francis-Williams, 1996). In London she worked as a clinical Psychologist in both Cane Hill hospital and Guy's Hospital.

By the late 1950s Kaldegg had become a member of the British Rorschach Forum and in 1958 became an official society committee member (Francis-Williams, 1996). During the 1960s Kaldegg was central in the activities of the British Rorschach Forum and their journal; she continued to publish in the journal and present her work at the annual conferences (e.g. Kaldegg 1964). She was especially keen on the Rorschach as well as other projective tests such as the Lowenfeld Mosaic Test (see Kaldegg, 1966). She reported that "There are even people who enjoy taking the Rorschach test!" In 1965 Kaldegg became Honorary Vice Chair of the committee, a position she held until her retirement in 1967. In 1969 she published a popular short comment in *British Journal of Projective Psychology and Personality Study* about bizarre and curious incidences that had occurred to her when conducting Rorschach tests. In 1973 she and Lady Jessie Francis-Williams were made Honorary Fellows of the British Society for Projective Psychology and Personality Study.

Kaldegg's life, including an openness to her living arrangements with another woman, demonstrate a self-sufficiency and resilience echoed in Hopkins' lesbian personality description (1969). For example, in 1975 at age 76, Kaldegg passed A-level Italian and in 1977 she reported her address had changed as she had moved, with Joyce Ridding, to South West London (Francis-Williams, 1996). Similarly, in accordance with Kaldegg's bohemian lifestyle and unconventionality she flew over the Himalayas to celebrate her 80th birthday and a decade later went on a cruise to New York on the QE2 and flew back on the Concorde. She died six years later, on 8th December 1995 at the age of 96. Her obituary described Kaldegg as strict but warm and referred to Joyce Ridding as her 'close friend'. Unfortunately, however, the original obituary called her 'Janet' and a correction had to be submitted in the next issue. Joyce Ridding, who was twelve years younger than Kaldegg, died in 2006 in Wandsworth, London.

The similarities between the lives of Ann Kaldegg and Charlotte Wolff are uncanny. They both came from middle-class or upper-class Jewish families, both narrowly escaped Berlin and travelled to Paris and ended up in Britain working in psychological research. They also had important relationships with women which they were relatively open about. Kaldegg certainly defied convention as she published information about her living with another woman and clearly those who knew her were aware of her and Joyce Ridding 'setting up house together'. Brennan (2011; Brennan & Hegarty, 2010; Brennan & Hegarty, 2012) has described Wolff as living a 'marginal' or 'liminal' life and it is easy to see how such application can also be made to Kaldegg. Wolff went on to write two psychologically informed books on lesbian and bisexual women (1971, 1979), and most significantly used the Minorities Research Group as research participants in the same way Hopkins did (see Chapter 5). In all, Kaldegg can certainly be described as being independent, resilient, and bohemian. She lived a fascinating life and spent around 50 years living with Joyce Ridding in their own home having moved to London together.

Effie Lilian Hutton

Though not directly involved with the British Rorschach Forum or the associated journal, Effie Lilian Hutton was interested in personality as were many of the projective users (see Hutton, 1945). She was born March 25, 1904 and trained at the Royal Free Hospital London in 1928. Her early psychiatric experience was obtained at Harton Hospital, near Newcastle and at Rainhill Hospital, Liverpool (Nicol & Golla, 1956). In 1933 she began work at Horton Hospital in Epsom as the first medical officer to receive a clinical research appointment under the London Country Council. Here she worked at a clinic treating neurosyphilis. In 1939 she left and joined the Burden Neurological Institute where she worked until her death. The increase in patients following the Second World War meant she focused more on physiological psychology. At the Burden Neurological Institute, she assisted in the introduction of electronic convulsive therapy and lobotomy into Britain. However, her faith in psychosurgery quickly waned and she began research indicating the negative side effects of such procedures (e.g. Hutton, 1942, 1945, 1947; Hutton & Bassett, 1948).[6] In order to show the effects of lobotomy on patients she used projective tests to detect personality changes (Hutton, 1947) and problems with creativity (Hutton & Bassett, 1948). Specifically, she used the Rorschach, the TAT, and the drawings of patients. The results of her research led to the end of the use of psychosurgery at the Burden Neurological Institute. However, in 1959, three years following Hutton's death, they reinstated the use of lobotomy.

In contrast to the physiological emphasis on her work, Hutton had a rather more holistic approach to neurosis. Hutton was deeply religious and felt psychotherapy could only succeed if one took into account the patient's spiritual difficulties. She subscribed to Jung's idea that neurosis is the seeking of the soul but argued that the process is somewhat more 'activistic' than suggested by Jung (Nicol & Golla, 1956). She spiritually believed that to love, rather than to be loved, was the ultimate goal and that psychological medicine required the inclusion of religion. She was said to have 'remarkable success' with those suffering neurosis and despite publishing little, began to gain an international reputation (Nicol & Golla, 1956).

In her obituary she was described as a 'remarkable' person and her life certainly was unconventional (Nicol & Golla, 1956). Single and living with her mother until her death Hutton did not appear to be a typical educated woman of the 1950s. As shown by her portrait (see Figure 4.1) she presented as a masculine figure in a time of great gender conformity and rejected notions of gendered social convention.

Her short-cropped hair and shirt convey a masculine style and confidence that would surely have not gone unnoticed in the 1950s. Hutton's sense of style including shirts and a lack of feminine adornments is similar to that of Charlotte Wolff, whose clothing was very much recognised as deviant (Brennan & Hegarty, 2010). Hutton's masculinity is also captured in a caricature by a patient (see Figure 4.2).

When identifying Hutton in this image many people wrongly assume she is the smaller, feminine figure on the right. She is actually the figure on the left and is shown as tall, masculine, short-haired, and confident. Again, it is unclear as to who is saying: "Wasn't Rorschach Wonderful?" and perhaps the 'joke' in the cartoon is that

FIGURE 4.1 Effie Lilian Hutton (1904–1956)

The image is courtesy of The Science Museum. The copyright owner could not be identi-fied by The Science Museum and investigation for authorization is ongoing. If the owner sees the image can they come forward and contact The Science Museum, so they can amend their records and credit the copyright.

FIGURE 4.2 Drawing of Effie Lilian Hutton

Reproduced here with permission from © The Science Museum.

the psychologist is being tested rather than the patient. In fact, by depicting her in a lab coat, a symbol in many ways of scientific masculinity in the mid-20th century, Hutton is certainly portrayed as unconventional, different, and arguably queer.

Hutton died at the young age of 52 on 8th August 1956. Her obituary reported that "her death at the height of her powers is a severe loss to psychological medicine" (Nicol & Golla, 1956). Hutton's great belief in love was also conveyed in the obituary:

> She was loved by her patients and loved and admired by her colleagues. Those who knew her only as a physician mourn the loss in the fullness of her powers of a very great teacher and healer, and it is nothing short of a calamity that her early death has prevented her views from becoming made widely known.
>
> *(Nicol & Golla, 1956)*

The lesbian personality

The women I have presented here were pioneering in their careers and were central to the projective test movement. As noted, Hopkins (1969, 1970) concluded that the lesbian personality has seven key features, which distinguishes it from the heterosexual personality. Lesbian women are more: independent, resilient, reserved, dominant, bohemian, self-sufficient, and composed. I argue that all of the features or 'signs' can be identified in the biographies of these three women.

First, Hopkins argued that lesbian women are more independent, more resilient, and more self-sufficient. In regards to the projective test, and women's independence, resilience, and self-sufficiency, it is clear that all of the women took some risk in advancing as they did in Psychology against the barriers of sexism that were rife in Psychology at the time. Of the women I am drawing upon in this analysis, all were unmarried and none had children. Here I exclude June Hopkins herself as she later divorced and said she and her husband were married despite them both knowing she was a lesbian. This is perhaps unsurprising due to the pressures on women to choose *either* a family or a career in the early 20th century (Furumoto & Scarborough, 1986; Milar, 2000). It is possible they may have forgone marriage in order to fulfil their careers, yet this is dramatically in contrast with the gendered expectations of women from the early- to mid-20th century and is suggestive of a resistance to societal expectations, especially for middle- and upper-class women. It also goes some way to demonstrate they were self-sufficient as they received their own salaries and forged their own lives and careers. Illustrating their independence, both Margaret Lowenfeld and Ann Kaldegg were described in their obituaries as 'revolting' against their fathers or 'insisting' upon further education and careers despite being from wealthy families and thus were not expected to work. While these features are not necessarily indicative of sexuality, they are indicative of feminist values.

Second, Hopkins argued that the lesbian personality was more reserved and more dominant. Several of the women were described in certain ways indicating a more reserved and dominant personality. Ann Kaldegg was described by students in her obituary as being harsh or relatively strict, but also as warm or loving (Francis-Williams, 1996). This illustrates a tension between simultaneous traditionally masculine and feminine traits and echoes the gendering of obituaries in Psychology (Radtke et al., 2000). Equally, Lowenfeld has been remembered as distinctly dominant and confident in her approach to children's psychology and the development of her career and the ICP, yet as simultaneously fragile and reserved. Effie Lililan Hutton also fits within this more reserved but dominant description. These features of the women as reserved and dominant appear to be best reflected in certain masculinities they present. They were certainly unconventional given the socio-historical contexts of the mid-20th century. Brennan and Hegarty (2010) deal with the potential claim that masculine dress, including shirts, suit jackets, a lack of jewellery and/or clear feminine clothing, could perhaps be due to the professional status of such women or more fashionable 'flapper' looks from the 1920s. Instead they suggest that such visible signals extend beyond the norm of this time. In fact, Charlotte Wolff claimed it was exactly her 'dressing like a man' and her masculine hair that almost had her arrested in Berlin in 1933 by the Gestapo (Brennan & Hegarty, 2010). This indicates a particular deviance of androgynous dress beyond that of 1920s women's fashion. The biography and work of Charlotte Wolff is especially comparable to Ann Kaldegg and Effie Hutton and is further explored in Chapter 5.

Finally, Hopkins (1969) found that the lesbian personality was more composed and bohemian. As argued throughout, these women within the projective test movement were certainly unconventional. Kaldegg certainly appears to have more bohemian interests, for example, her ambitious travelling in her old age and Hutton outwardly presented herself in an unconventional manner. Lowenfeld was described as a very successful career women and a pioneer of child psychology, indicating a relatively well-composed personality and approach. Like Margaret Mead, Lowenfeld never outwardly described her sexual identity, but did have a close and likely romantic relationship with another woman (Banner, 2010). Ville Anderson is described as Lowenfeld's 'close friend and living companion' supporting much of Lowenfeld's later work. Similarly, Kaldegg and her 'close friend' Joyce Ridding also 'set up house together'. The women's unconventional or 'bohemian' lifestyles and their composure in living them aligns with Hopkins' (1969) findings.

The three women I have presented here were pioneering in their careers and were central to the projective test movement in Britain. These women had other women in their lives and little personal contact with men; in some cases they lived, worked, and I believe loved other women. They were all unmarried despite the pressure to do so in their lifetimes and were all highly educated, again something rather surprising and limited for women at this time. Indeed, both Lowenfeld and Kaldegg were from rather high-class families who were told they did not require an education past a certain point, and they rebelled against their families (mainly their fathers) and dedicated themselves to postgraduate educations. There is indeed an important intersection here with class. None of these women as far as I can tell have come from working-class families and they were clearly provided for during their learning and early careers. Also there is the concern that women were given the choice of either careers or marriages and it is possible these women chose careers. However, my interview with another player in this field described how having her psychiatrist husband assisted her career, rather than dampened it. This is somewhat unsurprising as Rossiter (1982) argued that marriage sometimes acted as a strategy for academic recognition. Equally, Hegarty (2003a) discusses the publications of married couples on topics such as homosexuality, which he recognised as an attempt to separate themselves from the subject itself, or to be 'pure' as Hooker described it. Relationships between those who were not married did also occur in the projective test movement; the creators of the TAT for example, Christiana Morgan and Henry Murrey, were lovers (Josselson, 2013). The reduction of these women as 'just choosing' careers then seems a little short-sighted and prevents the reading of their lives as distinctly queer.

However, there is one figure in this movement who I introduced earlier which complicates this narrative somewhat. Theodora Alcock was another unmarried woman working within this field and she too shares a number of traits and qualities with the women outlined here. She was well connected to psychoanalytic circles and clearly knew Lowenfeld from working at the ICP. There is also evidence she knew Anna Freud personally as she sent a letter of condolences to her upon the death of her father Sigmund.[7] Her links to queer women's networks is therefore compelling as is her own biography (see Chapter 2) and personality. However very little is known about her despite her large contributions to the projective test movement in Britain.

In many ways Alcock fulfils the description of the lesbian personality from Hopkins (1969). Her history is one of defiance, confidence, and pioneering spirit. Moira Quinlan, who knew Alcock in Ireland and was one of the executers of her will, reported that Alcock's determinant nature had not gone in her old age; instead she continued to wear contact lenses despite cataract operations and drove her 1967 mini 'held together by faith' until she was hospitalised shortly before her death. In fact, her erratic yet confident driving was one of the things most reminisced about in her obituary (Phillipson, 1981). Dr Geoffrey Barker (who had previously conducted research on 'female homosexuals' at Tooting Bec Hospital, see Chapter 3) provided the following anecdote:

> She drove us at high speed in her open left-hand drive sports car. Her immense enthusiasm and zest for living were well illustrated on this occasion by a dramatic application of the brakes, a swerve through a gate into a field where, beside a stream, grew magnificent bulrushes. From the pocket of her car appeared, as if by magic a pair of secateurs, and we continued our journey triumphant with some splendid decoration for her consulting room.

Alcock died on the 1st June 1980. Described as a pioneer, she is often thought to be the life force behind the Rorschach in Britain (McCarthy Woods, 2008). As a pioneer she is said to have been loyal, and have boundless energy and a spirit of independence (Phillipson, 1981).

Alcock's attributes frame the question which runs through this chapter rather concisely: was Alcock an independent autonomous (heterosexual) woman *or* can we interpret her independent autonomy in a queer way? In many ways Alcock fulfils broad definitions of lesbianism and she shares many characteristic with the women outlined above. She was working with women in a small part of British Psychology which appeared to be particularly encouraging for women's careers and was central in the development of the Rorschach Newsletter and the society. She also has the personality traits described by Hopkins (1969) which identified lesbian women at this time. She was described as 'harsh but warm' illustrating the somewhat gendered nature of obituaries in Psychology and the apparent conflict of describing women who conduct themselves in more masculine assertive ways (see Stevens & Gardner, 1982).

Yet, fewer personal details are known about Alcock, unlike the other women I've described here. We do know she was not married. This is aligned with the queer women I identified but of course not being married (or being married for that matter, in the case of June Hopkins) does not always indicate sexuality (see Tooth Murphy, 2013). In early- to mid-century Psychology women were effectively told they had a choice of careers *or* marriage. This decision was enforced via both social expectations and literally in marriage bans in the US, which were also attempted in some places in Britain. These decisions around whether to have a career or marry were only forced upon women – men could have both, without question. However, in what ways can we queer the career–marriage debate? Did Alcock simply choose career out of these two options? Or by assuming this choice by these women are we in effect eradicating queer histories – to what extent do these women not choose a career over marriage but they were not able to marry the people they wanted to and were under extreme pressure and conflicts in a discipline which pathologised their sexualities?

Of the other women I identified certain relationships with other women and other queer indicators were clear and so this interpersonal evidence gave me more confidence in naming them as queer subjects. However, my reluctance to include Alcock as a reclaimed queer psychologist remains. I fear that I run the risk of doing either one of two things by ignoring Alcock in these types of analysis. On the one hand, by naming her queer I run the risk of describing someone in a way they may have absolutely rejected. On the other hand, by excluding her history I run the risk of contributing to an already heteronormative queerless history which ignores the contributions and actions of queer people. In answer to these ongoing questions I have provided details about Alcock alongside issues of conducting queer histories and about projection in hope that you yourselves can choose whether to project queerness onto Alcock. In the same way we can also project a feminist ideology onto her, which again may or may not have been something she rejected (see Hubbard, 2018).

In drawing upon Alcock's life and work briefly here, I aim to illustrate how some of these women also knew each other and were aware of each other's work. Alcock worked for Lowenfeld at the ICP in the early 1930s and Kaldegg reviewed Alcock's book in *The British Journal of Psychiatry*; they both would have likely known about the work of Hopkins after she presented her research at the society's AGM on 1st October 1969. The links and networks to other women living similar lives, for example, Theodora Alcock, Margaret Mead, and Magdalen Vernon all suggest a network of similarly minded women working in the same field.

These women also had some shared interests and experiences, beyond that of their careers and lifestyles. For one, spirituality or religious belief is another core theme which links all of these women. Lowenfeld shared a great spiritual belief in the afterlife with her sister; Kaldegg was Jewish, though it is unknown whether she practised the religion in Britain; and Hutton's religious belief extended into her thinking about Psychology. Hopkins was married to a Chief Methodist minister and Alcock converted to Roman Catholicism. This point is worthy of note, though I will not delve much further into it except to say that belief in the spirit world was especially common after the Second World War and this tied in very much with Psychology as a discipline (see Lamont, 2013; Valentine, 2010).

Another link which relates to a number of these women is the ways in which their relationships with their mothers has become known. Lowenfeld is reported to have had a difficult relationship with her own (Evans, 1986; Urwin & Hood-Williams, 2013), experiencing what was deemed 'deprivations of the rich'. In contrast Hutton was very close to her mother; she was the only non-professional referenced in her obituary and they lived together. Hopkins also thanked her mother in her acknowledgments of her 1969 paper for assisting her with the coding of the data, suggesting a close relationship. Psychoanalytic theories of homosexuality rebounding at the time most laid blame for homosexuality at the feet of mothers. In fact, psychoanalytic mother-blaming theories were very common in the mid-20th century.[8] Interestingly it was Eva Bene (1965a, 1965b), who like Hopkins collected data from the Minorities Research Group, who countered many psychoanalytic claims at the time that homosexuality was due to overprotective or domineering mothers. However, she instead suggested responsibility lie instead with fathers. This was for both gay men (Bene, 1965a) and lesbian women (Bene, 1965b). The similarities between these women, whether that be their spiritual beliefs or their parental relationships, are not identified in order to explain their sexuality or lives as described here. Instead, they shed further light on the contexts in which these women were living, that is, a time of widespread cultural interest in spirituality and a period of post-war psychoanalytic mother-blaming as an attempt to explain 'homosexuality'.

In conducting queer histories there is the continual problem of 'projecting' identities onto people of the past who would not have conceptualised their lives in such a way. Dealing with such presentist issues are especially difficult when conducting histories that are hidden, especially in Psychology where 'deviant' sexualities were symptomatic and considered evidence of mental illness. But, as I described in Chapter 1, a fear of anachronism surrounds the history of sexuality as if there is something inherently offensive in misidentifying a person of the past as queer. Here, I have focused on projection as a key topic and used relevant projective Psychology to frame and understand their personalities as lesbian using the information available about their lives. Thus, I have presented a nuanced and specific form of analysis whereby I rely on the Psychology these women contributed to, to analyse their lives rather than focus on identity per se (see Scott, 1991). Specifically, I have adopted Hopkins as a theorist and attempted to reclaim some of the Rorschach's history as affirmative by framing the lives of Margaret Lowenfeld, Ann Kaldegg, and Effie Lillian Hutton according to Hopkins' (1969, 1970) descriptions of the lesbian personality. Work to include queer histories into feminist thinking in Psychology is ongoing and such work contributes to the reclamation of queer history in Psychology.

Notes

1 Both Margaret Lowenfeld and Helena Wright were very much interested in the Fourth Dimension and the paranormal. When Margaret died, Helena, who was with her at the time, believed despite Margaret being in a coma, that she was able to communicate to her that she was about to be accepted in her 'place of rest' (Evans, 1984). This spiritual interest is very much in keeping with early 20th-century cultural interests (Valentine, 2012).
2 A joint biography of the two sisters had been originally under consideration, but was changed to just be about Helena (Evans, 1984).
3 The note is open access and available to researchers to view in the Wellcome Library, the file from which the extracts were obtained is catalogued under the reference PP/LOW/I.5.
4 Recorded in an edited history of the ICP by Ville Anderson, Lowenfeld archive, Wellcome library code PP/LOW/F.2
5 There are substantial archived materials related to Margaret Lowenfeld (and her sister Helena Wright) at the Wellcome Library, London. See collection PP/LOW. For correspondence specifically between Margaret Lowenfeld and Magdalen Vernon see PP/LOW/P/12b:Box 34.
6 The Burden Neurological Institute was the first in Britain to do such surgeries. See Casey (2015) for a review of the controversy of psychosurgery in the 1970s.
7 The letter itself is archived at the Freud Museum, London. In the letter Alcock refers to Anna Freud's close relationship with her father stating: "for you who have been so infinitely close to him, this loss must be beyond all measure." Alcock finished the short letter by saying that Sigmund Freud's book (which one is not stated) "lies the chief hope for this troubled world."
8 Another example of a literature which ties together lesbian women, famous psychoanalysts, and relationship with mothers is the graphic novel *Are You My Mother?* by Alison Bechdel (2012, see also Bauer, 2014 and *Fun Home*). Bechdel particularly adopts Donald Winnicott's work and his ideas about mother-child relationships, as well as the works of Jacques Lecan, Virginia Woolf, and Sigmund Freud in *Are you my mother?* I draw this to the foreground because another key example where Psychology has entered the world of graphic novels is in *Watchmen*, where Rorschach is actually an ink blot-masked vigilante (see Hubbard & Hegarty, 2017).

The original 10 ink blots as presented by Hermann Rorschach (1921) in
Psychodiagnostik.

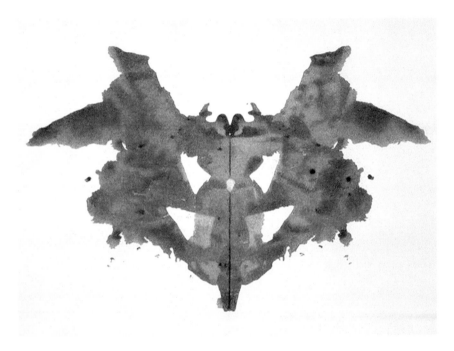

PLATE 1   Rorschach Ink Blot I

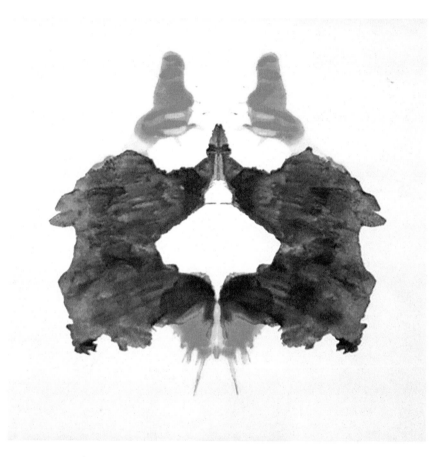

PLATE 2 Rorschach Ink Blot II

PLATE 3   Rorschach Ink Blot III

PLATE 4 Rorschach Ink Blot IV

PLATE 5 Rorschach Ink Blot V

PLATE 6   Rorschach Ink Blot VI

PLATE 7 Rorschach Ink Blot VII

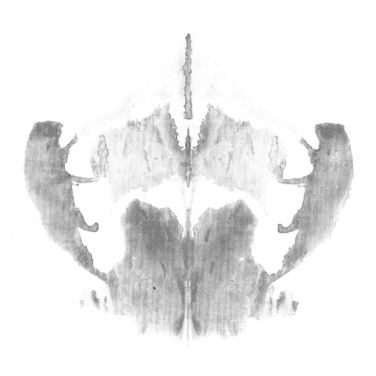

PLATE 8 Rorschach Ink Blot VIII

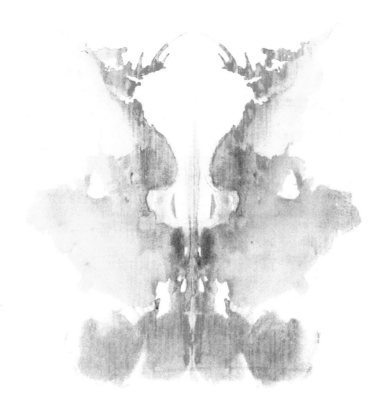

PLATE 9   Rorschach Ink Blot IX

PLATE 10   Rorschach Ink Blot X

5

QUEER RESEARCH AND LESBIAN LIBERATION

And we all assembled at some hall, some medical center in Bloomsbury and we were asked to strip off. I think maybe we were allowed to keep our knickers on. And it was all extremely embarrassing. And somebody remarked that it was the most uninhibited party they'd ever been to. And we also had to bring along a 24-hour specimen of urine and we, they took photographs of us, and they measured us and they measured the sub-cutaneous fat and, oh they took some buccal smears – which is, buccal being the inside of the cheek – apparently that shows hormone levels or shows something. I don't know, it all took about an hour and a half, and also, I think that, as far as I remember, we all took a psychological test, answering some psychological questionnaire. And then we all dressed and went home.

(see Jennings 2006, 2007a; Inventing Ourselves Lesbian Life Stories, 1989)

This is the description of one research project conducted in London on lesbian women in the 1960s/1970s as described by Diana Chapman, one of the founding members of the Minorities Research Group. While the preceding was likely to be after her involvement with the Minorities Research Group, they regularly took part in psychological and sociological research with the aim to provide non-clinical participants in the hopes to convince the medical world that lesbians were not sick.

In this chapter I focuses less on Psychology as a discipline and more on the activists fighting against pathologisation. Here, I outline the important role of the Minorities Research Group and the effect they had on the blurred boundary between activism and research. As a lesbian group they maintained that they would actively take part in research in order to quash the notion in scientific literature that lesbian women were neurotic and pathological. Importantly, it was the Minorities Research Group who volunteered as the lesbian sample for June Hopkins' Rorschach and personality research. They were highly aware of what Psychology was saying about them – that is about lesbians and gay men more generally, and took part in nine studies in total, some of which involved aspects of projective psychology.

This chapter begins with an introduction to the Minorities Research Group and British lesbian culture of the 1960s, followed by an in-depth look into the ways the group, in their publication *Arena Three*, presented Psychology and engaged with psychological research. In understanding the blurred boundary between Psychology and the social world, it is of course important to remember that the groups themselves are not distinct. Rather, there is evidence some members of the Minorities Research Group were psychologists themselves. It is true that some had membership because of their research interests and not their sexualities, but this is not true for all members who were psychologists. The story of June Hopkins alone (see Chapter 3) demonstrates the complicated nature of making assumptions of heterosexuality and separating research interests from lived experiences. Another psychologist who identified as queer in some way and also engaged with the Minorities Research Group was Charlotte Wolff. In the final section of this chapter I describe the life and work of Wolff and her links to the group for her research for her book *Love Between Women* (1971). Wolff is another fascinating figure who overlaps a number of the topics covered in the previous chapters, including similarities with the women discussed in Chapter 4.[1]

This chapter therefore begins to bleed out of Psychology, in the same way that an ink blot bleeds out onto paper. It is also evidence of the porous membrane between research and activism; between Psychology and social justice. It provides just one example in the history of Psychology which demonstrates that the idea that Psychology is apolitical is a mere myth. Instead, Psychology is integrated into societal ideas about what is/is not acceptable and acts as a controller of mental lives and experiences. This is demonstrated by the use of aversion therapy on queer people (gay men usually) as well as how some individuals used Psychology as a powerful governmental discipline to turn the tide away from pathologisation. This chapter shows the early stages of this for lesbian women particularly in Britain and their use of queer research and their activism around lesbian liberation.

The Minorities Research Group

On May 10th, 1963 Esme Langley wrote to Anthony Grey, the secretary of the Homosexual Law Reform Society, asking some central questions about establishing a lesbian group and publishing a newsletter "by, for and about Lesbians, inverts, their problems, the historical background, the social perspective and so on and forth." She requested information about the legal situation regarding such an endeavour, questioning whether it was in fact illegal for "lesbians, hermaphrodites, male homosexuals etc. etc. to found their own clubs if they wish to assert a perfectly understandable sense of community? And, if it *is* illegal, why was [she] able to join a club in Chelsea several months ago with almost exclusive Lesbian membership?" They agreed to meet to discuss on the 24th May: "If you bring some sandwiches, I can provide a cup of tea!"[2]

The Minorities Research Group was officially founded by five lesbian women in July 1963 when they met in Langley's flat in London. Of the first founding members, one was of course Esme Langley, the somewhat dominating force behind establishing Britain's first lesbian group and publication. Langley is said to have been angered by an article written in *Twentieth Century* entitled 'A quick look at lesbians' but impressed by a retort written by 'A Lesbian'. She then contacted 'A Lesbian' and met with her upon her return from London (Jennings, 2007a). Her name was Diane Chapman and she became romantically involved with Langley and ended up financially supporting her while Langley devoted herself full-time to establishing the Minorities Research Group (Jennings, 2007a). Two other women, Cynthia Reid and Julie Switsur, were connected to Langley via introductions from Langley's letter to Anthony Grey, and the fifth woman was known as 'Paddy' Dunkley, though she dropped out of the organisation not long after it had started (Jennings, 2007a). Later on, the founding members' occupations outside of the organisation were described as: an engineer, a sociologist, a writer/journalist, a librarian, and a trades-woman. Langley was the group's secretary and main editor of their publication *Arena Three* which began monthly circulation in January 1964. The title *Arena* was initially chosen because its aim was to provide lesbian women a space to discuss and be open about their sexualities. But Langley discovered two other magazines with the same title so added *Three* to avoid confusion (see Jennings, 2007a, chapter 5).

The Minorities Research Group stressed: "all those prepared honestly to endorse these aims and objects were admitted to membership, whether their interest was directly personal or sociological, or from disinterested good will." Their more open membership was directly related to their intention to "free female homosexuality from the prurience, sensationalism and vulgar voyeurism with which it is associated in some minds."

The objections of the group were as follows:

1   To provide a centre wherein homosexual women can meet others for discussion of their differing views, problems, and interests. It is now becoming generally recognised that isolation is a potent factor in inducing neurosis.
2   To provide material for medico-social research workers and writers who wish to investigate the condition.
3   To seek ways of improving the public image of the Lesbian by familiarising this fairly common condition, and of removing from it the aura of social stigma.
4   To publish and circulate monthly to members the magazine *Arena Three*, in which items of particular concern to homosexual women can be discussed, but which will also publish material of more general interest.
5   To arrange meetings, debates, lectures, and conferences and to promote intelligent and properly informed press and radio comment in relation to this minority group.

In the first year *Arena Three* had to overcome a number of barriers – the largest one that continued to plague the group was regarding funding. They found that very few newspapers would carry their advertisements, and some paper shops would not stock their publication. Eventually some newspapers did carry advertisements 'although with the honourable exception of one Welsh newspaper' all had been London-based. Following the publishing of a report in the Manchester Evening Standard (27th November 1965) about apparent 'cures' for homosexuality at Crumpsall Hospital using aversion therapy an *Arena Three* writer commented:

> Our local rag having refused your advertising, I wonder how they could be such daring little devils as to publish this news? And how in the name of all that is good and holy can "cures" be claimed for experiments which on begun *here* a year ago? I would be more impressed if the patients' inclinations remained in a so-called 'cured' state twenty years hence.

While advertising space was sometimes hard to come by for the out lesbian group, several newspapers were willing to talk to the Minorities Research Group for interviews and articles of their own. One such example, materialised on 13th December 1964 in the *News of the World*. In fact, it was precisely the Minority Research Group's advert in the *Sunday Telegraph* that alerted the journalist to the group in the first place. In this article Langley, described as wearing slacks with short-cropped hair, who smoked heavily throughout the interview, described the aims of the group and the loneliness plaguing thousands of lesbian women nationally. The article appears keen to reassure readers that the group did not 'promote' homosexuality or endanger marriages. While Langley acknowledged that around 40 percent of their members were married, the Minorities Research Group insisted on having husbands' signatures to confirm their wives could join.[3] Similarly, anyone under the age of 21 needed to obtain the signature of a parent, doctor, or clergyman.

The December 1964 press release to members of the Minorities Research Group echoed similar themes found in the newspaper article. Towards the end of its first year of running the group was made up of over 500 members and almost twice as many non-subscribing supporters. Not all members, the press release was careful to state, were those with 'active or inactive homosexual make-up' but instead interested parties who joined out of goodwill. However, the staff of the Minorities Research Group did struggle in the early days with some people requesting information who did not have such 'healthy or socially responsible motives'. It appears that several men who called, wrote to, or arrived at the offices of the group had misinterpreted the meaning behind the group and sought sexually illicit materials. Staff discouraged such behaviour and encouraged these men 'to regard women, including lesbian women, as whole human beings rather than mere sex-objects'. Upon finding out that the Minorities Research Group were not 'suppliers of pornographic materials, had no interest in sadism, masochism, leather goods, rubberwear or in sexual perversion of any sort' they tended to lose interest with the group. Of course what is rather interesting here is the positioning of lesbianism as outside of sexual perversion, which for many at this time, it was squarely in the middle of.

Alongside monthly copies of *Arena Three*, members also had access to monthly pub meet ups where they held debates, discussions, and lectures, as well as providing a social environment for women often isolated and struggling with social stigmatisation. While the main hub of activity was in London (in the Hampstead home of Diana Chapman and Esme Langley and in West End pubs) other regional groups sprouted up as the Minority Research Group recognised that isolation was especially negative on members in rural areas.

Following the burst of membership and the constant stream of letters to the Minority Research Group headquarters it quickly became apparent that additional resources were needed for many of the women seeking their help. They reported that they had been inundated with requests for information, help, and advice from all sorts of people including lesbians or 'women who fearfully suspect themselves of being lesbian'. Other groups included relatives, physicians, psychiatrists, and social workers as well as members of the press and the general public. Personal counselling services and postal correspondence to individuals became key work and this was apparent across a number of 'homophile' groups at this time. This was initially called the 'Bureau' of advisors and worked in collaboration with social and medical agencies who were sympatric to the aims of the Minorities Research Group. The group became somewhere for health and social services to direct queer women to and the demand for the network and supportive friendships demonstrated the group's argument that such an organisation was needed to counter the isolation, fear, and worry of many, especially remote, lesbian women.

The 1964 press release and newspaper article argued that the experiences of isolation for lesbian women and gay men was particularly acute compared to other marginalised groups. They compared themselves in particular to black and Jewish people, arguing that it was harder and more isolating for queer people because sexuality is more invisible than race and there is less of a community. The distinction between race and sexuality and lack of intersectional thinking here is stark, as is the belief that sexual minorities experienced the worst form of social exclusion in 1960s Britain.

> our research during the year confirmed that almost every woman homosexual, no matter how intelligent, well-balanced and integrated, is subject to stresses not imposed on members of any other sizeable minority groups. Analogies are sometimes made with the Jewish or Negro minority groups. But no Jew or Negro is a) reared from infancy, willy-nilly, as if he or she were Gentile or White b) obliged to conceal, even from his mother and father, the fundamental fact of his Jewishness or colour. Even the illegitimate child or adults (another member of a 'sexual minority') shares knowledge of his difficulties with relatives, if no-one else. In this respect the situation of the homosexual, from puberty onwards, often begets a feeling of unique isolation, of 'having to go it alone'. Again, a Jew or Negro refused employment in one

> place may reasonably hope to find it within his own community if not else-where, and has no difficulty in finding his fellows and in comparing notes and news with them. The homosexual has no such comforts. Despite the popular myth, homosexuals so not "recognise one another" at a glance, and may often work side by side in the same building for years without self-disclosure.

The language in the preceding paragraph is reflective of language in the 1960s though it does demonstrate a very niche perspective. The use of 'he/his' to denote all people despite the publication here being for and by lesbian women seems somewhat ironic and lacking in reflexivity. The apparent distinction between les-bian women and Jewish and black people also does little to hide the ignorance or even the possibility of queer Jewish and black people. This demonstrates the white nature of the Minority Research Group and their distinctly white feminist perspec-tive. Such issues of intersectionality became more apparent in the 1970s/1980s in British queer movements and is referred to again in Chapter 6; however, this goes to show that the history contained within this book continues to be about white people working for white people as I explained in the introduction. To solidify the queer people vs people of colour distinction apparent here, an article appeared in *Arena Three* in August 1966 entitled 'The Negro and Us'.

The careful separation made by the Minorities Research Group between them-selves and black people, Jewish people and, as previously shown, people interested in kink, is likely to have had the intention and effect of building a sense of appar-ent respectability around white lesbian women. Explicitly arguing they were not interested in sexual perversion of any sort when lesbianism would have largely been considered a perversion, carefully aligns these women with a heterosexual norm. They were careful to not to rock the boat of heterosexual marriage, reassuring *News of the World* readers that many married women members "are still leading normal married lives" (see Tooth Murphy, 2013). As mentioned earlier, married members had to have their husband's signatures and under 21s also needed a responsible adult to confirm their membership, thus adding to the 'respectability' of the group and perhaps to separate it as much as possible from the predatory and paedophilic stereotype which rebounded around queer people in the mid-20th century. Diane Chapman remembered:

> We hadn't realised that there was this interest in lesbianism in pornography and we found that quite shocking. . . . We were very concerned that it should be a proper, decent magazine and that there should be no overt sex, nothing that could be remotely described as titillating. Just up the road from Broad-hurst Gardens, our flat, lived Anthony Grey and he used to appear, uttering terrible warnings that we might get prosecuted for 'uttering an obscene libel', so we had to be very careful in the climate of the time that is was fearfully respectable . . . we had one or two letters from raving husbands more of less threatening to sue us for alienation of affection.
>
> *(Inventing Ourselves Lesbian Life Stories, p. 53)*

The Minorities Research Group carefully crafted a representation of themselves as being respectable and decent women, who happened to be lesbians. The group represented a largely white middle-class group, though of course it is likely subscribers and membership itself was rather varied. Class, however, is evident in personals sent to the correspondence section. Jennings (2007a) identified the following as being representative of *Arena Three* readership when seeking other similar women:

> Is there someone civilised, with mature mind, not too neurotic, who wants constructive relationship? Any replies treated in strict confidence.
>
> *(p. 155)*

The implications of decency and discretion are central in the portrayal of respectability these women were framing themselves and other (white, middle-class) lesbian women as. Indeed, after the second meeting it was noted in the editorial:

> We must also regretfully voice a complaint. A good many members who have attended the first two MRG meetings have been somewhat piqued by the exhibitionist tendency of one or two others, and want to know if it is really absolutely necessary to turn up to these meetings dressed in what is popularly known as "full drag". As the majority of women homosexuals are not "transvestites" . . . we shall be glad if at future meetings there will be no further cause for wounded sensibilities.
>
> *(see Jennings, 2007a, p. 158)*[4]

A heated debate ensued in the subsequent pages of *Arena Three* but it was clear the majority of members did not feel butch women and masculine dress, which was a major signifier of queerness in mid-20th century, was not welcome in the reputable circles of the Minorities Research Group.

However, that is not to say butch or femme women did not still get involved with the group. Letters published in *Arena Three* included some from women exasperated that these such 'undesirables' had not yet weeded themselves out. Described as "a collection of morons, dyed blonde hard faced 'Tarts' and betrousered fat tough guys" (Jennings, 2007a, p. 162). Langley herself was described as notably masculine in the *News of the World* article and friends described her not dressing 'properly'. Langley was described as looking 'peculiar' and her dressing in motorcycle gear was criticised as improper given her position as trying to legitimise lesbians (see Hamer, 2013). As the Editor she also replied to a letter published which described butch lesbians 'as revolting as men' with the following: "Never you mind, love. If our Editorial Board went in for high heels, frills and lipstick, we'd never get A3 out at all" (see also Hamer, 2013, p. 167). There was also encouragement from other replies arguing that "there are plenty of feminine ladies who prefer their butch partners to be as masculine as possible" (see Jennings, 2007a, p. 165).

The intersection of butch/femme identities and dress with class appears to be of particular tension in the Minorities Research Group. In many ways butch women were presumed (and often were) working class and this presented a tension of interests for the group. Hamer (2013) described the tension and perceptions of butch queer women in *Arena Three* thus:

> 'Butch' working-class lesbians were blatantly sexual and dangerously stupid because they did not care what straight society thought of them. Straight-acting middle-class lesbians were 'decent people', i.e. not 'butch', not working-class, and not dangerous. They could not afford to be recognised as lesbians, and did not wish to be seen as sharing a common identity with 'butch dykes'.

As Editor, Langley also denied the group was middle-class when it was criticised as such by Brian Magee in 1965. Magee had worked with the group to develop a TV show the previous year (see Jennings, 2007a). However, as Hamer (2013) argued the majority of members continued to be described as having middle-class roles and there is evidence that some working-class lesbian women felt ignored. The tension therefore in presenting as 'respectable' to wider society appeared in contrast to queer presentations of some individuals. Assimilation was key for some lesbian women – the trick was to *not look like a lesbian* in order to have lesbianism accepted.

In fact, the name 'Minorities Research Group' was chosen precisely because 'research' 'lent a certain air of respectability' and it did not directly state it was a queer organisation (Jennings, 2007a). Initially the group was therefore keen to portray themselves as just 'normal' women – which in 1960s Britain essentially boiled down to white, middle-class, feminine women – who were lesbians. In rejecting the 'outside the norm' positioning of lesbian women, the group argued they had been unfairly socially stigmatised which led to isolation and suffering. Lesbians thus required sympathy, not social exclusion.

In effort to counter medical and psychological explanations of homosexuality, the Minorities Research Group were clear to highlight that the issues lesbian women were facing, including their psychological distress at being queer, was not their sexualities *per se* but rather the social impact such a realisation had. They positioned the cause of such distress squarely at the feet of prejudice, discrimination, and social exclusion. This was also argued with somewhat more political force by the Gay Liberation Front in the 1970s (see Chapter 6). They also identified how good psychological intervention can help with such distress, though of course this was plagued with difficulty as the majority of psychologists and psychiatrists would have considered lesbianism as a form of mental illness in and of itself in the 1960s. The Minority Research Group explained how just like public attitudes towards lesbians varied, so too does "the lesbian's view of herself [vary] widely, from self-acceptance-sometimes achieved only after decades of lonely emotional conflict, sometimes through the good offices of a psychiatrists – to suicidal despair. The conflicts are not inherent in the homosexual condition: they are the products of ignorance and hostile social pressures." They argued that such feelings were then made worse by friends' and family's reactions, isolation from other queer people, the lack of a central advice bureau and well-meaning but misguided advice from others without experience or understanding.

They noted that while, unlike gay men, lesbian sex was not penalised by criminal law, lesbian women did still feel the effects of 'punitive' treatment metered out in other contexts', for example, dismissal from employment, emotional blackmail, and repressive methods "*whether or not* the women concerned were actively homosexual." Being an 'active' lesbian was therefore positioned as particularly dangerous, as June Hopkins was clear to point out in her married life she wasn't an 'active lesbian' but one in her own mind. The Minorities Research Group also estimated that there are more than one million women with lesbian 'tendencies' though most do not 'necessarily practise as such'. Understandings of lesbians were therefore constrained and constricted by legal and medical frameworks but the work of groups like the Minorities Research Group and the Homosexual Law Reform Society highlighted the social aspects of queer experience and worked to counter such legal discrimination and medical pathologisation.

By the end of 1964 a great deal had happened in the past year and the Minorities Research Group was well established in a short period of time. For the future they were establishing a counselling service primarily in London and hoping to secure salaries to pay staff as they had been working on a purely voluntary basis.

In issues of *Arena Three* the group showed particular interest in articles on queer history, the social and lived experiences of lesbian women, and engagement with lesbian representation in the media and in literature. They also demonstrated particular interest in what was being said about them in psychological literature and were engaged in research about lesbian women, but more on that in the following section. Queer women's interest in their queer feminist history is therefore not a recent phenomenon by any stretch of the imagination. The stories of lesbian murderers from the 18th century, famous lesbians of the past such as the Queen Christina of Sweden and the ladies of Llangollen (Sarah Ponsonby and Lady Eleanor Butler) were favourites, as was what we might now understand to be trans histories. For example, the lives of Colonel Barker and Dr James Barry (see Jennings, 2007b).

As the Minorities Research Group expanded so did the sub-groups and special interest groups. There was a social activities register with groups such as the Literary Circle/Society and indoor and outdoor games, though it was announced the music group was disbanding in 1965 due to a lack of interest. By 1966 there was a Chinese Supper Club, a Photography Group, and a Chess Club. The Minorities Research Group supplied a central book service, correspondence sections of *Arena Three*, and the MRG sound library. Book lists were sent out with copies of *Arena Three* and included the *Mattachine Review*, Freud's *Leonardo da Vinci, A Memory of His Childhood*, and Virginia Woolf's *Mrs Dalloway*. Other literature which was available to readers and reviewed included other psychological literature as well as legal, for example the Wolfenden Report (1957), as was lesbian-specific journalism, such as *The Grapevine: A Report on the Secret World of the Lesbian* by Jess Stearn. This list continually expanded and multiple copies of the same texts were available. In 1965 Djuna Barnes' *Nightwood* was added as well as six Radcliffe Hall books including two copies of *The Well of Loneliness*. The Literary Society certainly did seem to have great deal of fun in the mid-1960s; a report from this time to members suggests they were a rather rowdy lot where people would arrive in 'full drag' and they received neighbour complaints for their literary parties which included members being 'eloquent and persuasive about Iris Murdoch'. (Murdoch incidentally is likely to have been a subscriber to *Arena Three*, see Chapter 6 and Jennings, 2007a, p. 167).

In 1965 one of the specific geographical sub-groups of the Minorities Research Group – the Surrey and South West London group – became 'disquieted with its running by Esme Langley' and so a splinter group formed, which became known as Kenric (so called because most of the members came from Kensington and Richmond). This also somewhat coincided with the breakup of Langley and Chapman. Kenric is still running today and is now the longest running lesbian group in Britain. Disputes that caused the split were centred around the intertwined finances of the Minorities Research Group and the personal accounts of Esme Langley. Langley had also registered *Arena Three* as a public limited company in her name in response to the growing tension. Kenric wanted a greater socially focused democratically organised group and were less concerned about the research aspects of the Minorities Research Group. While the Minorities Research Group were not directly political (compared to, say, the Homosexual Law Reform Society, or the later Gay Liberation Front), Kenric was even less politically engaged, though as argued by Hamer (1996), they never set out to be.

Letters published in *Arena Three* also suggest a distancing from the Minorities Research Group and the queer London club scene of the 1960s. London clubs, such as the lesbian club the Gateways, were rarely discussed and in one letter described as 'vice' (although meetings were eventually held there from 1966). The Gateways was a central location for lesbian culture and activity in the 1960s and became more widely known from 1968 after the release of the film 'The Killing of Sister George' in which the club was featured (Gardiner, 2003; Jennings, 2006). Outside of the club scene, other regional groups also cropped up and had their own socials, though stayed a part of the Minorities Research Group. In spite of the Kenric rift, additional groups formed in the Midlands, Yorkshire, Hampshire, and Lancashire as well as specific London-based groups like the Essex and East London and North West and North London sub-groups.

In 1966 members were reminded of the origins of the group as well as the aims to remedy the isolation of the homosexual woman, promote better informed public opinions/services and press, collaborate in unprejudiced research, collaborate with international 'homophile groups', and to oppose unenforceable laws and obsolete legislation in relation to homosexuals' civil rights. Members were asked to detach and sign a form to confirm they agreed. Despite the split, the Minorities Research Group also continued with their commitment to be engaged with research and the legal frameworks which discriminated against gay men and lesbian women.

By 1967 they continued to have significant financial difficulties and other more politically active groups such as the Homosexual Law Reform Society and the Albany Trust, as well as the Campaign for Homosexual Equality began to gain a stronger hold on the issues they were tackling. From such efforts the Sexual Offenses Act (1967) decriminalised the sex between two men over the age of 21 from having sex in private. In 1968, in response to a number of problems, the Minorities Research Group became a registered charity and therefore was transformed into the Minorities Research Trust. *Arena Three* continued to be published until 1972 at which time *Arena Three* writer Jackie Forster then established the magazine *Sappho* alongside Angela Chilton. Other members joined, or were already working with, the Gay Liberation Front and the Campaign for Homosexual Equality, though these were at times criticised for being less welcoming to women (see Chapter 6, Jennings, 2007a).

Research and the MRG

The Minorities Research Group's thinking about their sexualities was directly informed by medical understandings of homosexuality. Such discourses were entrenched into their own writing in *Arena Three*. What is perhaps rather interesting is their positioning of their sexualities as a 'condition' and the descriptions of how such social pressures can lead to loneliness, unhappiness, and *neurosis*. The psychological framework used to describe the group and their definition of themselves as a minority illustrated that the only discourses available in the 1960s to think about sexuality were medical ones. This began to shift at the end of the 1960s as queer people were somewhat reconceptualised in Britain and the US as a minority social group (see Chapter 6).

It was particularly difficult to break away from medicalised understandings of queer sexualities as 'homosexuality' was conceptualised as 'deviant' and pathological at this time. For gay men, there was another dimension to their 'deviancy' as sex between men was, of course, illegal until 1967 (from which time it was legal for two consenting adults over the age of 21 outside of the military). Issues of blackmail and social exclusion were rife and Psychology and Psychiatry were responsible for some of the abhorrent 'treatments' for queer people (see Dickinson, 2015; Minton, 2002). While some psychologists appeared to have helped some queer people, there remained a risk for queer people approaching medical professionals. This was a particular risk for men due to the criminal consequences. From the 1960s onwards men's homosexuality especially became more firmly understood as a 'sickness' instead of a criminal issue (Dickinson, 2015).

Queer women were rather invisible in medico-scientific writing though the sickness model was applied to them in the sense that much of psychological thought was actually about men but applied to women. Diana Chapman in her oral history interview held at the Hall-Carpenter archives recognised the impact psychological texts had on lesbian women:

> I thought I was a lesbian but then I saw that it was ridiculous and awful and every book on psychology I ever read (and I had a stack of those blue Pelicans) told me that it was immature and that I should really get my act together and reconcile myself to my femininity and find myself a good man and have children.
>
> *(also see Inventing Ourselves Lesbian Life Stories, 1989, p. 50)*

Aversion therapy and other 'treatments' for homosexuality were primarily targeted towards gay men. However, that is not to say lesbian women were not invited or advised to undergo such interventions. In 1967 MacCulloch and Feldman published 'Aversion Therapy in Management of 43 Homosexuals' in the *British Medical Journal*. This research included two lesbian women in the sample who at the time were 'practicing heterosexual intercourse'. The authors described the outcomes for these women as having 'made a very good improvement and neither displayed any homosexual fantasy, interest or practice'. They also highlighted how one woman was now experiencing heterosexual intercourse with greater pleasure than before, and while the other did not engage in intercourse she did maintain a fairly stable relationship with a man. An aforementioned writer for *Arena Three* also commented on this research as it was reported in the *Manchester Evening News*. Upon reading the newspaper report they expressed their critical views on such research and the outcomes for those who had undergone such treatment in *Arena Three*. It is also worth noting that the vast majority of those who underwent such treatment did so voluntarily. In the preceding study, of those approached with the opportunity to take part, only two of the 45 people declined (see Dickinson, 2015, Chapter 6). Such is the power of fear, stigmatisation, and pathologisation.[5]

The Minorities Research Group reported how some lesbian women had "in fact been refereed to MRG by psychiatrists, hospital and other social workers, and church and other agencies" or had otherwise been helped by psychological intervention. Such positive experiences however were framed as relatively rare, as psychologists and researchers who 'want to collaborate in the fight against ignorance' were considered a comparative minority. A journalist member of the Minorities Research Group wrote in 1966 to *Arena Three* that she had asked several psychiatrists why they had so few lesbian patients. They had responded that this was because being a lesbian was merely an 'adolescent phase' and they were not interested in such things.

Psychological discourse and research was, however, regularly used by the Minorities Research Group to legitimise their perspective and experiences. For example, the 1966 report starts with the quote from Sigmund Freud: "Homosexuality is assuredly no advantage but it is nothing to be ashamed of, no vice, no degradation: it cannot be classified as an illness." While Psychological discourses as a whole were disparaging towards queer people, the group had faith that good research could turn things around. They seemed to have held the belief that the psy disciplines and social sciences held the power to change societal beliefs. If made to realise how lesbian women were not pathological because of their sexualities alone, research would convince and transform society thus removing the stigmatisation, fear, and isolation of many lesbian women. To this end, they reported on some psychological and sociological research, reviewed academic style books and actively volunteered to take part in research.

Before explaining the research that the Minority Research Group took part in, I will now outline three places where *Arena Three* presented psychological and sociological research and their reactions to it. First, in an international news round in 1966 the writers note a few developments in psychological and sociological circles as well as legal. In the section on Canada the author describes an article provided by the Association for Social Knowledge entitled 'What turns women to lesbianism?' by Mrs Renate Wilson. While noting the 'curious' title they appear somewhat pleased with the article despite its occasionally ill-informed stereotyped conjectures about lesbians. Mrs Wilson reported that:

> At the Forensic Service, researchers describe certain typical lesbian characteristics: excessive jealousy and possessiveness – lesbians may actually become suicidal if their partner leaves them.

The author of the news roundup also highlights the constant contradiction that doctors and psychiatrists often informed the world about lesbians but also identified the lack of knowledge about lesbians as a central issue.

> Mrs Wilson quotes extensively from Canadian doctors and psychiatrists, with evident respect for their views; this makes of her article yet another demonstration of the absurd readiness of the "experts" to make categorical pronouncements on the subject while blithely admitting their own total ignorance of it. If the psychiatric world wishes to earn the respect and confidence of the homosexual communities – in Canada or elsewhere – it will have to do better than this. As Mrs Wilson notes, the lesbians she met "rejected much of the 'textbook lesbianism'." Small wonder. They happen to know something about it!

Second, in another article published in 1967, 'Hippocamp' wrote about 'Healthy Homosexuality' adopting the aims of psychotherapy according to Cohen (1964). In this four-page article they argued that the broad aim of therapy is to be about reduction of neurotic anxiety but suggested that lesbians were making their neurosis worse by being overly cautious and concerned. They suggested that fears about what people might think or do were usually disproportionate and even if worst fears were realised 'there are other homes, other jobs, other friends'. Instead they suggest that "the first step towards a healthy attitude to one's own homosexuality is not to canter about the landscape 'telling'; but merely to start in a small way, by discussing the subject, sensibly and honestly, in completely impersonal terms." Despite the borrowing of psychological terms and theory, however, the author remained critical of therapists who treated homosexuality as if it were pathological in and of itself. Hippocamp made the remark that as reduction in 'Stereotyped thinking' was one of the aims of psychotherapy and this was, according to Hans Eysenck, linked to authoritarian mindsets, "this aim might well be taken first of all to heart by those therapists themselves before setting out to put the homosexuals' house in order."

Third, Langley wrote an extensive book review of Michael Schofield's *Sociological Aspects of Homosexuality* (1965). Scholfield was himself gay, and initially wrote under the pseudonym Gordon Westwood. He was also involved in the Homosexual Law Reform Society and although he was a sociologist with an interest in law, he held a degree in Psychology from Cambridge. The book received a glowing review in *Arena Three*; it seemed to be the research they had been so desperate for, and its rare affirmative perspective was noted. Once again using a matched-pairs design, just like Evelyn Hooker and June Hopkins (see Chapter 4), he demonstrated how in contrast to most of the medical research about homosexuality, there was little to distinguish homosexual well-adjusted men and heterosexual well-adjusted men. There were greater similarities between men (straight and gay) in psychiatric clinics, in prisons, and those in neither, than between straight men and gay men across the three groups. The review ended with a quote from Schofield which described "The idea that doctors can rid the world of homosexuality [is] . . . a medical fantasy."

Arena Three therefore was not only a magazine, but the product of a group highly attuned to the attitudes of psychologists and medical professionals about their sexualities. *Arena Three* was used to advertise recruitment calls from researchers who had been in contact with the Editorial Board as well as inform readers about research being published about them. At times the Minorities Research Group and some individuals reported being sceptical about the ways their data was being used; such scepticism arose from 1965 onwards. Still, they purposely agreed to nine studies in total in order to dispel pathological beliefs in the medical world about homosexuality (Jennings, 2007a).

Of the nine studies, there is some variation of how much is known about each one, and they ranged across the lifespan of the Minorities Research Group from 1964 to the early 1970s. The first researcher to approach the Minorities Research Group was Dr Eva Bene, who was interested in the genesis of homosexuality. The second was an unnamed psychiatric social worker (a member of the Minorities Research Group themselves) who suggested they collaborate on research about mental health (Jennings, 2012). Less is known about this project compared to the others. The third researcher was June Hopkins who is introduced in Chapter 3 and used the Rorschach. Dr F.E. Kenyon was the fourth researcher who later did follow-up research just with the 'predominantly homosexual' women who had previously filled in a questionnaire (the follow-up study included a physical examination). The fifth was Dr D Stanley Jones who was interested in 'the unmarried lesbian' and their maternal instincts, and later contributed articles to *Arena Three*. Dr Charlotte Wolff was the sixth researcher and I expand more upon her in the following section of this chapter. The seventh researcher was Mrs Morwenna Jones on behalf of an unnamed American Psychologist who was interested in the erotic imagination of lesbians (Jennings, 2007a). The eighth researcher was Mary Cecil who did a study on handwriting and wrote twice in *Arena Three* about her work. The ninth and final researcher was Marvin Siegelman, associate professor at City University (New York) who was interested in personality, attitudes, and parental background of both straight and lesbian/gay people (Jennings, 2007a).

This small range of research goes some way to demonstrate the interests of researchers investigating lesbian women in the 1960s. Key themes here include projection, in the Rorschach and handwriting studies, as well as thinking about the 'causes' of homosexuality. Parenting of queer people and their own feelings about parenting was also a central concern, as was personality. These largely reflect how lesbians were framed in Psychology and the social sciences at this time. Siegelman's work, as well as Bene's, also adds to the collection of matched-pairs studies that were particularly popular in this context. In her early work with the Minorities Research Group, Eva Bene stayed at the house of Esme Langley and was later involved with some of the activities of the group until 1966 (Jennings, 2007a). She tested the claim from psychoanalytic circles in Psychology and psychiatry that family child-parent relations were the 'cause' of lesbian women, i.e. the presence of a weak father with whom the daughter cannot relate.

Bene was a member of the British Society for Projective Techniques and had earlier developed the Bene-Anthony family relations projective test (Bene & Anthony, 1957; see Parkin, 2001). The Bene-Anthony Family Relations Test is a projective test whereby children have to allocate phrases to each family member by putting the statement in a post box that represents them. Bene modified the test slightly for use in adult samples and described it in her papers on homosexuality as a 'semi-projective test yielding objective, quantifiable scores' (1965a). The test has since been revised in 1978 and reprinted in 1985.[6] This projective test was argued to measures feelings of like/dislike, love/hate towards both the parents from the child and vice versa as well as overindulgence and overprotection. It was this test that Bene used on members of the Minorities Research Group and the Albany Trust.

Bene (1965a, 1965b) countered some psychoanalytic claims that domineering and smothering mothers were to blame for homosexuality, but continued to use psychoanalysis to suggest fathers were more responsible for the production of gay men and lesbians. *Arena Three* reported on Bene's findings as well as recruited participants for the study. They seemed particularly pleased that Bene acknowledged them in her paper (1965b). "Members who kindly volunteered to help Dr. Eva Bene with her research project last year will be glad to know her paper, 'On the Genesis of Female Homosexuality' (pub. Brit. Journal of Psychiatry, Sept. 1965) includes an acknowledgment to 'the Minorities Research Group for their kind help in finding subjects for the sample of this investigation'." They also quoted Bene's findings from the paper which argued that the lesbian group, who were compared to married (thus presumed to be heterosexual) women, were more hostile and afraid of their fathers.[7] The 37 lesbian woman from London also considered their fathers to be weaker and more incompetent than the 80 married women. Bene also argued that her results indicated how there was a correlation between wishing for a son and having a lesbian daughter.

In a strikingly similar vein, Bene also conducted work on gay men. Her research on lesbians was considered a sequel to her corresponding paper 'On the Genesis of Male Homosexuality: An Attempt at Clarifying the Role of the Parents' which was published the same year (1965a). In this paper she recruited gay men via the Albany Trust and again compared their results on the Family Relations Test to married men. Once again, she argued that it was not over-emotional attachment to the mother that was the 'cause' of homosexuality in men, but rather the lack of good role modelling by the father. Extrapolating her findings further and maintaining a psychoanalytical perspective, she suggested:

> It seems that much could be done toward the prevention of homosexuality if more attention were paid to the relationships young boys have with their fathers; and if those who are in need of father figures would be given opportunities for finding them
>
> *(1965a, p. 813)*

At the end of 1966 Bene's interest in the 'prevention' of homosexuality was evidenced once again. *Arena Three* included a short article on a 'Another 1967 Project Treatment Follow-Up Research' in which Bene was introduced as the 'research psychologist whose recent papers on the genesis of homosexuality have aroused world wide interest'. Bene was once again recruiting participants from the Minorities Research Group and the Albany Trust. This time she was asking "as many people as possible who had undergone treatment (medical, psychiatric or psychological) either because of their homosexuality, or in the course of which homosexual tendencies were considered" to complete an anonymous questionnaire. In order to take part, the 'treatments' had to have ended already and a snowball sampling technique was used, meaning participants were asked to request as many questionnaires as they wanted if they had friends who could also take part. It seems this request was in collaboration with the Albany Trust as it was highlighted that the research was of great assistance to the researchers as well as the Albany Trust in getting 'a clearer picture of how best to help the many people who seek our assistance'.

The next research project the Minorities Research Group were involved with was the Rorschach study conducted by June Hopkins. This study was outlined in detail in Chapter 3 and so here I will describe how the study was presented by the Minorities Research Group.[8] In re-introducing the research and participant opportunity to members and subscribers of *Arena Three*, the editor was keen to emphasise its usefulness to the group and the enjoyment of taking the Rorschach test.

> "Mrs. Hopkins is starting her research tests again this month and still needs a few more subjects. The tests are great fun to do. (We were so delighted with the 'ink-blots' we hope to run one soon as an A3 cover design.)" If you'd like to help, do write to Mrs Hopkins . . . and she'll be happy to explain further. (N.B. – Mrs. Hopkins is doing this project entirely at her own expense, and she's giving up a vast amount of her own time to it, and she devoutly hopes that it will be of great value and help to *us*.)

Hopkins' altruism and her devotion to the research, as well as her intention for it to assist in the depathologisation of homosexuality is therefore clear. She had conveyed this clearly to the Minorities Research Group and they were clearly fascinated with the ink blots as well. In keeping the promise of an ink blot cover, Figure 5.1 was printed as the image of the February (Vol 3 No. 2) 1966 issue of *Arena Three*.

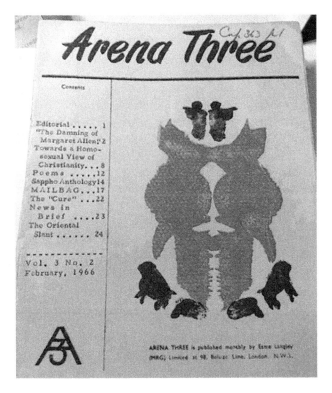

FIGURE 5.1 *Arena Three* ink blot cover February 1966 created by Carol Potter having inspired by taking part in the research of June Hopkins

Reproduced here with permission from the copyright holder, Cynthia Reid.

This front cover, which matches Card 2 and 3 of the Rorschach ink blots with its red and black design, does more than represent Hopkins' research and involvement with the Minorities Research Group. This image demonstrates the thread of this book from the Rorschach in the early 1920s, to its involvement with academic research fighting pathologisation. The presentation of an ink blot on the front cover of the first British lesbian magazine goes some way to show the sometimes bizarre history of the Rorschach and its ability to bleed into the most unlikely of places. In the Editorial of this issue Langley explains that the cover design was created by Carol Potter having been:

> inspired by our visit to Mrs. Hopkins to undergo her fascinating tests, including the Rorschach ("ink-blot") cards. We are happy to say that there was a very good response to the appeal for more volunteers, and our latest news is that only two more were needed to make up the hundred.[9]

Within this issue there was also an article titled: The 'Cure' written by 'Hilary Benno' – believed to be an alias of Esme Langley (Hamer, 2013). In this article the writer describes a deeply tongue-in-cheek satirical hunt for the 'cure' for homosexuality. Again, highlighting the knowledge of Psychology and Psychiatry's attempts to prevent, control, and treat homosexuality, the writer cites four 'cures'. These include the apparently happy-ever-after stories of consulting room therapies by which women (only in the late teens to mid-twenties age range) are said to be curable. Cure B can be identified as aversion therapy specifically on gay men ("as if they hadn't enough to put up with already"). Aversion therapy was described both as a "weirdly nasty version of the mediaeval 'cure by disgust' suddenly re-invented" and as being directly linked to Pavlovian Psychology. Parallels were also drawn between its practice and Communist 'brainwashing', including starvation, continuous interrupted sleep, incessant mental propaganda, solitary confinement, and other forms of psychological torture. The writer explains the methods of aversion therapy as "bouts of artificially induced nausea in association with all that he has previously held dear" (that is, patients were shown erotic images of men), the results of which the writer is understandably scathing.

A few months later, in August 1966, a psychologist who was conducting research with the Minorities Research Group wrote in *Arena Three*:

> Here is one psychologist who *knows* that you and the MRG are doing a marvellous job . . . You have brought so much hope and mental relief to so many people – I know because I have talked to them and heard their testimony . . . I will let you know how the (research) project is progressing . . . if it doesn't do any more than stimulate other research, we will have accomplished something very important.

This was later quoted in *Arena Three* as evidence of there being supportive and affirmative psychologists out there. While it's unknown if this was June Hopkins or not, it is very much within the time frame she was conducting her research and they were engaged with her project. Perhaps as further evidence, Hopkins sent regular donations to the Minorities Research Group throughout its existence.

It was particularly difficult for the editorial team to manage interest in their members as recruitable participants in research projects given the overall homophobic and non-affirming approach of the social sciences in the 1960s. Indeed, readers did not always respond positively to the publications produced after research was conducted with them. The editorial team, however, were keen to assure members and subscribers that they vetted the researchers. In a 1965 article entitled 'Psychology and the homosexual' Cynthia Reid highlighted how they had turned down researchers if they did not appear satisfactorily sincere, qualified, or have appropriate methods or respect of confidence (Jennings, 2007a). Dr Kenyon's work, for example, had a mixed response, and as Jennings (2007a) describes, Julie Switsue in her Hall-Carpenter oral history remembered that "He did a dreadful bit of research that we all hated him for" (p. 144). However, one researcher who seemed to have a good relationship with the Minorities Research Group was Dr D. Stanley Jones. He had originally proposed research into the 'unmarried lesbian' and seemed to hold the view that everyone is bisexual, well the 'wholesome adult' anyway (Charlotte Wolff who we will consider in the next section had a similar argument). Stanley Jones wrote a couple of articles for *Arena Three*, donated five relevant medical texts to the Minorities Research Group book service, and was invited to speak at a London meeting of the group.

While Kenric, the splinter group, were not as actively involved in research as the Minorities Research Group, they were still occasionally invited to take part in research as a non-clinical sample of queer women. This is evidenced in Diane Chapman's quote at the very beginning of this chapter. In the abridged version in *Inventing Ourselves Lesbian Life Stories*, Chapman recalled:

> I remember in, I think, 1971, a group of doctors form the Maudsley raised about fifty volunteers from Kenric because they were concerned to discover whether there were any measurable anatomical psychological differences between lesbians and straight women.

Such physiological and anatomical concern with bodies was also replicated in other studies of this period. Another study, by Dr Fraser Roberts at Guy's Hospital, that was circulated to Kenric members by Cynthia Reid involved similar testing.[10] The testing for this study was to be conducted by Dr R. Huntsman at the Lambeth Hospital. Reid also managed to piggyback somewhat on this recruitment as she recruited for her own study at the same time for her thesis to be submitted in 1968 to the University of London. The testing procedure included a blood sample, a buccal smear (from the inside of the cheek), a urine sample, and:

> A superficial medical examination (not a vaginal examination) to forestall any possible criticism that the results could have come from male transvestites without the doctors' knowledge.[11]

This research was being conducted with the chief aim to further understand the 'sexing of babies born with genital and chromosomal abnormalities'. Understanding lesbian chromosomes was thought be useful in 'making the tremendously far-reaching decision as to whether a baby is to be regarded as a boy or a girl'. This highlights how the pathologisation of sexuality is weaved through intersex and trans histories also. Medical understandings of 'deviancies', 'pathologies', and 'abnormalities' around sex, sexuality, and gender were lumped together at times, and separated at others, as medical and psychological disciplines tried to grapple with them. In the *British Journal of Projective Psychology and Personality Study* Ralph Pickford published an article titled 'Four Paintings by a Transexualist' and described the art work of a trans woman, along with her commentary about the work – two of which were produced before her transition and two afterwards. While Pickford is clear to distinguish between 'homosexuals', 'transvestites' and 'transexualists', he continued to equate all three as having the same type of essential 'error'. I also must note that this sort of language to describe trans people is very outdated and inappropriate nowadays – though Pickford did use the correct pronouns when referring to the painter, albeit only when describing her after medical procedures had taken place to affirm her gender.

Research conducted on queer people in the past has often conflated, collapsed, and confused what we might now consider to be distinct groups. In some ways this can be used to justify more umbrella terms like 'queer', 'trans', and acronyms such as LGBTQI (lesbian, gay, bisexual, trans, queer, intersex), as these recognise the complexities of the history. It also goes to show how complex our conceptualisations of sex, sexuality, and gender are and how they have changed throughout history. In this next section I will describe the life and work of one final researcher who used the Minorities Research Group as participants and her fascinating story of resistance as another queer psychologist.

Charlotte Wolff

Charlotte Wolff (1897–1986) was an (originally) German Jewish queer woman who became engaged with some of the aforementioned lesbian groups in Britain in the 1960s.[12] However, before she arrived in Britain she first lived in various German cities,[13] then in Paris to which she had fled in May 1933 due to the rise of the Nazi regime. Prior to the rise of the Nazis Wolff had gained her Medical Degree in 1928 in Berlin, though she also had substantial interest in philosophy and poetry (Wolff, 1980). After gaining her degree, she worked at a Family Planning Clinic as a Welfare Doctor. This work aligned her closely with feminist principles and practices as she deliberately sought to help poorer women and advocated for the removal of paragraph 218, the anti-abortion law (Brennan & Hegarty, 2009). Wolff argued that there was little to distinguish feminism and lesbianism and viewed feminism and lesbianism as inseparable to some extent (Brennan & Hegarty, 2012).

She reflects on this time in her two autobiographies *On the Way to Myself* (1969) and *Hindsight* (1980) and remembers her early realisation that she was romantically interested in women. While she did not 'name' this as such at this time, she suggests this is perhaps because of the support from her family and the lack of marginalisation she experienced her early years about her sexuality.

> Love for women has always been my natural inclination ever since I can remember. I did not think of myself as someone on sidelines because nobody ever questioned me about my erotic preference. It was taken for granted by my parents, relatives and the circle in which I moved . . . I was pleasantly surprised when my aunt Bertha once remarked "I think you are in love with Mrs X." I answered: "Not in love, but very attracted." She smiled. My uncle had always looked on me as a boy, and never expected that I would fall in with the conventional pattern. The prejudiced patterns of society didn't affect me because I was unaware of them.
>
> *(1980, p. 71)*[14]

The confidence Wolff gained in this period later assisted her when she experienced 'nagging doubts about [her] way of loving'. As did, as we can imagine, nights spent in the lesbian bars of Berlin in the 1920s. Despite such a thriving queer sub-culture, however, Wolff became very aware that the vast majority of society was not as supportive of her loving women.

As the Nazis came to power, it also became increasingly clear her being Jewish was also not accepted. However, she seemed to have experienced limited discrimination prior to the 1930s (see Brennan & Hegarty, 2009). In 1931 she was advised to leave the Health Service for 'political reasons', following a shift to a less visible position in electro-physical therapy Wolff recalled:

> But all too soon I was shaken to the core on seeing young men in Nazi Uniform, marching through the streets of Berlin, and banners stretching across streets which read: "Death to the Jews". Katherine [Wolff's partner at the time] came into her own at the beginning of Nazi unrule. She was with me body and soul, protecting my Jewish face with her Aryan Beauty when we had to leave the comparative safety of our flat.

Katherine and Wolff were then taking a course in chirology together organised by Julius Spier, renowned 'hand-reader'. This skill in reading hands and providing a psychological and personality analysis was later to come in very useful for Wolff and inspired much of her later research.

In 1933, like all Jewish employees in public service, Wolff was informed she no longer had a job. Upon her return to work to say goodbye to colleagues, Wolff was arrested by the Gestapo.

> I went as usual by underground. But I was arrested before the train reached the station Hasenheide. This outrage revived my spirits rather than paralyzing them. I asked the Gestapo officer to show me his warrant, which he did. I asked why I was being treated like this: "You are a women dressed as a man and a spy." I laughed in his face, sternly telling him to leave me alone.
>
> *(Wolff, 1980, p. 110)*

The Gestapo officer did not leave her alone, but instead took her to the guard at the next stop. Luckily, however, the Guard recognised Wolff as his wife's doctor and she was released.

Wolff's attire, her 'dressing as a man', particularly highlights the non-normative nature of such appearance. Wolff herself recognised her own dress as being linked to her sexuality and also stated "Fashion has come to the aid of both the female and male homosexual" (1971, p. 164). Such fashion choices and masculine dress is also evident in the photograph of Effie Lillian Hutton (see Chapter 4) and there seems to be marked similarly in both women's presentation as distinctly masculine. Chapman recalled how in the 1940s "you didn't walk around with cropped hair and trousers, not unless you wanted to be pointed out in the street." Therefore, while some masculine features of dressing might be viewed as 'professional' for women at this time, there remains a distinctly queer component (see also Brennan & Hegarty, 2010, for a fuller discussion).

Three days after the near arrest, Wolff's flat was searched, ostensibly for bombs because she had been identified as a 'dangerous communist'. Her maid had warned her and so she had given any 'dangerous' material (some of her books and papers) to a nearby patient. Gaining a five-year passport Wolff departed in May 1933, and while Katherine's father had persuaded her to breakup with Wolff precisely because she was Jewish, Katherine arrived at the train station to see her leave. When she arrived in Paris, having been allowed to pass by the steely eyed Nazi official who stared at her and her passport, Wolff had only a single suitcase and soon learned that she was stripped of her German citizenship and that her qualifications were not recognised in France.

In Paris, Wolff eventually found herself in intellectual circles and relied upon her knowledge of hand reading. Magnus Hirschfeld, the famous Jewish and gay sexologist, was in Paris at the same time, but the two never met. Hirschfeld was to later have great influence on Wolff, and inspired her work on sexology in the 1960s onwards. Her last major work was also a biography of him.[15] In this time, Wolff met a number of very influential bohemian intellectuals. She became friends with and posed for artist Man Ray and was indebted to Aldous and Maria Huxley for their help in securing her later relocation to London. In her work reading hands of the rich and sometimes famous (including a member of the French Royal family), Wolff managed to secure her living. In her meetings with the surrealists of the era, she recounts sitting at the same table in Café de Flore as 'the burly Picasso' who 'hardly said a word' (1980, p. 122).

In 1936, Wolff left Paris and identified herself as an exile. Aldous Huxley's brother assisted in Wolff's departure from Paris and organised her taking hand prints of primates in London Zoo. She was also given access to patients at Caterham Hospital in Surrey. Wolff's aim was to demonstrate the scientific value of hand reading and dissociated it with palmistry. This accumulated into a number of books such as *The Human Hand* (1943) and *The Hand in Psychological Diagnosis* (1951) and some key papers describing the hands of apes (1937), 'Mongolian imbeciles' (1942), and 'mental defectives' (1944).

The similarities between the lives of Ann Kaldegg (who features in Chapter 4), and Charlotte Wolff are uncanny. They both came from middle-class or upper-class Jewish families, both narrowly escaped Berlin and travelled to Paris and ended up in Britain working in psychological research. They also had important relationships with women and lived what Brennan and Hegarty (2010) termed 'marginal' or 'liminal' lives. Unlike Kaldegg, however, Wolff remained an independent scholar and did not hold an institutional position. She was, however, made a Fellow of the British Psychological Society in 1945. Upon her death in 1986 Wolff left all of her papers to the BPS archive and so continued her legacy and seemed to recognise the importance of her own history. Her autobiographies and biography of Hirschfeld also demonstrate her value to queer history as well as how she valued it (Brennan & Hegarty, 2009).

In the 1960s, Wolff began her next endeavour – researching lesbian and bisexual women. In May 1968 she approached the Minorities Research Group (then Trust) having heard about the TV show made by Brian Magee in 1965. Wolff asked participants to complete 'an emotional autobiography' providing a sketch of their lives and their beliefs about the origins of their 'homosexual feelings', some participants were also interviewed (Jennings, 2007a). Wolff similarly recruited via Kenric and the Albany Trust, whom she used again in the early 1970s for her sequel *Bisexuality* (1979). In all she interviewed and received questionnaires from 108 lesbians and 125 'controls' (aka straight people). Wolff demonstrated a keen awareness of the research already being conducted using the Minorities Research Group and in *Love Between Women* (1971), the first book to emerge out of this sexuality focused research, she cited Dr Eva Bene, Dr June Hopkins, and Dr F Kenyon.

In *Love Between Women* Wolff outlined previous thought about lesbianism and hoped to outline a new theory encompassing biological, psychological, and psychoanalytic approaches. In a similar vein to Hopkins' description of the lesbian personality, Wolff described lesbians as having certain characteristics. The most pronounced was aggression, which was coupled with extreme shyness, difficulty in adapting, and high levels of stress. In reflecting on this time, Wolff recognised a certain prejudice she felt towards organised lesbian groups.

> A friend of mine had joined the first lesbian collective in this country founded in 1963 and known as Minorities Research Group. She regularly passed on to me their monthly publication Arena Three. But I have to admit that I had not been particularly interested in either. I was probably rather prejudiced against lesbian groups which, in my view, were bound to lead to a ghetto. And nothing was more alien to me than a "professional lesbian" – the likely result of forming groups of this kind. It seemed to me insensitive and uncivilized to make a focal point of a perfectly natural way of loving and living.
>
> *(Wolff, 1980, p. 215)*

Some members of the Minorities Research Group shared such feelings of animosity. While an initial review of *Love Between Women* in *Arena Three* had been very positive, a later letter published was much less impressed by the book.

> When Dr Wolff was doing her research for Love Between Women, we were to be interviewed, glad to think some attempt was being made to dispute popular "myth" about lesbians. Having just read her book we now wonder how far our image has been helped by the writing of it.
>
> *(Jennings, 2007a, p. 145)*

There was also some annoyance at a number of incorrect details about the Minorities Research Group. For example, that it had shut down in 1968 rather than become a registered charitable Trust. Wolff wrote a note explaining that as these facts had come to light, they would be amended in future editions.

In an appendix of *Love Between Women* Wolff outlined the 'New Developments in Homosexual Organization' and effectively provide a list of activist groups and organisations, along with their publications. This inclusion goes to show the embedded nature of her work within activism – whether she recognised it as such or not.

In *Bisexuality* (1979) Wolff once again used extensive interviews and passages from her interviews to 'speak for themselves' in the text (see Brennan & Hegarty, 2012). Her arguments in *Bisexuality*, though sometimes contradictory, suggested the need for a bisexual society which removes ideas of binaries and simultaneously attempts to highlight the importance of recognising bisexual identities (see also Steakley & Wolff, 1981). In this book, Brennan and Hegarty (2012) argue that Wolff challenged the possibility for objectivity in Psychology and importantly recognised the value in people's own experiences vis a vis feminist approaches (see Kitzinger, 1987). However, her entrenched position as a Psychologist and her sometimes overstretching of the word bisexuality meant that her arguments were not that effective. Brennan and Hegarty (2010) have since suggested that, viewed as precursor to queer theory, Wolff can be seen as pioneering, and in adopting the writing of Audre Lorde stated: "Wolff's effort could be seen a valiant ultimately doomed attempt to dismantle the master's house with the master's tools" (p. 161).

By this time, Wolff was acutely aware of activism and social movements towards liberation. She had become friends with Anthony Grey and began to see the value in collective action and 'professional' gay and lesbian groups. Nonetheless, she continued to have such faith in the psychological frameworks and academic institutions that she struggled to become absolutely involved in British activism. For example, she was a patron of the magazine *Sappho* developed by writer Jackie Forster and Angela Chilton following the end of *Arena Three* in the early 1970s, but withdrew from it several years later because of members' hostility towards psychiatrists. Similarly, she felt the Gay Liberation Front's attitude towards Psychiatry and Psychology was excessively broad as she argued that not all psychologists were trying to 'cure' homosexuality (see Brennan, 2011).

Despite this, she did later recognise the value in the Gay Liberation Front and attributed activist groups, including the Albany Trust, as central in her recognition of her sexuality as something with which to identify. Whereas previously she felt it should not be worn 'like a banner' she later recognised the importance of naming oneself and aligning with collective action. In 1969 Wolff's first autobiography *On the Way to Myself* was published, which proved to be a critical point in this change of heart (Brennan, 2011). Upon the invite of Diane Chapman, she then gave a talk about her life to Kenric members. In 1976, Wolff also wrote *An Older Love*, an arguably semi-autobiographical novel about women who love one another. Just as Hopkins has been reclaimed as a pioneering lesbian psychologist, so too has Charlotte Wolff (Brennan, 2011).

These histories discussed in this chapter, of queer individuals whether they be psychologists or members of activist groups (or both), demonstrate the compelling nature of queer history. The language and available discourses might have changed but the early signs of valuing social research as one of the prongs by which to manage and shift social beliefs is clear. It has been through the bizarre bleeding between the two that we can see the actions of queer researchers do affirmative research and activists generate social collectivity.

Notes

1 This chapter does not, and cannot, present the wealth of rich lesbian history in Britain during this time. Instead, I try to provide enough detail in order to contextualise the psychological meaning of the activism which took place and explore the intricate details of movements towards lesbian liberation in relation to pathologisation. For further reading on lesbian history and culture at this time I strongly recommend the brilliant work of Rebecca Jennings (2006, 2007a, 2007b) who has been so kind and useful in my own research. I also suggest reading Dickinson (2015), Hamer (2013), the Lesbian History Sourcebook compiled by Oram and Turnbull (2001), *Inventing Ourselves Lesbian Life Stories*, 1989; Gardiner (2013); Lewis (2013, which includes very useful chapters by Amy Tooth Murphy, Chris Waters, and Laura Doan); and Weeks (1977/2016). For more on depathologisation from within Psychology, see Minton (2002) and the always wonderful Peter Hegarty (2018). There have also been some wonderfully rich books which draw on oral history and the life stories of those involved in this lesbian scene. These include some of the aforementioned texts but also Summerskill (2012) and Traies (2018).
2 The club Langley is referring to is most likely the Gateways in Chelsea. For a more extensive history of the Gateways see Gardiner (2003) and also Jennings (2006, 2007a, 2007b, 2008). Also please note that 'hermaphrodite' is no longer appropriate terminology to describe people who are intersex or have variations of sex characteristics.
3 See Tooth Murphy's (2013) account of lesbian domesticity which centrally considers the experiences of married lesbian women in the British post-war era.
4 Distinctions between 'butch', 'femme', 'lesbian', and 'transvestite' here appear to work hard to distinguish (apparently separate) types of being. From Magnus Hirschfeld's work 'transvestite' distinguished between gender variance from sexual variance. While it remains a contested term its history is integrated in interesting ways as sexologists, psychologists, and other medical professionals attempted to untangle sex, gender, and sexuality. See Pearce (2018) Chapter 2 for a provided historical account of the term 'transvestite' and its relationship with the history of diagnosis in trans health care.
5 This research was conducted at the Crumpsall Hospital, Manchester following donations of between £6,000 and £7,000 to set up a unit specifically for the purpose of 'curing' homosexuals. I recommend Dickinson (2015) for a more extensive history of the use of such treatments and an oral history of mental health nurses and the people who underwent aversion therapies.
6 Parkin (2001) argued that the test was not reliable enough for research purposes but was useful in therapeutic settings; his conclusion alludes to the idea that he himself was developing a solution to the issues raised in his review of the test.
7 The presumption that married women were heterosexual can of course be questioned (see Tooth Murphy, 2013). Considering it was also estimated that 40% of the Minorities Research Group members were married to men and there is evidence of substantial pressure for women to marry in the 1960s, this assumption that marriage equals heterosexual can be questioned.
8 While Hopkins' work (1969, 1970) was not initially considered in high regard (see Morin, 1977) and it was later that the pioneering aspects of her research were to be accounted for (see special issue of *Lesbian and Gay Psychology Review*, 2002, Volume 3, part 2), her 1969 research with the Minorities Research Group is included in the Lesbian History Sourcebook compiled by Oram and Turnbull (2001), as is the research by Dr Kenyon and Dr D Stanley Jones.

 9 Despite eventually collecting data from 100 lesbian women from the Minorities Research Group, only 24 women were compared to heterosexual women because of the difficulty in recruiting heterosexual women for the study (see Chapter 3).

10 Information regarding this study can be found in the archive of Mary McIntosh (at the London School of Economics Library) who features more heavily in Chapter 6.

11 It is possible this study is the same as the one described by Diane Chapman as they have striking similarities (e.g. the urine test and buccal smear), however both descriptions include differing details about the location of testing and the institutions responsible, so I have reported them as separate in this chapter.

12 Charlotte Wolff's (1897–1986) materials are available in the BPS archive at the Wellcome Library, London.

13 I have a fond memory of managing to pick up my own copy of Wolff's second autobiography *Hindsight* in Heidelberg – one of very few books in English in a beautiful, crammed second-hand book shop. The notes on the inside indicate several owners in London prior to the book's travels to Germany before I brought it back to Britain, following Wolff's own trajectory.

14 Wolff (1980) recalls how her father had identified her as a boy to the family upon her birth despite the announcement by the midwife she was a girl. Such stories tie in closely to psychoanalytic theories about parental desires for boys leading to lesbian daughters which was exemplified by Bene (1965a, 1965b) as discussed earlier in the chapter.

15 See Brennan and Hegarty (2009) for more details about Wolff and Hirschfeld and her 'portrait' of him. Hirschfeld established the famous Institute for Sexual Science in 1919 – the first institute to scientifically study sexuality. Hirschfeld had been travelling for a lecture tour when he was advised not to return to Germany in the early 1930s. The Institute was destroyed by Nazi storm troopers and its libraries were burned in the famous book burning at the Opernplatz.

6

QUEER ACTIVISM AND ACADEMIA

In the mid-1960s Maureen Duffy began to conduct her own research. As a queer woman who was involved in the lesbian scene in Britain she wanted more representation of real lesbian women to be available. She went out, using her own links to the Gateways, and conducted 'life-story' interviews. Such oral history approaches and opportunistic snowballing methods are now very popular in academic work of this kind. Duffy intended on writing a non-fiction book about the broad spectrum of queer women in Britain (see Gardiner, 2003). She also reflected on her own experiences as a working class, educated woman:

> I don't remember how many women I interviewed. I wanted a wide a spectrum as possible. Partly because I was aware of all these divisions; partly because of the underlying ethos of what I wanted to present which was a microcosm. I also wanted to point out that it is not confined to any one age or class or culture or necessarily even straightforward sexuality.
>
> *(as cited in Gardiner, 2003, pp. 104–105)*

But Duffy was told it was not possible to publish the work as non-fiction. She was not considered qualified to produce such a book as she was neither a sociologist or psychologist. It was therefore transformed into fiction and while there were concerns about people being identifiable in the novel and about the obscenity law, *The Microcosm* was published in 1966.

This chapter aims to answer the question of which sociologists *were* doing something akin to Duffy's research. In the previous chapter the actions of psychologists were the focal point, but here instead we consider the life and work of one sociologist who was deeply involved in both academia and activism in the 1960s and 1970s: Mary McIntosh. *The Microcosm* became a very popular book, especially for queer women, and it was around this time Duffy became notable as an out gay woman in British public life. She was active in gay liberation, involved in nuclear disarmament, and active in efforts for authors' rights and animal rights. *The Microcosm* was also remembered fondly by Mary McIntosh. Gardiner quotes McIntosh's response to *The Microcosm*:

> I just saw *The Microcosm* as life as it is, at last. It really captured a lot of the Gateways for me, the sense that you met a lot of varied people. It was brilliant.
>
> *(p. 104)*

Mary McIntosh (1936–2013) was a British lesbian sociologist who frequented the Gateways and conducted her own research about the homophile movements in the US and in Britain. She was very involved in the Gay Liberation Front from 1970 and at the core of all of her activism and academic work was her Marxist feminism, her perspective as a queer woman, and her recognition of research and activism not being all that distinct.

Once again, then, it appears that popular literature and public life are entangled with that of academic thought. Just as Evelyn Hooker had a close friendship with Christopher Isherwood, McIntosh knew Maureen Duffy and Iris Murdoch, another queer author. As explored in Chapter 5, the links between researchers and the Minorities Research Group are also evidence of the blurring of this boundary. Charlotte Wolff, for example, met Virginia Woolf and read her hands, as previously mentioned. She also knew the Surrealists in Paris, including Man Ray and was great friends with Aldous and Maria Huxley who helped her settle in Britain. There is evidence of psychologists themselves being members of the Minorities Research Group and of course of queer women like June Hopkins doing affirmative work with the Rorschach with their members. Wolff's research notes for her book *Bisexuality* also indicate she had women who were academics in her research. For example, one participant seemed to know Wolff personally and provided additional information to her previous responses and spoke of their experiences speaking at conferences.[1]

Queer people have of course existed in all areas of public life, so its unsurprising we can find evidence of queer lives across the borders of academia and activism. However, what is interesting here is that these people were working and living at a time of pathologisation and criminalisation in some cases. 'Homosexuals' were considered both socially and psychologically sick and so to work within such a field as queer people and to be active in efforts against such thinking was undoubtedly challenging.

Dickinson (2015) explored in detail the intricacies of queer mental health nurses who administered aversion therapy to fellow queer people, usually gay men. In order to understand this apparent paradox, he argued that it's important to understand identity boundaries, cultures, and communities at work. Notably, he argued that there were prominent lesbian and gay sub-cultures within some mental health hospitals. Of the gay nurses Dickinson interviewed all had administered treatments to 'cure' patients of the same 'illness' they had (2015). The medical, social, and psychological sciences were engrained with thinking that LGBT people were 'sick', ill and pathological, and capable of 'cure'.

Sociologists, as well as psychologists, therefore had a particular role to play in the fight for gay liberation and depathologisation. This chapter will concentrate on the work of sociologist Mary McIntosh to demonstrate how individuals positioned as both academics and activists have made substantial change in the fight for equality and social justice. First, I outline the early life and work of McIntosh, including her own involvement with the Minorities Research Group, Kenric, and other more political groups (see Figure 6.1). Next, I will outline her first major paper 'The Homosexual Role' and the impact it had on shifting ideas around the positioning of homosexuality in society. Her paper is particularly interesting given it was developed alongside advice given by Evelyn Hooker. Finally, I will explore McIntosh's work in the Gay Liberation Front and how she was particularly involved in the sub-group fighting against the pathologisation of queer people in Psychology and Psychiatry.

Mary McIntosh

Mary Susan McIntosh (1936–2013) was born in Hampstead, London. Her upbringing was surrounded by socialism and she was at one point a member of the Communist party (see Weeks, 2013; Roe, 2013). She studied Philosophy, Politics, and Economics at Oxford at St Anne's College where she met author Iris Murdoch, with whom she had an ongoing correspondence. It was at this time that McIntosh was beginning to come to terms with her sexuality. Her reading of Simone de Beauvoir's 'The Second Sex' in her student days was pivotal in both her feminist and queer understanding. After Oxford she went to the University of California, Berkeley, as a graduate student and became involved in protests and activism against the House of Un-American Activities and McCarthyism. Despite being deported from the US in 1960 because of her involvement in protests, McIntosh's activism showed no signs of stopping.

Upon her return to Britain McIntosh first worked at the Home Office and then at the University of Leicester until 1975. Following this, she began working as a Lecturer at the Sociology department at the University of Essex, here she spent the next 26 years as a Senior Lecturer following promotion in 1980. In 1986 she became the department's first woman Head of Department. She also was one of the founding editors of *Feminist Review*. At the age of 60 McIntosh retired from academia and pursued work at a Citizens Advice Bureau in London. Following her death in 2013, she was remembered in various obituaries as a pioneer, an excellent speaker, a kind mentor, and most of all a prominent feminist and socialist activist (see Smart, 2003).

In many ways Mary McIntosh is one of the names most synonymous with British Sociology, especially in queer studies. Yet, she is situated in a somewhat unusual position in that she is both remembered and recognised; but has not been widely celebrated as one might expect. For one, she was not fully academically awarded in her lifetime as arguably she should have been (for example, she never received a professorship, see Weeks, 2013). There are of course particular difficulties in conducting more recent histories, but the archive and materials surrounding McIntosh are plentiful and certainly deserve more attention by historians and social scientists.[2] As a queer, feminist, and highly political woman she did not play by the rules of British academia for the most part, especially given the time in which she was working.

The 1960s and early 1970s was a particularly fascinating time in McIntosh's life, which I will focus on here. It was during this time that McIntosh first felt more affirmed in her sexuality and began to get increasingly involved in gay liberation and later women's liberation movements.

> The realisation came on me during, I suppose, particularly when I was a student and read Simone de Beauvoir and later during the sixties when I read *The Golden Notebook*, that women were just not at all the equals of men and that men saw us, as Simone de Beauvoir put it, as other. We served to define men and masculinity but we didn't exist in our own right, according to them, and so I saw it then as quite difficult for women to define themselves. But then, in addition, there was the fact of being a lesbian which took me, I think, really a long time to come to terms with. Probably not until I was about twenty-four did I realise that it was not a bad thing to be a lesbian. Before that, if I was a lesbian it was as a form of suffering and it meant to me definitely that you couldn't be a mother. It probably meant unhappiness and that you couldn't ever have a rewarding relationship and it wasn't until the sixties that I did start to have a rewarding lesbian relationship, with Elizabeth Wilson in fact as it turned out.[3]

McIntosh and Wilson's relationship is also remembered by Wilson in her published works:

> I told some of the women in my college [at Oxford University] that I thought I was a lesbian and was upset and humiliated when they reacted with either brushing it aside as a phase, or else by looking on me as neurotic rather than sinful. This attitude of "you are sick" rather than "you are wicked" which actually the more undermining of the two. . . . When I did finally meet and start an affair with another woman I immediately became very dependent on her, because, believing as I did that homosexuals were all doomed to misery (since that is what you read in all the books on the subject) a happy relationship was something to cling to as hard as you could.
>
> *(Wilson, 1986, as cited in* Lesbian Sourcebook, *2001, p. 268)*

The two of them 'drifted towards Marxism' and became increasingly involved in the lesbian social scene in London. McIntosh recalled: "I just loved being at the Gateways. It gave me a huge buzz to be there when it was crowded and there was just a sea of women like us" (Gardiner, 2003, p. 79).

McIntosh was also involved in the Minorities Research Group and their publication *Arena Three* (see Figure 6.1 for her joint membership card with Elizabeth

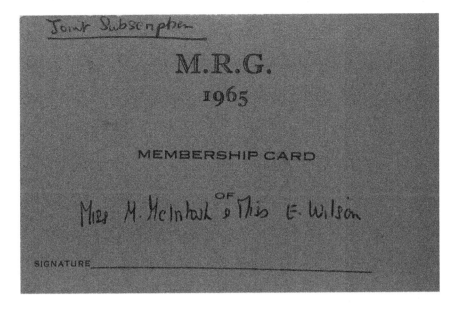

FIGURE 6.1 The joint Minorities Research Group membership card of Mary McIntosh and Elizabeth Wilson

Reproduced here with permission from the London School of Economics Library.

Wilson). As a group they were certainly invested in Sociology as a discipline which had the potential to assist in their broader goals. The founding members' occupations outside of the organisation were described as: an engineer, *a sociologist*, a writer/journalist, a librarian, and a trades-women. While McIntosh was not one of the five founders, it does seem a sociologist was influential. It is unclear at times who occupied these positions, as some founding members such as Paddy Dunkley quickly withdrew from involvement whereas others increased their participation. Another clue to suggest there was a deliberate inclusion of sociological interest is the group being for "all those prepared honestly to endorse these aims and objects were admitted to membership, whether their interest was directly personal or *sociological*, or from disinterested good will" (my emphasis).

Letters between Esme Langley, the groups instigator and editor of *Arena Three*, and McIntosh suggest they knew each other from March 1964 when McIntosh wrote to the Minorities Research Group to subscribe having seen an advertisement in *The Observer*.

McIntosh also contributed an article to *Arena Three*. Having written to one another, Langley and McIntosh met in person and discussed the progress of the Minorities Research Group. McIntosh also provided some comments on a published article in *Arena Three* by Langley's 'friend' D.M.C. entitled 'Bent or Straight mates?' In a follow-up letter in May 1964 McIntosh provided a written response which was then published in the June issue. This was entitled: "'Bent or straight mates?' A Sociologist's views." The response in effect criticised the simplicity of the original article which provided an outline of psychological and medical theories about the causes of homosexuality in contrast to potential biological explanations about sexuality being 'in born'. D.M.C. had highlighted how psychiatrists considered homosexuality to be an 'acquired neurosis' and how those with a psychoanalytical perspective considered it to be caused by under – or over – identification with one's father.

McIntosh's response complicated some of the statements made and particularly showed a deep understanding of psychoanalytical theory and the life of Radcliffe Hall. She was most critical however of the suggestion that if indeed homosexuality was the result of neurosis or mental disorder then it could be 'eliminated'; this was in contrast to the 'in born' argument which was utilised to demonstrate how ineffective such 'cures' are. McIntosh stated: "What is curious about DMC's argument is her assumption that *if* lesbianism is curable or preventable, *then*, as a value judgment, it should be cured, or prevented." In providing clear objection, McIntosh argued that lesbianism should not be assumed to be a) undesirable and b) easily banished, even if the unlikely event a 'cure' or method was found to prevent lesbianism.

In following letters McIntosh also requested the November and December 1964 issues of *Arena Three* which had not yet been delivered by January 1965. The reply from Langley emphasised the growth of the group in only a year and the frantic nature of their last London meeting where 150 people descended upon the Bull's Head pub.

The McIntosh archive collection contains copies of *Arena Three* from 1964 and 1965 very consistently with then a much more sporadic collection, until there are some more copies from 1970 onwards. The issues in McIntosh's collection demonstrate she would have known about the work being conducted by researchers with the Minorities Research Group, for example, June Hopkins, Eva Bene, and later Charlotte Wolff. The relative dearth of *Arena Three* copies towards the end of the 1960s is also demonstrative of McIntosh being more involved with the splinter group Kenric. It was through their correspondence that she found out about other studies such as the one by Roberts and Huntsman who were interested in the genetic makeup of lesbian woman to assist in the categorisation of intersex infants (see Griffiths, 2018a, 2018b, for further information regarding histories of intersex in Britain).

It was at this point in time that McIntosh began to develop an interest in studying gay society from a more sociological perspective. She began to conduct her research along a similar vein to that which Duffy had been doing at roughly the same time in the mid-1960s. The year before *The Microcosm* was published McIntosh wrote to Duffy explaining some of her intentions and asked to meet. McIntosh outlined her research interests thus:

> I am a sociologist, and I am doing research into the social situation of homosexuals. As part of this I have been studying the so-called 'homophile' organisations and the law reform movement, particularly in America but also in this

country. So far most of my information has been gleaned from the magazine published by these organisations and from various people I know. But I am beginning to feel that the picture I am getting is rather one-sided: I have found out a good deal about the reasons why people support the movements and what they are trying to do but I have not heard the point of view of people who do not support it, or even oppose it.

The reason I am writing to you is that I have heard that when the Minorities Research Group was founded in London you were not in favour of this idea. I should be most interested to hear what your reasons were and whether you still hold this view.

(Letter from McIntosh to Duffy dated 25th June 1965)[4]

In response Duffy agreed to meet, stating this account was 'garbled', though critique of the Minorities Research Group was clear. As Gardiner (2003) outlines, many queer women found comfort in *The Microcosm* and wrote to Duffy for advice.

I got more letters in response to *The Microcosm* than for any other novel, letters of such recorded misery, and relief that someone was putting in into the public domain. . . . In a lot of cases it was a matter of pointing them towards the various clubs and pubs and such literature as was available. There was *Arena Three* and *The Ladder*, to both of which I contributed. With all its limitations there was MRG.[5]

McIntosh's interest in the sociology of queer organisations and individuals was therefore founded. It was at the precise time that she was engaged with these groups that she began to study them, having been involved with the Minorities Research Group and Kenric. Her research on organisations both in Britain and also in the US led her to write to a number of interesting and influential people in advance of speaking to Duffy – some of whom had used Rorschach ink blots for a very similar purpose.

Hooker and the homosexual role

On 14th August 1964, mere months after joining the Minorities Research Group, McIntosh wrote to Dr Evelyn Hooker. Citing her Rorschach research, McIntosh outlined her interests in conducting research on the 'functions of homosexual groups' and the experiences of individuals involved in homosexual groups. She outlines her plan to interview 20–30 'homosexuals' but requests further guidance on how best to recruit participants aside from being in touch with groups in Britain akin to the Mattachine Society.

As outlined in Chapter 3 both Hooker and Hopkins used 'homophile' groups in order to recruit their participants. Hooker used the Mattachine Society in the US – which later published a copy of her scientific article in their magazine *The Mattachine Review* – and Hopkins used the Minorities Research Group in Britain (see Chapters 3 and 5). Both researchers also relied upon the influence of their friends for the research. Hooker was deeply influenced by a student, then friend, Sam From who is said to have begged her to do the research and introduced her to his gay friends and the gay scene in Los Angeles. Hopkins reported she had been outraged by attitudes towards lesbian women as those she knew from the US Air Force were 'absolutely smashing, and not at all neurotic' (Clarke & Hopkins, 2002). These two studies link up to McIntosh in important ways. She too was influenced and supported by queer networks for her academic work and, like Hopkins, was a queer woman navigating a pathologising academic culture. She also would have known about the Hopkins research, and was clearly knowledgeable about Rorschach research in this field. She paid particular attention to the advice of Hooker.

In her reply of 1st October 1964 Hooker was very encouraging of McIntosh's work. She provided a full publication list of her work on the subject, of course including her Rorschach work, and gave specific advice on McIntosh's project. First, she outlined that unlike in her (1957) research where she recruited only men who considered themselves a six (exclusively homosexual) on the Kinsey scale, McIntosh would probably not need to stipulate such strict criteria at the outset of her work. Second, Hooker warned against being 'taken in' by information provided by participants due to the varied nature of their reasoning for wanting to take part in such research. She argued that the motivations for taking part were varied and included some being "militantly defensive about the homosexual way of life and see the research as a way of obtaining a platform to the larger public." Others did so because they wanted help from a psychologist because they were unhappy with their (homo)sexualities; whereas others simply believed in the importance of knowledge about the subject.

Hooker also alluded to her knowing many of her participants personally, all of whom knew that they would not experience 'damnation or devaluation' from her. She states that initially the Mattachine Society was very useful but snowballing methods of being introduced to friends was the largest method of recruitment by 'following up social invitations to dinners, parties, etc.' Hooker remarks "I cannot tell from your letter whether you have any such contacts" and reassured McIntosh that she is likely to gain good cooperation from the homosexual community. Yet, that it is important that one's own attitude is of complete acceptance that they are assured the researchers interest in them in a genuine way. This reassurance goes some way to demonstrate a slight heteronormativity at work here and also the inability for McIntosh to out herself even to a researcher she knows is working against homophobic pathologisation.

Finally, Hooker suggested the use of standardised measures to look at the opinions and attitudes of participants. She advised against a broad interview plan but recommended a careful design which identified the areas of interest more specifically. In recognising McIntosh's plan she described it as excellent and in a most neglected area, meaning there was also little literature Hooker was able to recommend, especially of 'sociological value'. However, she did flag Leznoff and Westley's

(1956) article about the characteristics of Canadian gay men's social groups and the individuals involved in them which was published in *Social Problems*. It was then this precise journal that McIntosh eventually published her 1968 paper 'The Homosexual Role', based on the research she discussed with Hooker.

Another key source of advice about this paper and her ongoing research was Iris Murdoch. Once again, this relationship demonstrates the links between some queer research at this time and authors and writers outside of academia, similar to that of Hooker and Isherwood. Murdoch and McIntosh met while they were both at Oxford University, and in a letter dated 23rd August 1964 McIntosh refers to Murdoch as her 'moral tutor' most likely because of her teaching Philosophy at St Anne's college. In this letter McIntosh outlined her research plans and her sociological approach but crucially wanted advice on whether this was 'the right time to talk about these aspects of homosexuality'. McIntosh cites her awareness of the law reform movements and the Minorities Research Group as key but seemed somewhat concerned that such a study could be misinterpreted by those who agreed sex between men should be illegal and who considered it a 'wicked perversion'. Hand-written letters and postcards from Murdoch evidence that the two then met in person to discuss McIntosh's plans.

By 1965 the research continued but progress was slow. In March 1965 McIntosh wrote to the Mattachine Society to request documents and histories of their organisation as well as information about any other similar groups. She also got back in touch with Murdoch and Hooker in August that year to explain the progress of the research. To Murdoch she explained she was not only busy conducting interviews in London but was also now the secretary for a Campaign for Racial Equality group. Notably, she commented how the British homophile organisations were 'tame' compared to the American ones. Such a note of frustration in regards to this somewhat foreshadows her later involvement with the Gay Liberation Front, a group known for their public and political activism. To Hooker, McIntosh wrote that she had taken her advice to have clearer variables in her interviews and avoid the broader unstructured approach. To both letters she attached an early paper presented to the Sociology Department at Leicester University which included thoughts from some exploratory interviews.

In 1968 McIntosh's 'The Homosexual Role' was published in *Social Problems*. This paper proved pivotal (Weeks, 1998), though occasionally overlooked for other prominent queer theorists. This paper cemented McIntosh's perspective as a queer affirmative person within a difficult British scene. In 'The Homosexual Role', McIntosh argued vehemently that "the homosexual should be seen as playing a social role rather than having a condition" (p. 184) opposing the then-prominent view of 'homosexuality' as a mental illness, sickness, or otherwise deviancy. As Weeks (2013) recollected:

> At the time, these insights were revelatory and central to rethinking homosexuality (and sexuality more generally) as a historical and sociological rather than a biologically or psychologically fixed phenomenon.

McIntosh therefore foreshadowed a turn in lesbian and gay studies and affirmative queer approaches in academia, including Sociology as well as Psychology. Her specifically Marxist feminist queer perspective remained integral to her approach to Sociology. In her later work about pornography, the 'family' (or 'the household'), criminality, and further work on sexuality, McIntosh's personal beliefs about injustice, multiple oppressions, and intersecting issues were central. This blending of her personal and academic work fills in the exact gap which is often presented as a chasm in some academic circles.

McIntosh's engagement with queer groups and individuals was for both personal and professional reasons. Her politics, her activism, and her academic research are intertwined. 'The Homosexual Role' was pivotal and sits across the bridge of her academic and activist life. It also sits across a disciplinary gap considering the valued advice and guidance from both Evelyn Hooker, a psychologist and Iris Murdoch, a writer and philosopher.

In fact, McIntosh described Hooker as 'the great pioneer of research on homosexual life' in her *Lunch* article (the publication of the Campaign for Homosexual Equality from 1970–1974). The letters between Hooker and McIntosh indicate that Hooker was very influential on the work of McIntosh, recommending she use standardised measures rather than unstructured interviews in her research. Hooker also identified alienation as a key construct to consider, the Mattachine Society as a central organisation who could help with her research, and even highlighted *Social Problems* as a key journal for the topic. Despite Hooker's influence however, the discipline of Psychology was not as progressive as Sociology at this time. Despite the legal shift in 1967 meaning the Sexual Offenses Act decriminalised sex between two men in private over the age of 21,[6] Psychology for the most part continued to treat queer people as mentally ill. Gay men especially were 'cured' by aversion treatments as a form of 'reparative' therapy (Dickinson, 2013; King, 2003; King & Bartlett, 1999; King et al., 2004).

In all, 'The Homosexual Role' was pivotal in the history of lesbian and gay rights (Weeks, 1981), and Waters (2012; see also Waters, 2013) argued that McIntosh was central in the move from understanding 'the homosexual' as a social problem to a social group. He also referred to McIntosh's use of Hooker (1957) to evidence the beginnings of more valuable research materialising about homosexuality. The paper has been remembered by Weeks (1998) as being particularly significant in providing the realisation that it was better to consider queer sexualities as distinctly social rather than focus on the so-called 'causes' as had been very common in thinking of 'homosexuality' as deviance. In doing so McIntosh began asking new types of questions and thus quietly contributed to the origins of queer theory, to social constructionist approaches to sexuality and to critical perspectives on the psy-disciplines pathologisation of queer people. Alongside this theoretical contribution, however, she also made very practical moves in effort to depathologise homosexuality.

The Gay Liberation Front

The Stonewall Riot in 1969 led to a shift in thinking in the British movements that McIntosh had described as 'tame' compared to those in the US. The rioting began in the early hours of 28th June 1969 in response to a police raid on the Stonewall Inn – one of the more popular gay bars in Greenwich Village, New York City. Such raids were relatively common and this was not the first time violence had ensured after a raid on an LGBT venue (see Weeks, 1977/2016). While the Stonewall Riots may be the best known, earlier examples include the Cooper Do-nuts riot in Los Angeles in 1959 and Compton's Cafeteria riot in 1966 in San Francisco. Like Stonewall, these riots also represent examples where poorer and more marginalised queer people in particular (including drag queens, trans women, butches, people of colour, and sex workers) fought back against police discrimination and oppression (see Rivera, 2002; Stryker, 2008).

In the autumn of 1970, the British Gay Liberation Front was formed by Aubrey Walter and Bob Mellors who was a Sociology student at the London School of Economics (LSE). Having been especially influenced by the growth of gay liberation in the US, they were keen to get something similar moving in Britain (Weeks, 1977/2016). British homophile organisations had not been in existence as long as US organisations such as The Mattachine Society and the Daughters of Bilitis. There was also a substantially different context in which British activists were working. As outlined in Chapter 5, the Minorities Research Group, the Campaign for Homosexual Equality, and the Homosexual Law Reform Society were all relatively conservative in their approach to social change.[7] The 1967 Sexual Offenses Act showed their work was making a difference, but their approach was careful and considered. The British Gay Liberation Front however was inspired by the radical responses to oppression by activists in the US following the Stonewall Riots. Based on a left political stance, with core ethos of pride, coming out, and fighting oppression via loud demonstration, the Gay Liberation Front became perhaps the best-known gay liberation group in the UK. In the first meeting there were nine people. Within a month word had spread and there were 200 people in attendance. They had to move locations from the LSE to a Parish Hall, where 400–500 people attended weekly meetings. Despite the fact the group only lasted for two years, their legacy has endured to this day. To read more about this, Jeffrey Weeks, a member of the Gay Liberation Front himself who knew Mary McIntosh personally, describes the Gay Liberation Front in fascinating detail in his book of British LGBT history *Coming Out,* now in its 3rd edition, and I fully recommend it.

The Gay Liberation Front were radical and confrontational, unlike other groups at the time (see Figure 6.2 for the front page of their Manifesto). They argued that oppression towards gay and lesbian people was directly related to gender roles and strict gendered boundaries in society. They explained how queer people are oppressed via the family, the schooling system, the church, the media, and in employment. Not only did they describe discourses around homosexuality as contributors to oppression, they

FIGURE 6.2 The Gay Liberation Front Manifesto 1971

Reproduced here with permission from the London School of Economics Library.

specifically outlined the legal system, psychiatry, and the threat of physical violence as systematic institutionalised homophobia. They were also critical about 'self-oppression', that is the act of being critical of other queer people or distinguishing oneself away from 'undesirable' lesbian or gay people. This demonstrated a real shift in the ways in which queer groups were thinking as this is in contrast to the approach by the Minorities Research Group (as outlined in Chapter 5).

The Gay Liberation Front Manifesto was published and available in 1971 (see Figure 6.3 for their demands leaflet). In the introduction they stated: "Homosexuals who have been oppressed by physical violence and by ideology and psychological attacks at every level of social interaction, are at last becoming angry." In line with their 'righteous anger', as they described it, they outlined a number of demands. These were not to be interpreted as requests: "We do not intend to ask for anything. *We intend to stand firm and assert our basic rights.* If this involves violence, it will not be we who initiate this, but those who attempt to stand in our way to freedom" (emphasis original, p. 16 GLF Manifesto). The demands were as follows:

- That all discrimination against gay people, male and female, by the law, by employers, and by society at large, should end.

- That all people who feel attracted to a member of their own sex be taught that such feeling are perfectly valid.
- That sex education in schools should stop being exclusivity heterosexual.
- That psychiatrists stop treating homosexuality as though it were a sickness, thereby giving gay people senseless guilt complexes.
- That gay people be as legally free to contact other gay people, throughout newspaper ads, on the streets and by any other means they may want, as are heterosexuals, and that police harassment should cease right now.
- That employers should no longer be allowed to discriminate against anyone on account of their sexual preferences.
- That the age of consent for gay men be reduced to the same as for heterosexuals.
- That gay people be free to hold hands and kiss in public, as are heterosexuals.

In all, the Gay Liberation Front changed the face of queer activism in Britain and were much more aligned with traditional activist approaches. No strangers to demonstrations, protests (for example, at the Gateways), and street performances, they utilised a whole tool box of action. In town hall meetings hundreds of people would attend and the political underpinning to the group meant that they were

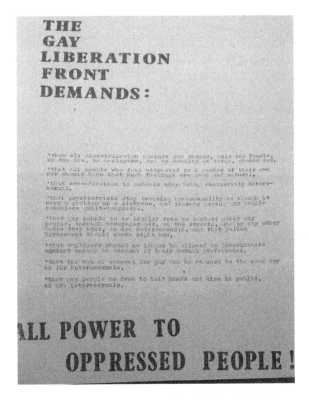

FIGURE 6.3 The Gay Liberation Front Demands leaflet from 1971

Reproduced here with permission from the London School of Economics Library.

highly aware of gender, race, and class politics (with varying degrees of success). This led to regular changes to the main committee as to avoid only certain voices being heard. Sub-groups became focused on specific issues. For example, the GLF Youth Group were tasked with liberating school sex education and for lowering the age of consent for sex between men from 21. The Action group were responsible for 'coordinating activity against harassment and entrapment by queer-bashers and the police'. There was a regular publication *Come Together* and 'gay-ins' in public parks, designed to develop solidarity among the queer community and also to be visible to society at large. The language used in *Come Together* and other leaflets/pamphlets and publications show a shift in efforts to be a community. For example, they often describing one another as 'brothers' and 'sisters'. Similarly, having a heightened awareness of other group identities beyond sexuality, and intersecting forms of oppression, the Gay Liberation Front had a political agenda beyond previous groups. Acting in the aftermath of increased empowerment from the Stonewall Riots, they (literally) demonstrated how solidarity in the community was able to make waves for lesbian and gay rights in Britain.

Adopting the American terminology, they encouraged lesbian and gay people to 'come out of the closet' and no longer hide who they were. Wilson remembered the effects of such slogans in the early 1960s and how they contrasted with the ethos of gay movements in the 1960s:

> in its beginnings the great, explosive, positive thing about gay liberation was the feelings that there were hundreds of homosexuals who were not afraid to assert their homosexuality. It no longer had to be discreetly hidden. That was a truly liberating experience, and although perhaps gay liberation was essentially a liberal movement, its slogans "gay is good" and "gay is proud" are important in challenging the oppression of homosexuals. Gay people really are oppressed although their oppression is a peculiar one since it rests partly on the possibility of always remaining hidden and invisible. This was the reasons for the stress on "coming out" in gay liberation.
>
> *(Wilson, 1986 as extracted in Oram &Turnbull, 2001, p. 270)*[8]

Grounded on Marxist, anarchist, and anti-imperialist perspectives, the group sparked thinking about how the 'personal is political' (Hamer, 2013). Because of their deep political awareness which contrasted occasionally with actions of its members, the group was rather fragmented. For example, as Weeks (1977, p. 200) noted "many women felt that sexist attitudes were as prevalent among men in the gay movement as outside." Eventually many women in the Gay Liberation Front became more involved in women's liberation movements, especially after the main Gay Liberation Front group dissolved in 1972.

Mary McIntosh and her partner at the time, Elizabeth Wilson, were involved in the Gay Liberation Front from the beginning. McIntosh reflected how she was able to follow this mantra of coming out: "I was probably one of the few who felt able to come out in her job because I was in a particularly liberal occupation.

Most of the middle-class ones didn't come out and had they done so, they might have well been sacked especially the social workers" (as quoted in Gardiner, 2003, p. 194). Both McIntosh and Wilson also remembered how the Gay Liberation Front contrasted with the lesbian scene at the Gateways which was engrained within the earlier 1950s–1960s ethos of queer lifestyles.

> Gay liberation was complexly glamorous, crazy and outrageous and for me it made the Gateways instantly out of date.
>
> *– Elizabeth Wilson*

> Part of the GLF philosophy was that we should try and change what we called the straight gay scene and make it into a liberationist scene. We had a big ball in Kensington Town Hall. A ball was not too politicized way of getting people to come along and see how wonderful GFL was.
>
> *– Mary McIntosh (Gardiner, 2003, p. 179)*

Following the distribution of leaflets advertising the ball at the Gateways, a skirmish with one of the managers ensued and they were chucked out. McIntosh was later involved in a protest against the Gateways and an ongoing feud continued on the basis of the political agenda of the Gay Liberation Front in contrast to the relative apolitical perspective of the Gateways and Kenric (who had nights regularly at the venue, see Gardiner, 2003 for a full history of the Gateways).

The psychological component to oppression was central in the thinking of the Gay Liberation Front, as were the actions of sociologists like Mary McIntosh and Jeffrey Weeks. In fact, it was at McIntosh's house in London that the Gay Liberation Front counter-psychiatry sub-group was established in London (Jennings, 2008). This group had several aims and objectives which directly fed into the Gay Liberations Front's demands, which included "that psychiatrists stop treating homosexuality as though it were a problem or a sickness, and hereby giving gay people senseless guilt-complexes" (1971, GLF Demands). They were particularly active against the publication of the book *Everything You Always Wanted to Know About Sex (But Were Too Afraid to Ask)* by psychiatrist Dr Reubens (1969). They demonstrated outside of the publishers, wrote leaflets, and made the newspapers with their protests. This book, they argued, was deeply and 'viciously' prejudiced and problematic – they argued it was libellous against gay people, 'hysterical', and generalised gay sexual behaviours in very unhelpful ways – especially to young people coming to terms with their (homo) sexualities.

The sub-group wrote to individual GPs providing them advice on how to respond to patients concerned about their homosexuality. They cited their members' own experience of aversion therapy and its ineffectiveness and recommended that doctors respond with reassurance that they are capable of living full, happy lives. "This positive attitude substituted for attempts to provide treatment and cure will spare many from intense and undue suffering" (Dickinson, 2015, p. 200).

McIntosh personally wrote letters to organisations asking about their discriminatory practices and collected anecdotal evidence about gay people who had undergone behavioural or psychoanalytic therapeutic practices to 'cure' their sexualities. The counter-psychiatry group (perhaps more accurately, sometimes referred to as the anti-psychiatry group) accused psychiatrists of slander and paid particular attention to reports of aversion therapies and the use of Electroconvulsive Therapy (ECT, or 'shock treatment'). McIntosh collected information about individuals who had undergone such 'treatment' as well as information on the lectures given to Psychiatrists and Social Workers about such practices. For example – she collected individual accounts of aversion therapy. One man reported experiencing regular 'treatment' from 1963–1965. He concluded that it was a 'complete and utter failure' leading to exhaustion, episodes of panic, and suicidal tendencies. McIntosh also collected information on which hospitals were providing aversion therapy (e.g. High Croft Hospital in the West Midlands) and those which were not (e.g. the Birmingham Group of hospitals). It was also interestingly noted that a member of the Management Committee for the Birmingham group described aversion therapy as 'cruel' and so they had discontinued its use – this member of the committee was also identified as gay himself. For a full oral history account of aversion therapy in Britain see Dickinson (2015; also King & Bartlett, 1999; Smith et al., 2004).

McIntosh was also involved with the Campaign for Homosexual Equality (CHE) and their publication *Lunch*. This was despite the fact that both the Gay Liberation Front and CHE were criticised for being less welcoming to women (Jennings, 2008). McIntosh wrote a book review and an article entitled 'GaySpeak' for *Lunch* in 1973. The article began with a quote from Karl Marx, and considered the language and speech expressions of the gay community and the variations in meaning across context and across women's and men's scenes. While CHE had been criticised for being rather more conservative, androcentric, and less activist, it did occasionally engage with some key lesbian issues. They published a woman's account of her life called 'A Homosexual Woman's Story', published two of Maureen Duffy's poems, and reviewed an Iris Murdoch book in issues throughout 1973.

The counter-psychiatry sub-group of the Gay Liberation Front were later responsible for demonstrations at medical institutions like the Tavistock, which acted as the institutional home for the Rorschach. Nettie Pollard, a friend of McIntosh's whose oral history is at the British Library Sound Archive, joined the GLF in 1971 and also remembered the ongoing activism that the group did (also see Jennings, 2007a, 2007b, 2007c):

> I started, I joined, something called the, the counter-psychiatry group, which was something I was particularly interested in, trying to bash psychiatric theories about gayness and lesbianism . . . and then I got involved in organising a conference that we held at LSE which was actually held for people in medical professions, quite interesting . . . funnily enough quite a few of them did come along, come and listen to us.

The Gay Liberation Front had further influence on psychologists. It was such action which inspired Charlotte Wolff to be more open about her sexuality (1965). Groups involved in gay liberation in the 1970s therefore had a profound effect on the history of Psychology (Minton, 2002). Minton (2002) discussed how these groups reclaimed this influence and actively rejected the 'deviant' and 'sick' models of homosexuality resounding in Psychology and Psychiatry.

Depathologisation per se

Efforts by gay liberation movements and activists in Britain, and especially in the US, led to the eventual removal of 'homosexuality' as a mental illness '*per se*' in the Diagnostic Statistical Manual (DSM) in 1973. This messy and complex history is well narrated by Minton (2002) and includes of course people working within, as well as outside of, Psychology. Minton especially identified the Rorschach research of Hooker as pivotal in this history. Gay Liberation activists in the US were disrupting Psychology and Psychiatry conference sessions about homosexuality (as it was being presented as a mental illness, sickness, or perversion) from 1970 starting with the American Psychological Association meeting. According to Minton (2002) they chanted: "Stop talking *about* us and start talking *with* us" (emphasis original, p. 256). In a session about aversion therapy the heckling became so disruptive the chairperson halted the talk. Perhaps in the most succinct description of the issues at play between psychologists and activists is the following exchange described by Minton, which begins with a justification by Irving Bieber, justifying his position that homosexuality is an illness:

> "I never said homosexuals were sick, what I said was that they have displaced sexual adjustment." In response a protestor retorted, "That's the same thing, motherfucker".
>
> *(p. 256)*

Following the protest by activists, Kent Robinson, a sympathetic psychiatrist, discussed the issue with Larry Littlejohn, one of the protest organisers, and learned they wished to represent themselves. A panel was then formed, including Frank Kameny, entitled 'Lifestyles of Non-Patient Homosexuals' alongside an exhibit entitled 'Gay, Proud, and Healthy: The Homosexual Community Speaks'. This action encouraged gay psychiatrists to get in touch with the activists. At the end of this conference in 1971, Kameny and Littlejohn made clear to Robinson that they wished to instigate a demand for the deletion of 'homosexuality' as a mental disorder (see Minton, 2002). The following year a presence of gay activists was once again on the conference proceedings, but also included, for the first time, a panel which included a gay psychiatrist. 'Dr Henry Anonymous' was disguised by large suit, wig, mask, and a voice distorting microphone for the session and described the suffocating difficulty in being gay in a profession in which to be out spelled 'doom'. John Fryer, 'came out' as it were, as Dr Anonymous in 1994 (Minton, 2002).

Following further debate and discussion, which included whether 'homosexuality' was indeed a perversion or a mental illness, both, or neither, the APA committee eventually held a vote in 1973. With a vote of 13 to 0 (2 abstentions) 'homosexuality' was deleted from the DSM. However, Sexual Orientation Disturbance was added, including 'ego-dystonic homosexuality' (Minton, 2002). It is this precise reason why many consider this as the removal of homosexuality *per se*. Psychologists and psychiatrists were still able to 'treat' or indeed attempt to 'cure' homosexuality under this version of the DSM – if patients were unhappy with their sexualities psychologists would offer therapies, be they behavioural or therapeutic, to alter it. Ongoing activism inside and outside of Psychology led to removal of 'ego-dystonic homosexuality' in 1986. It wasn't until 1990 that the World Health Organization removed homosexuality from their International Classification of Diseases. Conversion therapies and therapeutic offerings still continued despite the de-classification.

Certainly from the 1980s the use of therapies trying to 'cure' homosexuality had dramatically decreased. However, Lowenstein and Lowenstein (1984) in their review of research on homosexuality after 1978 in Britain indicated some researchers still promoted the use of 'treatments' including 'exceptional methods' (e.g. exorcism, religious conversion, and castration). They also reported other psychologists who alluded to social prejudice impacting the lives of gay men rather than their sexuality directly (see also Dickinson, 2015).

King and Bartlett (1999) in their review of homosexuality and Psychiatry argued that the history of aversion therapies and institutionalised homophobia has "exposed the conservative social bias inherent in psychiatry and psychology, damaged the lives of gay men and lesbians and provided grounds for discrimination" (p. 111). King et al. (2004) in an oral history study of mental health professionals found a small minority would still assist patients 'becoming heterosexual' if the patient desired it. The same authors in 2009 also found in a survey study of mental health professionals that 55 (4%) of therapists would still attempt to change a client's sexual orientation and 222 (17%) had assisted someone in either reducing or changing their gay or lesbian feelings.

As explored in great depth by Dickinson (2015), for the most part the nurses and mental health professionals, including psychologists, did not deliberately set out to cause great distress and pain in those they 'treated'. Just as in Psychology, those nurses who conducted aversion therapies and other 'treatments', were occasionally themselves gay or lesbian, and the negotiations of this psychologically were often rather complex, with people often believing they were genuinely helping unhappy people. Some psychologists, for example Bancroft who wrote on the uses of aversion therapies in the same issue as Hopkins (1969) described the lesbian personality, later admitted he would no longer give aversion therapy, citing a shift in social attitude as well as the ineffectiveness of treatment (see King & Bartlett, 1999).

This history therefore shows the impact social attitudes and beliefs can have on apparently scientific, objective, and unbiased disciplines such as Psychology and vice versa. By looking closely at the gaps between disciplines, between the personal and the academic, it is possible to see just how blurred and indistinct this border actually is. These rather stubborn areas, which can be hard to historicise, are even harder to understand in the present. But by paying attention to how such borders have been crossed in the past, for example by Mary McIntosh, we can consider the ways in which we might best continue such social justice legacy in and outside of academia.

By paying attention to the gaps, the marginal, and the liminal we not only get information about the histories of oppression but also evidence of the resistances. McIntosh's work was centrally about injustice, resistance, and reaction. By paying closer attention to stubborn aspects of history – that is, the gaps and the marginalised – it might be possible to reconsider the more stubborn aspects of injustice in our present time in a way that might be more reflective of what McIntosh was doing in the latter end of the 20th century.

Notes

1 This participant also described some uncertainty about their gender identity at points in their letter and mentioned referring to themselves as a 'boy-girl' at some point. They also discuss their husband and another friend who would have liked to have taken part in the *Bisexuality* study but couldn't: "One person whom I've got to know recently would have been excellent subject for you, and wanted to contact you, but alas, Her husband created hell, and she decided that she ought to keep quiet. Such a shame, but she's in a delicate situation" (letter dated 14/5/1976, Wolff archive, Wellcome Library).
2 McIntosh's materials have been carefully curated and archived at the London School of Economics Library and she also has contributed to the Hall-Carpenter oral history collection. See the LSE Library blog here for more information about her deposit to the archive in 2001 http://blogs.lse.ac.uk/lsehistory/2018/02/07/mary-mcintosh-1936-2013/.
3 See McIntosh's interview in the Hall-Carpenter archive at the British Library for the collection 'Sisterhood and After: The Women's Liberation Oral History Project'. Also, it is worth noting that McIntosh did become a mother, despite the stereotype at this time that a lesbian trajectory was inevitably child-less. In his obituary Weeks (2013) described her as "survived by former partners, with whom she remained on good terms, Duncan Barrett, whom she co-parented with Michèle Barrett, and her partner of over 20 years, Angela Stewart-Park."
4 In folder MCINTOSH/M3765/3 in the McIntosh collection at the LSE archive, London.
5 *The Ladder* was the publication of the Daughters of Bilitis, the first Lesbian organisation in the United States of America. The ladder was published from 1956 to 1972, so 8 years before *Arena Three* but ending at the same time.
6 This change in law was upon the recommendation of the Wolfenden report in 1957. In 1994 it was lowered to 18 and in 2000 it was lowered to 16 to match the age of consent for sex between men and women.
7 The Homosexual Law Reform Society (later named the Sexual Law Reform Society) was the earliest of these British groups. It was established in 1958, the year after the Wolfenden Report had been released, due to the governments' reluctance to enact any of the recommendations of the report related to sex between men (see Weeks, 1977/2016). The Albany Trust was its charitable component and from 1962 this was championed and ran by Anthony Grey. Both the Campaign for Homosexual Equality and the Minorities Research Group were established in 1964 (see Chapter 5). In the US where the so-called homophile groups were established a little earlier, the Mattachine Society was established in 1950 and the Daughters of Bilitis in 1955.
8 Weeks (1977, p. 190) discussed how the Gay Liberation Front deliberately used 'gay' over 'queer' in the early 1970s as 'queer' represented the word of the oppressor whereas 'gay' fitted the mood of the time. Since the 1990s and the emergence of 'queer theory', 'queer' has gained particular popularity for being more inclusive and encompassing. It also represents a reclaiming of the word which was once oppressive (for further reading on this, I recommend Barker & Scheele, 2016).

7
CONCLUSION

After being tested in 2015 with the Rorschach, I did what a lot of 'well-adjusted' queer women who were tested in the 1960s by Hopkins did: I went home to be with my partner (well, immediately after, I went to the pub). In short, I continued to live my queer life. But this was not a possibility for lots of queer people. As explored across this book, the effects of being identified as queer by a psychological test (whether correctly or incorrectly), could be profound.

As outlined in Chapter 1, there are stark differences in the *contexts* in which I was tested compared to queer people tested in the 20th century. The experience of being tested with the Rorschach has a queer history that ties together: American men tested in officer selection for the US Army in the 1940s; the participants of Hooker's study in Los Angeles in the1950s; and those in Hopkins' study in the1960s, among many others. There are also, of course, the many queer people who underwent psychological testing to help 'cure' them of their (homo)sexualities, including treatments such as aversion/conversion therapies. Their tests and experiences of the ten ink blots are very different to my own as I was tested in a time when my sexuality was not considered to be evidence of a neurosis, a sickness, or a mental illness. Nonetheless, we are all connected by the bleeding threads of ink in the Rorschach cards.

Throughout this book I have outlined a history of the Rorschach which places women and queerness at the centre. In doing so I have covered a time range from about 1920s–1970s thus far. A transgression across the academic/activist border has occurred across the chapters. The early chapters were more focused on academia and Psychology 'proper' then moved across the boundary to focus on activism in the 1970s. The Rorschach has been used as a tool to access this queer history. In some ways I've continued with the tradition to use the Rorschach to detect queerness.

Chapter 1 provided a contextualising introduction which answered why a queer feminist history of the Rorschach is revealing. It also introduced some of the challenges that need to be addressed when doing queer history. Chapter 2 provided a brief history of the Rorschach in Britain as well as the US and explored what the gay signs were on the Rorschach and how 'homosexuality' was detected. It also deconstructed ideas around what testing *does* from a sociological perspective and how people responded to being tested. Chapter 3 introduced two women central to the use of the Rorschach for affirmative and non-pathologising ends: Evelyn Hooker and June Hopkins. Their research and approach was highlighted against a backdrop of pathologising research on queer people in the mid-20th century.

In Chapter 4, using the findings of Hopkins, we travelled somewhat back in time against the overall chronology of the book. Here, I considered the lives of three women who worked in the projective test movement who had particular queer 'signs' in their own lives. This chapter somewhat switched the lens from studying the people who were tested to studying those doing the testing. Chapter 5 more concretely moved us away from Psychology as a discipline and instead began to consider the ways in which activist groups in the 1960s began to fight against the sickness model of queer sexualities. In these early British lesbian liberation movements, there was a blending of activists and psychologists. Finally, Chapter 6 centralised Sociology more with particular reference to the work and life of Mary McIntosh. Rorschach work re-emerged here as Hooker proved influential and in turn McIntosh was influential in activist movements against pathologisation. Such activist action, especially in the US, then shifted Psychology's official conceptualisations away from the idea that 'homosexuality' was a mental disorder.

This border crossing from the academic to the activist demonstrates how blurred and indistinct it is in practice. The positioning of academia as separate and distinct from the social world is false, and belief in the clear distinction eradicates the actions of academics/activists. I seriously question the apparently strict boundary between academia and activism and suggest that this border is blurrier (and perhaps more like the edges of an ink blot) than it might first appear. The recognition of this blurry and messy border also means that we are able to recognise the actions of marginalised individuals who often get ignored in history-telling. By looking historically with a queer feminist lens, we are able to re-position the actions of women from both the past and present as deliberate, intentional, and empowered.

Since the history outlined here, there have been substantial changes to attitudes towards the Rorschach and towards queer people in Britain. As outlined in Chapter 2, while recently there have been a handful of people interested in the Rorschach for psychological and diagnostic purposes in the UK, there has largely been a distancing from it as a reliable psychological tool. Mirroring the Maudsley's beliefs in the mid-20th century, growing critique of the Rorschach grew to the extent that the Rorschach Society and journal ended in 1997. However, that is not to say such a pattern has been seen internationally (see Hubbard & Hegarty, 2016). In some areas of the US, France, and Italy the Rorschach continues to be a popular test – sometimes for therapeutic and counselling purposes as well for as clinical and forensic ends. There is an International Society for the Rorschach and Projective

Methods and corresponding journal entitled *Rorschachiana*. The Rorschach's history therefore continues and this book contributes to that in part.

Similarly, there have been substantial changes in Psychology's attitudes towards queer people in Britain since the 1970s. Extensive action has taken place with thanks to people inside and outside of Psychology. As explained towards the end of Chapter 6, in 1973 the APA removed 'homosexuality' as a mental illness from the DSM. Since this change, Division 44 of the APA was established, first named the 'Society for the Psychological Study of Lesbian and Gay Issues' in 1985.[1] Its British counterpart took somewhat more time to be (able to be) established. Having applied three times for such recognition in the British Psychological Society (BPS), lesbian and gay psychologists were finally given permission to develop a Lesbian and Gay Section at the end of 1998. This Section (now called the Psychology of Sexualities) celebrated its 20-year anniversary in 2018 and commemorated its earliest members, which included Sue Wilkinson, Celia Kitzinger, Martin Milton, and Adrian Coyle (see Jowett, 2018; Kitzinger, Coyle, Wilkinson, & Milton, 1998; Wilkinson, 1999).

The activism in academic work by people like Celia Kitzinger and Sue Wilkinson has received further recognition in anniversaries of their work for both feminist Psychology and LGBT Psychology; for example, their work in the Psychology of Women Section (established in 1987) and the earlier unofficial version of the Gay and Lesbian Section, which focused on the Psychology of Lesbians.[2] Kitzinger's (1987) *The Social Construction of Lesbianism* proved to be pivotal in the history of British Psychology, especially in relation to thinking about positions of lesbian women in the study of sexuality. For further history of these movements and the actions of psychologists in LGBT research see Clarke et al. (2010).

Overall, it's been argued that psychologists have shifted from trying to understanding what 'causes' and what could (apparently) 'cure' homosexuality to instead trying to understand prejudice towards LGBT people. This includes more consideration of the mental health of LGBT people due to social stigmatisation and marginalisation (see Coyle & Kitzinger, 2002). Equally, there has been greater consideration of the impacts of heterosexism and heteronormativity, including the impact it has within research as well as in wider society (e.g. see Herek, Kimmel, Amaro, & Melton, 1991). Substantial shifts have also occurred in the ways in which the positionality of researchers is considered. Feminist approaches in Psychology recognise the value in embodying a marginalised position when conducting 'insider' research in ways that were not possible in the times of Hopkins. From the early 2000s bisexuality became included within organisations which were originally thinking about lesbians and gay men only. Since then, trans issues have been included and at present intersex and broader diversities in gender and sexual identities are being introduced under the queer studies umbrella to a greater extent (see Griffiths, 2018b). This is somewhat exemplified by the terminology of 'sexualities' more broadly, thus including heterosexuality, in the BPS Section and APA's division 44 now being called the 'Society for the Psychology of Sexual Orientation and Gender Diversity'. For an extensive recent history of LGBT Psychology from the depathologisation of 'homosexuality' to the early 2000s see Hegarty (2018). This text eloquently covers the impacts HIV/

AIDS had on Psychology's understanding of LGBT people, particularly gay men. It also considers legal consequences and movements towards trans inclusion into LGBT Psychology.

There have also been dramatic changes in law and policy for British queer people (see Weeks, 1977, 2007, 2016). Perhaps the one which first comes to mind is the Marriage (Same-Sex Couples) Act which came into being in Britain in 2013. Other laws have also changed in this time which coincide with the demands from the Gay Liberation Front. For example, in 1994 the age of consent for sexual activity was lowered for men to have sex with men to 18 and in 2000 it was then lowered to 16 to match the age of consent for sex between women and men. Discrimination laws and hate crime statistics include sexual orientation and gender identity within their orbits, meaning that sexual orientation and gender identity are legally considered to be protected characteristics. Relatedly, equality and diversity programmes in organisations using the Equality Act (2010) as a framework attempt to deliberately ensure inclusion for LGBT people in the workplace and beyond. Such a world is very much in contrast to the way in which the Minorities Research Group and the Gay Liberation Front were describing working environments, discrimination, and oppression in the 1960s and 1970s.

However, while these movements towards liberation have been substantial, there remain significant problems for LGBT people inside and outside of Psychology. There is a time and place for recognition and celebration for such change, but there is still work to be done. King (2003) concluded that despite the DSM removing homosexuality as a mental illness in 1973 it had very little effect for lesbians and gay men in Britain. King (2003) cited the introduction of Section 28 in 1988 and the continuation of homosexuality as a mental illness in the International Classification of diseases (ICD) until the 1990s as indications that the DSM removal was not the end point of psychiatric and governmental control of homosexuality. Section 28, which made it illegal for local authorities to 'promote homosexuality', was finally repealed in 2000 in Scotland and in 2003 for the rest of the UK.

While a diagnosis of 'homosexuality' is not, in of itself, possible any more in Britain, psychologists and psychiatrists still act in many ways as gatekeepers for trans people seeking transition-based health care. For a full review of the present shape of trans health in the UK see Pearce (2018). Indeed, in order to receive such transition provisions in the UK, trans people require a diagnosis of 'Gender Dysphoria', a mental disorder included in the DSM-5, in order to receive referrals for treatments such as hormone therapy, hair removal, and chest or genital surgeries through NHS Gender Identity Clinics. An NHS England Report (2015, p. 9) noted that

> The trans community felt that the gender identity service should not be a psychiatry monopoly. Currently people referred for treatment fall under the umbrella of psychiatry and people tweeted that psychologists have too much power around decisions of people within the trans community, both medically and legally.
>
> (p. 9)

In the legal sphere, in order to receive a Gender Recognition Certificate individuals must supply evidence from medical practitioners, and applications are reviewed by an additional panel of medical professionals (Pearce, 2018). In addition, while the Same-Sex Marriage Act means couples who are (legally) the same sex can marry, it includes a spousal veto. This means spouses can prevent legal partners from receiving a Gender Recognition Certificate as long as they remain married. The civil rights of trans people, especially trans women, have also recently come under attack by some transphobic responses to a 2018 consultation on proposed reforms to the Gender Recognition Act. In the US, Hegarty (2018) comments that the present US administration appears to be 'unambiguous in their intent to undo the history described' in his book *A Recent History of Lesbian and Gay Psychology, From Homophobia to LGBT* (p. vii). This ongoing fight for the rights of trans people is particularly heartbreaking from a queer perspective given the long shared history of lesbian, gay, bisexual, *and* trans people: for instance, trans women of colour and drag queens played an important role in the Stonewall Riots, thereby helping to spark the Gay Liberation movement in the US and UK (see Stryker, 2008; Rivera, 2002). In spite of this long history of struggle, there remain considerable difficulties for trans people across a range of sectors, including in Psychology (e.g. see Ansara & Hegarty, 2014).

Outside of depathologisation, there continue to be major problems regarding the psychology of LGBT people. Findings from recent LGBT population surveys published by the British Government in 2018 demonstrate that LGBT people still face more difficulties in their mental health and social lives when compared to cis straight people. Findings included LGB people having lower life satisfaction (6.5/10) than the general UK population (7.7/10), with rates of satisfaction being lower still for trans people (5.4/10). Two in every five LGBT people had experienced verbal harassment or physical violence in the past year. Around a quarter of the more than 100,000 LGBT people who did the survey had accessed mental health services in the past year. Even more concerning was that 5 percent of respondents had been offered conversion therapy or reparative therapy in an attempt to 'cure' their sexual orientation and/or gender. Two percent had actually received such 'treatment' (see Dickinson, 2015, for an account of how conversion therapies have historically been experienced).

This book is sub-titled 'A Blotted History *Towards* Liberation' for precisely this reason. There remain many concerns which were raised by activists in the 1960s onwards that continue to be issues. In the LGBT survey mentioned above, one of the key findings was that "More than two thirds of LGBT respondents said they avoid holding hands with a same-sex partner for fear of a negative reaction from others" (2018, p. 3 Summary Report). This poignantly echoes one of the Gay Liberation Front's demands from 1971: "That gay people be free to hold hands and kiss in public, as are heterosexuals." In some aspects then, it looks as if we have not come all that far in nearly fifty years. Oppression towards queer people and the effects of marginalisation is therefore still very apparent.

In this book I have not intended to tell an unrealistically optimistic story about queer liberation. Likewise, here I do not wish to emphasise the negative. I am simply trying to provide an account of a queer feminist history which demonstrates how history is not as linear as it first appears. It provides another side of a history which is multi-faceted.

The past is confusing and uncontrollable but we create narratives to order them as much as possible. White (1973) argued that the 'facts' that historians uncover are constructed by the types of questions they posed in the first place. Historians create the historical narrative and so history does not accurately reflect what *actually* happened. Rather deliberately, I've tried to avoid telling an overly romantic or mechanistic story about this history. Instead, what I am trying to do is demonstrate a little of the messiness, the blurring, and the blending of history between projective testing and queer liberation.

The more marginalised histories (because, there are of course plural histories available) of (queer) women often get forgotten about, expunged from the regular narratives of Psychology. In *Psychology Constructs the Female* (1971) Naomi Weisstein argued that women were characterised by Psychology as emotionally unstable, weaker than men, nurturing and intuitive rather than intelligent. This, she argued, was because of the lack of understanding of the social contexts in which women live. Social context, therefore, became not only something historians of Psychology began to study about the past, but was also shown to be influential on the practices of Psychology in the present.

Incorporating more social context, Cherry (1995) used a feminist framework to consider the forgotten, or what she calls 'the stubborn particulars', in Psychology. Attention to the forgotten aspects of the history of Psychology is limited in general histories of Psychology; they provide simplified and falsified 'textbook stories', which can become myths of a discipline. Describing feminist work as 'liminal', Morawski (1994) aimed to highlight the importance of reflexivity in doing the history of Psychology (see also Morawski & Agronick, 1991). Feminist approaches in Psychology therefore moved from a re-placing project to a reflexive one which included women's history as central. Young (1966) had commented that the history of Psychology was, according to the history books, one of 'great men' and it was during the 1990s that feminist scholars such as Morawski began the project to highlight the gendered nature of the history of Psychology.

In the 21st century, historians of Psychology have continued to broaden the theoretical scope in which they consider Psychology. As with feminist approaches, a focus on social context and the public extended the possibilities of historical research in Psychology. For example, Hacking (2000) developed ideas about social constructionism in relation to what he calls 'human kinds', that is, categories by which people become organised. Hacking referenced the historically situated examples of hysteria, anorexia, the 'feeble-minded', and schizophrenia to argue, not that these illnesses are not 'real' *per se*, but that they are situated and constructed in specific contexts.

Another clear example of this can be seen in this book. The Rorschach was used to categorise and distinguish queer people from straight people in both pathologising and affirmative ways. This had major impacts on the ways in which queer people were treated (in some cases, literally) by psychologists. But as shown, the Rorschach has been implicated in histories of both homophobic and queer-affirming Psychology. There have also been some fascinating links to social activist groups. In this book, I have shown how the Rorschach was used with the 'other' in relation to gender and sexuality.

What this book has not explored in depth is how the Rorschach was used to categorise people along lines of culture and ethnicity. As noted in Chapter 1, the history presented here is a history of white, mostly middle-class, women. Projective tests, however, were used to consider the cultural 'other', as well as the sexual 'other', especially in the period of post-colonialism (see Lemov, 2011). Hermann Rorschach himself expressed a desire to test the Congolese using the Rorschach, exclaiming that "The test itself is technically so simple – it can be done through an interpreter – that it may be done with the most primitive Negro as easily as with a cultured European" (Rorschach, 1921, p. 97).

In Britain, Rorschach users raised questions about the use of the test with those from Britain's former empire. Jones and Jones' (1964) article 'Projective materials from a few West Indian subjects – The problem of assessment' and Herzberg's (1964) 'Can we Test Africans?' framed such questions directly. In the 1960s Rorschach researchers attempted to develop new norms for ethnic groups such as Greek children (Routsoni, 1965) and Bengalis (Zakia, 1964). Colonial thinking and racist stereotypes are clearly evident in this work. Herzberg likened Rorschach responses of British children to African adults and laid particular importance on breastfeeding practices in the formation of 'African personality'. Rorschach research on culture in both the US and Britain is characterised by an epistemological dilemma; the Rorschach was often imagined to be both a 'culture-fair' test that can access unconscious material *irrespective* of culture, and one that accesses unconscious material that is understood to be distinctly 'cultural'. The test both looks through, and at, 'culture' and in both the US and in Britain it allowed researchers to opine about cultures with the authority of experts, irrespective of the level of their cultural understanding. For perhaps this reason, projective tests were not only popular with psychologists, but also among anthropologists such as Margaret Mead and her lover Ruth Benedict (Banner, 2010). Benedict specifically used the Rorschach to test Japanese-Americans to gain an understanding of Japanese culture during the Second World War, whereas Mead later used Margaret Lowenfeld's projective tests (see Chapter 4, Mead, 1974). The actions of psychologists therefore need to be embedded into the broader social contexts which recognise the impacts of social beliefs about gender, race, colonialism, sexuality, and (dis)ability in order to avoid telling histories of Psychology which present it as having an unproblematic past.

The Rorschach emerged out of forms of popular culture and so to ignore the social world in such a history would be very limiting and this includes wider social beliefs and problematic applications of the test. As explored in Chapter 1 the Rorschach ink blot test emerged following centuries of fascination with intriguing ink blots. Leonardo da Vinci in the 15th century and Victor Hugo in the 19th century are said to have used ink blots as inspiration (Tulohin, 1940; Lemov, 2011). In 1857, a parlour game called 'Blotto', prompted players to make poetic associations to ink blots (Erdberg, 1990). Rorschach was aware of such games and was generally keen on how his patients responded and reacted to unusual stimuli (Akavia, 2013). He was also a keen artist and drew/painted the ten ink blots himself. It is perhaps not surprising then, that ink blots have continued to inspire other artists, for example, Andy Warhol.

Following the Rorschach's relative success in Britain and the US in the mid-20th century, it has continued to be popular in artistic circles. In many ways ink blots have looped back into popular culture following its time in Psychology. Now almost symbolic of Psychology and Psychiatry in some avenues, Rorschach ink blots can be seen in a whole variety of popular medias. One of the most fascinating, because of its close attention to the history of Psychology, is its use in the graphic novel *Watchmen* (Moore & Gibbons, 1987, there has also since been a film released). Here, 'Rorschach' is not just a test, but also an ink-blot masked vigilante super-hero, who at one point is even made to do the Rorschach ink blot test (Hubbard & Hegarty, 2017).[3] Public use and fascination with the Rorschach is therefore ongoing. In this book I have considered how the public in the form of activists in lesbian and gay organisations were engaged with Rorschach literature and research, especially that of Hopkins and Hooker. This history would be incomplete without such recognition of how the public reacted to and responded to being tested.

Throughout this book I have especially focused on how people both inside and outside of Psychology responded to, fought against, and worked with, the Rorschach to eventually shift Psychology's views of lesbians and gay men specifically. In doing this history I've shifted the focus a little from looking at those people who were tested to look at those who were doing the testing. With this mind, it's worth asking the question: In attempting to diagnose, treat, and cure homosexuals of their apparent sickness, did Psychology instead show itself to be sick? We might then ask, to what extent has Psychology and its wider social, historical-contextually bound world, since been 'cured'? At the crux of this history is power. It's about powerful groups across dimensions of gender, professional status, ethnicity, class, and sexuality whose power have led to some being able to *do* things with a powerful test, whether that be homophobic or queer affirmative.

I encourage you now to look a little more closely at some of the Rorschach ink blots. The blending and blurring edges. The colour mixing, the grey patches, and the white space. An ink blot is rather marvellously a brilliant metaphor for thinking about history. We can look at the same information and interpret it in different ways. Just as I interpret the ink blots and see a mask (card I); two women facing each other (card VII); and two blue crabs (Card X), I've also interpreted the history of this test. I've read the history in a particular way to explore feminist and queer themes in more depth than others.

Ink blots also work well for describing how inaccurate distinctions between academia and activism are. In reality, such borders are far more blended and messy as demonstrated in the actions of Hooker, Hopkins, the Minorities Research Group, Mary McIntosh, and the Gay Liberation Front, who frequently crossed borders between academia and activism. There are also those people who we might have made certain (heteronormative) presumptions about, such as the women described in Chapter 4, but when we look a little closer, they too show queer signs, just like those in an ink blot. Disciplinary boundaries have also been shown to not be all that distinct, but more indecipherable than first thought. The apparent borders between disciplines can also be thought of as inter-disciplinary cracks. These cracks are the best places to apply leverage and pry open potential space for queer inter-pretations. In using such inter-disciplinary leverage, we can shift the tectonic plates of heteronormativity and androcentric history-telling and reveal a greater number of rich queer histories. As shown throughout this book, ink blots have not been constrained or held in by boundaries of academic discipline. They have also flowed between being used for good and bad. If you make your own ink blot, just like Hermann Rorschach did in the early 20th century, you'll discover they can be inky, blurry, and smudged but strangely captivating. The history of the Rorschach in Britain is blotted and messy, but also has fascinating signs of queer liberation.

Notes

1 Division 44 is now titled the 'Society for the Psychology of Sexual Orientation and Gender Diversity'.
2 Originally called the Lesbians in Psychology Sisterhood (LIPS).
3 Hubbard and Hegarty (2017) for a full discussion on the history of the Rorschach, gender, and sexuality in *Watchmen*.

REFERENCES

Akavia, N. (2013). *Subjectivity in motion: Life, art and movement in the work of Hermann Rorschach*. East Sussex: Routledge.

Alcock, A. T. (1941). The bombed child and the Rorschach test. *British Medical Journal, 2*, 787.

Alcock, A. T. (1963). *The rorschach in practice*. Norwich: Tavistock Press.

American Psychological Association, American Educational Research Association, & National Council on Measurement in Education. (1954). *Technical recommendations for psychological tests and diagnostic techniques, 51*. Washington, DC: American Psychological Association.

Ansara, Y. G., & Hegarty, P. (2012). Cisgenderism in psychology: Pathologising and misgendering children from 1999 to 2008. *Psychology & Sexuality, 3*(2), 137–160.

Ansara, Y. G., & Hegarty, P. (2014). Methodologies of misgendering: Recommendations for reducing cisgenderism in psychological research. *Feminism & Psychology, 24*(2), 259–270.

Bancroft, J. (1969). Aversion therapy of homosexuality: A pilot study of 10 cases. *The British Journal of Psychiatry, 115*(529), 1417–1431.

Banner, L. W. (2010). *Intertwined lives: Margaret Mead, Ruth Benedict, and their circle*. New York, NY: Vintage.

Barkas, M. R. (1925). Psycho-diagnosis [psychodiagnostik] (1921) Rorschach, Hermann. *The British Journal of Psychiatry, 71*, 329–331.

Barker, G. B. (1970). The female homosexual in hospital. *British Journal of Projective Psychology and Personality Study, 15*(2), 2–6.

Barker, M. J., & Scheele, J. (2016). *Queer: A graphic history*. London: Icon Books.

Barnes, D. (1936). *Nightwood*. London: Faber and Faber.

Bauer, H. (2014). Vital lines drawn from books: Difficult feelings in Alison Bechdel's fun home and are you my mother? *Journal of lesbian studies, 18*(3), 266–281.

Bechdel, A. (2006). *Fun home: A family tragicomic*. London: Jonathan Cape.

Bechdel, A. (2012). *Are you my mother? A comic drama*. New York, NY: Houghton Mifflin Harcourt.

Beck, S. J. (1930). The Rorschach test and personality diagnosis: I. The feeble-minded. *American Journal of Psychiatry, 87*(1), 19–52.

Beloff, H. (2002). June Hopkins: Pioneering psychologist. *Lesbian & Gay Psychology Review*, *3*(2), 48–49.

Bene, E. (1965a). On the genesis of male homosexuality: An attempt at clarifying the role of the parents. *The British Journal of Psychiatry*, *111*(478), 803–813.

Bene, E. (1965b). On the genesis of female homosexuality. *The British Journal of Psychiatry*, *111*(478), 815–821.

Bene, E., & Anthony, J. (1957). *Manual for the family relations test*. London: National Foundation for Educational Research in England and Wales.

Bennett, J. M. (2000). "Lesbian-like" and the social history of lesbianisms. *Journal of the History of Sexuality*, *9*, 1–24.

Benno, H. (1964). Scouting for . . . The cure. *Arena Three*, February issue 3.

Bernstein, M. D., & Russo, N. F. (1974). The history of psychology revisited: Or, up with our foremothers. *American Psychologist*, *29*(2), 130.

Bérubé, A. (1989). Lesbians and gay gis. In M. B. Duberman, M. Vicinus, & G. Chauncey (Eds.), *Hidden from history: Reclaiming the gay and lesbian past*. London: Penguin Books.

Bérubé, A. (1990). *Coming out under fire: The history of gay men and women in WWII*. Chapel Hill, NC: The University of North Carolina Press.

Bogacz, T. (1989). War neurosis and cultural change in England, 1914–22: The work of the war office committee of enquiry into "shell-shock". *Journal of Contemporary History*, *24*(2), 227–256.

Bohan, J. S. (1990). Contextual history: A framework of re-placing women in the history of psychology. *Psychology of Women Quarterly*, *14*(2), 213–227.

Bourke, J. (2001). Psychology at war 1914–1945. In G. Bunn, A. D. Lovie, & G. D. Richards (Eds.), *Psychology in Britain, historical essays and personal reflections*. Leicester: The British Psychological Society.

Boyd, N. A. (2008). Who is the subject? Queer theory meets oral history. *Journal of the History of Sexuality*, *17*(2), 177–189.

Brennan, T. (2011). Charlotte Wolff (1897–1986): "Reluctant" pioneer lesbian feminist. *Feminism & Psychology*, *21*(2), 205–210.

Brennan, T., & Hegarty, P. (2009). Magnus Hirschfeld, his biographies and the possibilities and boundaries of "biography" as "doing history". *History of the Human Sciences*, *22*(5), 24–46.

Brennan, T., & Hegarty, P. (2010). Charlotte Wolff and lesbian history: Refiguring liminality in exile. *Journal of Lesbian Studies*, *14*(4), 338–358.

Brennan, T., & Hegarty, P. (2012). Charlotte Wolff's contribution to bisexual history and to (sexuality) theory and research: A reappraisal for queer times. *Journal of the History of Sexuality*, *21*(1), 141–161.

British Government. (2018). National LGBT survey report. *Government Equalities Office: Available Online*.

Brown, J. C. (1989). Lesbian sexuality in medieval and early modern Europe. In M. D. Duberman, M. Vicinus, & G. Chauncey (Eds.), *Hidden from history: Reclaiming the gay and lesbian past*. London: Penguin Books.

Brunner, J. (2001). "Oh those crazy cards again": A history of the debate on the Nazi Rorschachs, 1946–2001. *Political Psychology*, *22*(2), 233–261.

Buchanan, R. D. (1997). Ink blots or profile plots: The Rorschach versus the MMPI as the right tool for a science-based profession. *Science, Technology & Human Values*, *22*(2), 168–206.

Buchanan, R. D. (2003). Legislative warriors: American psychiatrists, psychologists, and competing claims over psychotherapy in the 1950s. *Journal of the History of the Behavioral Sciences*, *39*, 225–249.

Buchanan, R. D. (2010). *Playing with fire: The controversial career of Hans J. Eysenck.* New York, NY: Oxford University Press.

Bucknell, K. (Ed.). (1997). *Christopher Isherwood diaries, Volume 1, 1939–1960.* London: Vintage.

Buros, O. K. E. (Ed.). (1959). *The fifth mental measurements yearbook.* Highland Park, NJ: Gryphon Press.

Campo, V. (1993). Review in editorial of the 14th International Rorschach Congress. *British Journal of Projective Psychology, 39*(2).

Capshew, J. H. (1999). *Psychologists on the march: Science, practice, and professional identity in America, 1929–1969.* New York, NY: Cambridge University Press.

Casey, B. P. (2015). The surgical elimination of violence? Conflicting attitudes towards technology and science during the psychosurgery controversy of the 1970s. *Science in Context, 28*(1), 99–129.

Chambers, W. D. (1926). A visit to Zurich, with psychiatric notes. [Impresions psychiatriques d'un Sejour Zurich]. *British Journal of Psychiatry, 72,* 276–277.

Chapman, L. J., & Chapman, J. P. (1969). Illusory correlation as an obstacle to the use of valid psychodiagnostic signs. *Journal of Abnormal Psychology, 74*(3), 271.

Cherry, F. (1995). *The "stubborn particulars" of social psychology: Essays on the research process.* New York, NY: Routledge.

Clarke, V., Ellis, S. J., Peel, E., & Riggs, D. W. (2010). *Lesbian, gay, bisexual, trans and queer psychology: An introduction.* Cambridge: Cambridge University Press.

Clarke, V., & Hopkins, J. (2002). Victoria Clarke in conversation with June Hopkins. *Lesbian & Gay Psychology Review, 3*(2), 44–47.

Cook, B. W. (1979a). The historical denial of lesbianism. *Radical History Review, 20,* 60–65.

Cook, B. W. (1979b). "Women along stir my imagination": Lesbianism and the cultural tradition. *Signs, 4*(4), 718–739.

Coyle, A. E., & Kitzinger, C. E. (Eds.). (2002). *Lesbian and gay psychology: New perspectives.* Malden, MA: Blackwell Publishing.

Cronbach, L. J. (1949). Statistical methods applied to Rorschach scores: A review. *Psychological Bulletin, 46*(5), 393–429.

Cronbach, L. J., & Meehl, P. (1955). Construct validity in psychological tests. *Psychological Bulletin, 52*(4), 281–302.

Crossley, N. (1998). R. D. Laing and the British anti-psychiatry movement: A socio – Historical analysis. *Social Science & Medicine, 47*(7), 877–889.

Crozier, I. (2008). Nineteenth-century British psychiatric writing about homosexuality before Havelock Ellis: The missing story. *Journal of the History of Medicine and Allied Sciences, 63*(1), 65–102.

Danziger, K. (1994). *Constructing the subject: Historical origins of psychological research.* New York, NY: Cambridge University Press.

Derksen, M. (2001a). Science in the clinic: Clinical psychology at the Maudsley. In G. A. Bunn, A. D. Lovie, & G. D. Richards (Eds.), *Psychology in Britain, historical essays and personal reflections.* Leicester: The British Psychological Society.

Derksen, M. (2001b). Discipline, subjectivity and personality: An analysis of the manual of four psychological tests. *History of the Human Sciences, 14,* 25–47.

Dickinson, T. (2015). *Curing queers: Mental nurses and their patients, 1935–1974.* Manchester: Manchester University Press.

Dicks, H. V. (1970). *Fifty years of the Tavistock clinic.* London: Routledge & Kegan Paul.

Dimsdale, J. E. (2015). Use of Rorschach tests at the Nuremberg war crimes trial: A forgotten chapter in history of medicine. *Journal of Psychosomatic Research, 78*(6), 515–518.

Doan, L. L. (2006). Topsy-turvydom: Gender inversion, sapphism, and the great war. *GLQ: A Journal of Lesbian and Gay Studies, 12*(4), 517–542.

Doan, L. L. (2013a). *Disturbing practices: History, sexuality, and women's experience of modern war*. London: University of Chicago Press.

Doan, L. L. (2013b). "A peculiar obscure subject": The missing "case" of the heterosexual. In B. Lewis (Ed.), *British queer history*. New York, NY: Manchester University Press.

Donoghue, E. (1993). *Passions between women: British Lesbian culture 1668–1801*. London: Scarlett Press.

Downing, L. (2008). *The Cambridge introduction to Foucault*. Cambridge: Cambridge University Press.

Duberman, M. D., Vicinus, M., & Chauncey, G. (1989). *Hidden from history: Reclaiming the gay and lesbian past*. London: Penguin Books.

Dubrin, A. (1962). The Rorschach "eyes" hypothesis and paranoid schizophrenia. *Journal of Clinical Psychology, 18*(4), 468–471.

Due, F. O., & Wright, M. E. (1945). The use of content analysis in Rorschach interpretation: Differential characteristics of male homosexuals. *Rorschach Research Exchange, 9*(4), 169–177.

Duffy, M. (1966). *The microcosm*. London: Hutchinson & Co.

Duggan, L. (1993). The trials of Alice Mitchell: Sensationalism, sexology, and the lesbian subject in turn-of-the-century America. *Signs, 18*(4), 791–814.

Duggan, L. (2006). The discipline problem: Queer theory meets lesbian and gay history. In L. Duggan & N. D. Hunter (Eds.), *Sex wars: Sexual dissent and political culture*. New York, NY: Taylor & Francis.

Elias, J. (1989). The changing American scene in the use of projective techniques: An overview. *British Journal of Projective Psychology, 31*(2).

Ellenberger, H. (1954). The life and work of Hermann Rorschach (1884–1992). *Bulletin of Menninger Clinic, 18*, 173–219.

Ellis, H., & Symonds, J. A. (1897). *Studies in the psychology of sex: Volume 1 sexual inversion*. London: Wilson and Macmillan .

Erdberg, P. (1990). Rorschach assessment. In G. Goldstein & M. Hersen (Eds.), *Handbook of psychological assessment* (pp. 387–399). New York, NY: Pergamon.

Evans, B. (1984). *Freedom to choose: The life & work of Fr Helena Wright, pioneer of contraception*. London: The Bodley Head.

Exner, J. E. (1969). *The Rorschach systems*. New York, NY: Grune & Stratton.

Exner, J. E. (1993). *The Rorschach: A comprehensive system: Volume 1. Basic foundations* (3rd ed.). New York, NY: Wiley.

Exner, J. E. (2003). *The Rorschach, a comprehensive system: Volume 1, Basic foundations and principles* (4th ed.). Hoboken, NJ: Wiley.

Faderman, L. (1981). *Surpassing the love of men: Romantic friendship and love between women from the Renaissance to the present*. New York, NY: Morrow and Company Inc.

Faderman, L. (1991). *Odd girls and twilight lovers: A history of lesbian life in twentieth-century America*. New York, NY: Columbia University Press.

Faderman, L. (2011). A useable past? In N. Giffney, M. Sauer, & D. Watt (Eds.), *The lesbian premodern*. New York, NY: Palgrave Macmillan.

Fein, L. G. (1950). Rorschach signs of homosexuality in male college students. *Journal of Clinical Psychology, 6*(3), 248–253.

Fish, J. (2002). Personality differences research: A feminist perspective. *Lesbian & Gay Psychology Review, 3*(2), 56–58.

Foucault, M. (1975). In interview. In R. P. Droit (Ed.), (2004). Je suis un artificier. In *Michel foucault, entretiens*. Paris: Odile Jacob.

Foucault, M. (1975/1991). *Discipline and punish* (A. Sheridan, Trans.). Harmondsworth: Penguin Books.

Foucault, M. (1976/1990). The will to knowledge. In R. T. Hurley (Ed.), *The history of sexuality* (Vol. 1). Harmondsworth: Penguin Books.

Francis-Williams, J. (1996). Ann Kaldegg obituary. *British Journal of Projective Psychology*, *41*, 1.

Freud, S. (1910). *Leonardo da Vinci and a memory of his childhood [Original Essay Title: Eine Kindheitserinnerung des Leonardo da Vinci]*. London: WW Norton & Company.

Friedemann, A. (1968). The history of Rorschach. *British Journal of Projective Psychology and Personality Study*, *13*(1), 3.

Fromm, E. O., & Elonen, A. S. (1951). The use of projective techniques in the study of a case of female homosexuality. *Journal of Projective Techniques*, *15*, 185–230.

Furumoto, L. (2003). Beyond great men and great ideas: History of psychology in sociocultural context. In *Teaching gender and multicultural awareness: Resources for the psychology classroom* (pp. 113–124). Washington, DC: American Psychological Association.

Furumoto, L., & Scarborough, E. (1986). Placing woman in history of psychology: The first American women psychologists. *American Psychologist*, *41*, 35–42.

Galison, P. (2004). Image of self. In L. Daston (Ed.), *Things that talk: Object lessons from art and science*. New York, NY: MIT Press.

Gardiner, J. (2003). *From the closet to the screen: Women at the gateways club, 1945–1985*. London: Pandora Press.

Giffney, N., Sauer, M., & Watt, D. (Eds.). (2011). *The lesbian premodern*. New York, NY: Palgrave Macmillan.

Gillman, S. W. (1947). Methods of officer selection in the army. *The British Journal of Psychiatry*, *93*, 101–111.

Gluck, S. B., & Patai, D. (1991). *Women's words: The feminist practice of oral history*. New York, NY: Routledge.

Gould, S. J. (1996). *The mismeasure of man*. New York, NY: WW Norton & Company.

Griffiths, D. A. (2018a). Shifting syndromes: Sex chromosome variations and intersex classifications. *Social Studies of Science*, *48*(1), 125–148.

Griffiths, D. A. (2018b). Diagnosing sex: Intersex surgery and "sex change" in Britain 1930–1955. *Sexualities*, *21*(3), 476–495.

Grob, G. N. (1991). Origins of DSM-I: A study in appearance and reality. *American Journal of Psychiatry*, *148*(4), 421–431.

Hacking, I. (1986). Making up people. In T. C. Heller, M. Sonsa, & D. E. Wellbery (Eds.), *Reconstructing individualism: Autonomy, individuality and the self in western thought*. Stanford, CA: Stanford University Press.

Hacking, I. (1995). The looping effects of human kinds. In D. Sperber, D. Premack, & A. J. Premack (Eds.), *Causal cognition: A multidisciplinary debate*. Oxford: Claredom Press.

Hacking, I. (2000). *The social construction of what?* Cambridge, MA: Harvard University Press.

Hall Carpenter Archives. Lesbian Oral History Group. (1989). *Inventing ourselves: Lesbian life stories*. London: Routledge.

Hall, J. (2007a). The emergence of clinical psychology in Britain from 1943 to 1958. Part I: Core tasks and the professionalisation process. *History and Philosophy of Psychology*, *9*(1), 29–55.

Hall, J. (2007b). The emergence of clinical psychology in Britain from 1943 to 1958. Part II: Practice and research traditions. *History and Philosophy of Psychology*, *9*(2), 1–33.

Hall, R. (1928). *The well of loneliness*. London: Jonathon Cape.

Hamer, E. (2013). *Britannia's glory: A history of 20th century lesbians*. London: Bloomsbury.

Harding, S. (1986). *The science question in feminism*. London: Cornell University Press.

Harding, S. (Ed.). (1987). *Feminism and methodology: Social science issues*. Bloomington, IN: Indiana University Press.

Harding, S. (2008). *Sciences from below: Feminisms, postcolonialities, and modernities*. London: Duke University Press.

Harrower-Erickson, M. R., & Steiner, M. E. (1941). Modification of the Rorschach method for use as a group test. *Rorschach Research Exchange, 5*(3), 130–144.

Hayward, R. (2014). *The transformation of the psyche in British primary care 1880–1970*. London: Bloomsbury.

Hearnshaw, L. S. (1964). *A short history of British psychology, 1840–1940*. Oxford: Barnes & Noble.

Hegarty, P. (2003a). Homosexual signs and heterosexual silences: Rorschach research on male homosexuality from 1921 to 1969. *Journal of the History of Sexuality, 12*(3), 400–423.

Hegarty, P. (2003b). Contingent differences: A historical note on Evelyn Hooker's uses of significance testing. *Lesbian and Gay Review, 4*(1), 3–7.

Hegarty, P. (2007). Getting dirty: Psychology's history of power. *History of Psychology, 10*(2), 75–91.

Hegarty, P. (2013). *Gentlemen's disagreement: Alfred Kinsey, Lewis Terman, and the sexual politics of smart men*. London: University of Chicago Press.

Hegarty, P. (2018). *A recent history of lesbian and gay psychology: From homophobia to LGBT*. New York, NY: Routledge.

Hegarty, P., & Pratto, F. (2001). The effects of social category norms and stereotypes on explanations for intergroup differences. *Journal of Personality and Social Psychology, 80*(5), 223–235.

Herek, G. M., Kimmel, D. C., Amaro, H., & Melton, G. B. (1991). Avoiding heterosexist bias in psychological research. *American Psychologist, 46*(9), 957–963.

Herman, E. (1995). *The romance of American psychology: Political culture in the age of experts, 1940–1970*. London: University of California Press.

Hertz, M. R. (1992). Rorschachbound: A 50-year memoir. *Professional Psychology: Research and Practice, 23*(3), 168–171.

Herzberg, I. (1964). Can we test Africans? *The Rorschach Newsletter, 9*(2).

Hetherington, R. (1981). The changing role of the clinical psychologist. *Bulletin of the British Psychological Society, 34*, 12–14.

Hinshelwood, R. (1999). Psychoanalysis and history. *Psychoanalysis and History, 1*, 87–102.

Hooker, E. (1957). The adjustment of the male overt homosexual. *Journal of Projective Techniques, 21*(1), 18–31.

Hooker, E. (1958). Male homosexuality in the Rorschach. *Journal of Projective Techniques, 22*(1), 33–54.

Hooker, E. (1960). The fable. *Journal of Projective Techniques, 24*(3), 240–245.

Hooker, E. (1992). Reflections on a 40-year exploration: A scientific view of homosexuality. *American Psychologist, 48*, 450–453.

Hopkins, J. H. (1969). The lesbian personality. *The British Journal of Psychiatry, 115*, 1433–1436.

Hopkins, J. H. (1970). Lesbian signs on the Rorschach. *British Journal of Projective Psychology and Personality Study, 15*(2), 7–14.

Hopkins, J. H. (Eds.). (1984). *Perspectives on rape and sexual assault*. London: Butler and Tanner.

Hubbard, K. (2017a). Queer signs: The women of the British projective test movement. *Journal of the History of the Behavioral Sciences, 53*(3), 265–285.

Hubbard, K. (2017b). Treading on delicate ground: Comparing the lesbian and gay affirmative Rorschach research of June Hopkins and Evelyn Hooker. *Psychology of Women Section Review, 19*(1), 3–9.

Hubbard, K. (2018). The British projective test movement: Reflections on a queer feminist tale. *History and Philosophy of Psychology, 19*(1), 26–35.

Hubbard, K., & Hegarty, P. (2016). Blots and all: A history of the Rorschach ink blot test in Britain. *Journal of the History of the Behavioral Sciences, 52*(2), 146–166.

Hubbard, K., & Hegarty, P. (2017). Rorschach tests and Rorschach vigilantes: Queering the history of psychology in *Watchmen*. *History of the Human Sciences, 30*(4), 75–99.

Hutton, D. (2004). Margaret Lowenfeld's "world technique". *Clinical Child Psychology and Psychiatry, 9*(4), 605–612.

Hutton, E. L. (1942). The investigation of personality in patients treated by prefrontal leucotomy. *The British Journal of Psychiatry, 88*, 275–281.

Hutton, E. L. (1945). What is meant by personality? *The Journal of Mental Science, 91*(383), 153–165.

Hutton, E. L. (1947). Personality changes after leucotomy. *The Journal of Mental Science, 93*, 31–42.

Hutton, E. L., & Bassett, M. (1948). The effect of leucotomy on creative personality. *The British Journal of Psychiatry, 94*(395), 322–338.

İkiz, T. (2011). The history and development of the Rorschach test in Turkey. *Rorschachiana, 32*(1), 72–90.

Jennings, R. (2006). The gateways club and the emergence of a post-second world war lesbian subculture. *Social History, 31*(2), 206–225.

Jennings, R. (2007a). *Tomboys and bachelor girls: A lesbian history of post-war Britain, 1945–1971*. Manchester: Manchester University Press.

Jennings, R. (2007b). *A lesbian history of Britain: Love and sex between women since 1500*. Oxford: Greenwood World Publishing.

Jennings, R. (2007c). From "woman-loving woman" to "queer": Historiographical perspectives on twentieth-century British lesbian history. *History Compass, 5*(6), 1901–1920.

Jennings, R. (2008). "The most uninhibited party they'd ever been to": The postwar encounter between psychiatry and the British lesbian, 1945–1971. *The Journal of British Studies, 47*(4), 883–904.

Jennings, R. (2012). A room full of women: Lesbian bars and social spaces in postwar Sydney. *Women's History Review, 21*(5), 813–829.

Jennings, R. (2013). Sandra Willson: A case study in lesbian identities in 1950s and 1970s Australia. *History Australia, 10*(1), 99–124.

Jensen, A. R. (1989). Phillip Ewart Vernon (1905–1987). *American Psychologist, 44*, 844.

Jones, G. E., Fear, N., & Wessely, S. (2007). Shell shock and mild traumatic brain injury: A historical review. *American Journal of Psychiatry, 164*, 1641–1645.

Jones, G. E., & Jones, J. M. (1964). Projective materials from a few west Indian subjects – The problem of assessment. *The Rorschach Newsletter, 9*(2).

Josselson, R. (2013). Love in the narrative context: The relationship between Henry Murray and Christiana Morgan. *Qualitative Psychology, 1*, 77–94.

Jowett, A. (2018). Looking back: From lesbian and gay psychology to the psychology of sexualities over the last 20 years. *Psychology of Sexualities Review, 9*(1), 1–5.

Kaldegg, A. (1964). Book review. The Rorschach in practice, by Alcock, T. *British Journal of Psychiatry, 110*, 743–747.

Kaldegg, A. (1966). Vocational guidance in a mental hospital, with particular emphasis on the mosaic test. *The Rorschach Newsletter, 11*(1).

Kaldegg, A. (1969). A curious experience. *British Journal of Projective Psychology and Personality Study, 14*(1).

Katz, J. (1995). *The invention of heterosexuality*. Chicago: University of Chicago Press.

Kennedy, A. (2014). *Oscar & lucy*. United Kingdom: Lasserrade Press.

King, M. (2003). Dropping the diagnosis of homosexuality: Did it change the lot of gays and lesbians in Britain? *Australian and New Zealand Journal of Psychiatry, 37*(6), 684–688.

King, M., & Bartlett, A. (1999). British psychiatry and homosexuality. *The British Journal of Psychiatry, 175*(2), 106–113.

King, M., Smith, G., & Bartlett, A. (2004). Treatments of homosexuality in Britain since the 1950s – An oral history: The experience of professionals. *The British Medical Journal, 328*(7437), 1–3.

Kitzinger, C. (1987). *The social construction of lesbianism*. London: Sage.

Kitzinger, C. (2002). From deconstruction to incorporation: Two decades of engagement with "the lesbian personality". *Lesbian & Gay Psychology Review, 3*(2), 49–51.

Kitzinger, C., Coyle, A., Wilkinson, S., & Milton, M. (1998). Towards lesbian and gay psychology. *The Psychologist, 11*(11), 529–533.

Kitzinger, C., & Wilkinson, S. (1993). Theorizing heterosexuality. In S. Wilkinson & C. Kitzinger (Eds.), *Heterosexuality: A "feminism & psychology" reader* (pp. 1–32). London: Sage.

Koaureas, G. (2014). Researching (homo)sexualities: Working with military and war archives. In C. N. Phellas (Ed.), (2012). *Researching non-heterosexual sexualities*. Surrey: Ashgate.

Lamont, P. (2013). *Extraordinary beliefs: A historical approach to a psychological problem*. Cambridge: Cambridge University Press.

Lemov, R. (2011). X-rays of inner worlds: The mid-twentieth-century American projective test movement. *Journal of the History of the Behavioral Sciences, 47*(3), 251–278.

Leveille, J. L. (2002). Jurisdictional competition and the psychoanalytic dominance of American psychiatry. *Journal of Historical Sociology, 15*(2), 252–280.

Lewis, A. J. (1934). Melancholia: A clinical survey of depressive states. *The British Journal of Psychiatry, 80*, 277–378.

Lewis, B. (2013). *British queer history*. New York, NY: Manchester University Press.

Leznoff, M., & Westley, W. W. (1956). The homosexual community. *Social Problems, 3*, 257–263.

Lindner, R. M. (1946). Content analysis in Rorschach work. *Rorschach Research Exchange, 10*(4), 121–129.

Lochrie, K. (2011). Preface. In N. Giffney, M. Sauer, & Watt, D. (Eds.), *The lesbian premodern*. New York, NY: Palgrave Macmillan.

Lowenfeld, M. (1935). *Play in childhood*. London: V. Gollancz.

Lowenfeld, M. (1954). *The Lowenfeld mosaic test*. London: Newman-Meane.

Lowenfeld, M. (1979). *The world technique*. London: Allen & Unwin.

Lowenstein, L. F. (1987). Are projectives dead? *British Journal of Projective Psychology, 32*(2).

Lowenstein, L. F., & Lowenstein, K. B. (1984). Homosexuality – A review of the research between 1973–1983. *British Journal of Projective Psychology, 29*(2), 21–26.

Lutz, C. (1997). The psychological ethic and the spirit of containment. *Public Culture, 9*(2), 135–159.

MacCulloch, M. J., & Feldman, M. P. (1967). Aversion therapy in management of 43 homosexuals. *British Medical Journal, 2*(5552), 594.

Mahmood, Z. (1984). Review of 11th International Rorschach Congress. *British Journal of Projective Psychology and Personality Study, 29*(2).

Mahmood, Z. (1986). Editorial. *British and Journal of Projective Psychology Study, 31*(2).

Mahmood, Z. (1988). The projective science in the world at large: A blot on the landscape. *British Journal of Projective Psychology, 33*(2).

Malley, M. (2002). "I wish I'd written that": An appreciation of "the lesbian personality". *Lesbian & Gay Psychology Review, 3*(2), 54–56.

Manickam, L. S. S., & Dubey, B. L. (2006). Rorschach inkblot test in India: Historical review and perspectives for future action. *Somatic Inkblot Series Journal of Projective Psychology and Mental Health, 12,* 61–78.

Mattlar, C. E., & Fried, R. (1993). The Rorschach in Finland. *Rorschachiana, 18*(1), 105–125.

McCully, R. S. (1981). Theodora Alcock 1888–1980. *Journal of Personality Assessment, 45*(2), 115.

McCully, R. S., & Palmquist, K. (1968). The V11th International Congress of Rorschach and other projective techniques. *British Journal of Projective Psychology and Personality Study, 13*(2).

McIntosh, M. (1964). "Bent or straight mates" – A sociologists' views. *Arena Three, 1*(6).

McIntosh, M. (1968). The homosexual role. *Social Problems, 16*(2), 182–192.

McIntosh, M. (1972). Gayspeak. *Lunch:Campaign for Homosexual Equality, 16,* 7–9.

Mead, M. (1928). *Coming of age in samoa: A study of sex in primitive societies.* New York, NY: Morrow.

Mead, M. (1974). Margaret Lowenfeld 1890–1973. *Journal of Clinical Child Psychology, 3*(2), 56–57.

Meehl, P. E. (1954). *Clinical versus statistical prediction: A theoretical analysis and a review of evidence.* Minneapolis, MN: University of Minnesota Press.

Menninger, W. W. (2004). Contributions of Dr William C. Menninger to military psychiatry. *Bulletin of the Menninger Clinic, 68*(4), 277–296.

Milar, K. S. (2000). The first generation of women psychologists and the psychology of women. *American Psychologist, 55*(6), 616–619.

Million, T., Grossman, S. D., & Meagher, S. E. (2004). *Masters of the mind: Exploring the story of mental illness from ancient times to the new millennium.* Hoboken, NJ: John Wiley & Sons.

Minton, H. L. (1997). Queer theory historical roots and implications for psychology. *Theory & Psychology, 7*(3), 337–353.

Minton, H. L. (2002). *Departing from deviance: A history of homosexual rights and emancipatory science in America.* London: University of Chicago Press.

Moore, A., & Gibbons, D. (1987). *Watchmen.* New York, NY: DC Comics.

Morawski, J. G. (1994). *Practicing feminisms, reconstructing psychology: Notes on aliminal science.* Ann Arbor, MI: University of Michigan Press.

Morawski, J. G., & Agronick, G. (1991). A restive legacy: The history of feminist work in experimental and cognitive psychology. *Psychology of Women Quarterly, 15*(4), 567–579.

Morgan, C. D., & Murray, H. A. (1935). A method for investigating fantasies: The thematic apperception test. *Archives of Neurology and Psychiatry, 34*(2), 289.

Morin, S. F. (1977). Heterosexual bias in psychological research on lesbianism and male homosexuality. *American Psychologist, 32*(8), 235–243.

Murphy, J. (2008). War office selection boards 1942–1946. *History and Philosophy of Psychology, 10*(1), 16–31.

Myers, K. (2012). Contesting certification: Mental deficiency, families and the state in interwar England. *Paedagogica Historica: International Journal of the History of Education, 47,* 749–766.

National Health Service England Report. (2015). *Experiences of people from, and working with, transgender communities within the NHS – summary of findings, 2013/14.* Retrieved from https://www.england.nhs.uk/commissioning/wp-content/uploads/sites/12/2015/11/gend-ident-clnc-exprnc-rep-nov15.pdf

Newton, E. (1989). The mythic mannish lesbian: Radclyffe hall and the new woman. In M. D. Duberman, M. Vicinus, & G. Chauncey (Eds.), *Hidden from history: Reclaiming the gay and lesbian past.* London: Penguin Books.

Nicholson, I. (2011). "Shocking" masculinity: Stanley Milgram, "obedience to authority," and the "crisis of manhood" in cold war America. *Isis, 102*(2), 238–268.

Nicol, W. D., & Golla, F. L. (1956). Lilian Hutton M. B. D. P. M. Obituary. *British Medical Journal, 25*, 483.

O'Connor, N., & Ryan, L. (1993). *Lesbianism and psychoanalysis: Wild desires and mistaken identities.* London: Virago.

Oeser, O. A. (1932a). Some experiments on the abstraction of form and colour. I: Tachistoscopic experiments. *British Journal of Psychology, 22*(4), 200–215.

Oeser, O. A. (1932b). Some experiments on the abstraction of form and colour, II: Rorschach tests. *British Journal of Psychology, 22*(4), 287–323.

O'Kelly, E. (1972). The two houses test: Some preliminary work. *British Society for Projective Psychology and Personality Study, 17*(1).

Oram, A., & Turnbull, A. (2001). *The lesbian history sourcebook: Love and sex between women in Britain from 1780–1970.* London: Routledge.

Orford, E. (1965). Some thoughts on the use of projective tests in vocational guidance. *The Rorschach Newsletter, 10*(2), 7–14.

Parkin, A. (2001). The Bene-Anthony family relations test revisited: Directions in the assessment of children's perceptions of family relations. *British Journal of Medical Psychology, 74*(3), 323–349.

Pearce, R. (2018). *Understanding trans health: Discourse, power and possibility.* Bristol: Policy Press.

Peel, E. (2002). "The lesbian personality" three decades on. *Lesbian & Gay Psychology Review, 3*(2) 52–54.

Perrone, F. (1993). Women academics in England, 1870–1930. *History of Universities, 12*, 339–667.

Phillips, L., & Smith, J. G. (1953). *Rorschach interpretation: Advanced technique.* Oxford: Grune & Stratton.

Phillipson, H. (1955). *The object relations technique.* New York, NY: Free Press.

Phillipson, H. (1981). Miss Theodora Alcock. Obituary. *British Journal of Projective Psychology, 26*(1).

Pickford, R. W. (1977). Four paintings by a transexualist: The artists view of her pictures and personality development. *British Journal of Projective Psychology and Personality Study, 22*(2).

Pilgrim, D., & Treacher, A. (1992). *Clinical psychology observed.* London: Routledge.

Plummer, K. (Ed.). (1981). *The making of the modern homosexual.* London: Palgrave Macmillan.

Poortinga, Y. H., Coetsier, P., Meuris, G., Miller, K. M., Samsonowitz, V., Seisdedos, N., & Schlegel, J. (1982). A survey of attitudes towards tests among psychologists in six western European countries. *Applied Psychology, 31*(1), 7–33.

Portelli, A. (1997). *The battle of Valle Giulia: Oral history and the art of dialogue.* Madison, WI: University of Wisconsin Press.

Pruitt, J. A., Smith, M. C., Thelen, M. H., & Lubin, B. (1985). Attitudes of academic clinical psychologists toward projective techniques: 1968–1983. *Professional Psychology: Research and Practice, 16*(6), 781.

Psychology's Feminist Voices. Directed by Prof Alexandra Rutherford at York University, Canada. Retrieved from www.feministvoices.com

Radtke, H. L., Hunter, M., & Stam, H. J. (2000). In memoriam as in life: Gender and psychology in the obituaries of eminent psychologists. *Canadian Psychology/Psychologie Canadienne, 41*(4), 213.

Rapaport, D. (1942). Principles underlying projective techniques. *Journal of Personality, 10*(3), 213–219.

Reid, C. (1965, April 4). Psychology and the homosexual. *Arena Three, 2*, 10.

Reubens, D. (1969). *Everything you always wanted to know about sex (But were too afraid to ask).* London: McKay (WH Allen).

Rich, A. (1980). Compulsory heterosexuality and lesbian existence. *Signs, 5*(4), 631–660.

Rich, A. (1993). Compulsory heterosexuality and lesbian existence. In H. Abelove, M. A. Barale, & D. Halerpin (Eds.), *The lesbian and gay studies reader*. London: Routledge.

Richards, G. (2000). Britain on the couch: The popularization of psychoanalysis in Britain 1918–1940. *Science in Context, 13*, 183–230.

Richards, G. (2010). *Putting psychology in its place: A critical historical overview* (3rd ed.). East Sussex: Psychology Press.

Rivera, S. (2002). Queens in exile, the forgotten ones. In J. Nestle, C. Howell, & R. Wilchins (Eds.), *Genderqueer: Voices from beyond the sexual binary* (pp. 67–85). New York, NY: Alyson Books.

Roe, J. (2013). Mary McIntosh (1936–2013). *Australian Feminist Studies, 28*(77), 245–246.

Rollin, H. R. (1970). Measurement of handicap. *British Medical Journal, 4*, 543.

Rorschach, H. (1921). *Psychodiagnostics: A diagnostic test based on perception* (P. Lemkau & B. Kronenberg, Trans.). New York, NY: Grune & Stratton Inc.

Rose, N. (1999). *Governing the soul: The shaping of the private self* (2nd ed.). London: Free Association Books.

Rossiter, M. (1982). *Women scientists in America: Struggles and strategies to 1940* (Vol. 1). Baltimore, MD: Johns Hopkins University Press.

Routsoni, A. (1965). Rorschach responses on eight, nine, ten and eleven year old Greek children: A preliminary study. *The Rorschach Newsletter, 10*(2).

Rupp, L. J. (1989). "Imagine my surprise": Women's relationships in mid-twentieth century America. In M. D. Duberman, M. Vicinus, & G. Chauncey (Eds.), *Hidden from history: Reclaiming the gay and lesbian past*. London: Penguin Books.

Rutherford, A., & Pettit, M. (2015). Feminism and/in/as psychology: The public sciences of sex and gender. *History of Psychology, 18*(3), 223.

Rutherford, A., Vaughn-Blount, K., & Ball, L. C. (2010). Responsible opposition, disruptive voices: Science, social change, and the history of feminist psychology. *Psychology of Women Quarterly, 34*(4), 460–473.

Rutherford, A., Vaughn-Johnson, E., & Rodkey, E. (2015). Does psychology have a gender? *The Psychologist, 28*(6), 508–510.

Sangster, J. (1995). Beyond dichotomies re-assessing gender history and women's history in Canada. *Left History, 3*(1), 19–121.

Sayers, J. (1991). *Mothering psychoanalysis*. New York, NY: WW Norton & Company.

Scarborough, E. (2005). Constructing a women's history of psychology. *The Feminist Psychologist, 32*(1), 6.

Scarborough, E., & Furumoto, L. (1989). *Untold lives: The first generation of American women psychologists*. New York, NY: Columbia University Press.

Schafer, R. (1954). *Psychoanalytic interpretation in Rorschach testing*. New York, NY: Grune & Stratton.

Scott, B. (1965). Young heroin and cocaine dependant patients in hospital – Aspects of the Rorschach and the personality. *The Rorschach Newsletter, 10*(1).

Scott, J. W. (1991). The evidence of experience. *Critical Inquiry, 17*(4), 773–797.

Scull, A. (2015). Contending professions: Sciences of the brain and mind in the United States, 1850–2013. *Science in Context, 28*, 131–161.

Sedgwick, E. K. (1985). *Between men: English literature and male homosocial desire*. New York, NY: Columbia University Press.

Semeonoff, B. (1987). Philip E Vernon obituary. *British Journal of Projective Psychology, 32*(2).

Shephard, B. (1999). "Pitiless psychology": The role of prevention in British military psychiatry in the second world war. *History of Psychiatry, 10*(40), 491–524.

Shephard, B. (2002). *A war of nerves: Soldiers and psychiatrists, 1914–1994*. London: Pimlico.

Shields, S. A. (2007). Passionate men, emotional women: Psychology constructs gender difference in the late 19th century. *History of Psychology, 10*(2), 92–110.

Smart, C. (2003). A founder of feminist review Mary McIntosh, 1936–2013. *Radical Philosophy, 178*, 70–72.

Smith, G., Bartlett, A., & King, M. (2004). Treatments of homosexuality in Britain since the 1950s – An oral history: The experience of patients. *British Medical Journal, 328*(7437), 427–429.

Sorai, K., & Ohnuki, K. (2008). The development of the Rorschach in Japan. *Rorschachiana, 29*(1), 38.

Steakley, J. D., & Wolff, C. (1981). Love between women and love between men: Interview with Charlotte Wolff. *New German Critique, 23*, 73–81.

Stearn, J. (1965). *The grapevine: A report on the secret world of the lesbian.* New York, NY: Doubleday.

Stevens, G., & Gardner, S. (1982). *The women of psychology.* Cambridge, MA: Schenkman Publishing Co.

Stocking, G. W. (1965). On the limits of "presentism" and "historicism" in the historiography of the behavioral sciences. *Journal of the History of the Behavioral Sciences, 1*, 211–219.

Stryker, S. (2008). *Transgender history.* Berkeley, CA: Seal Press.

Suinn, R. M., & Oskamp, S. (1969). *The predictive validity of projective measures.* Oxford: Charles C Thomas.

Summerskill, C. (2013). *Gateway to heaven: Fifty years of lesbian and gay oral history.* London: Tollington Press.

Sundberg, N. D. (1961). The practice of psychological testing in clinical services in the United States. *American Psychologist, 16*(2), 79.

Thompson, P. (2000). *Voice of the past: Oral history.* Oxford: Oxford University Press.

Tooth, M. A. (2013). "I confirmed; I got married. It seemed like a good idea at the time": Domesticity in postwar lesbian oral history. In B. Lewis (Ed.), *British queer history* (pp. 165–187). New York, NY: Manchester University Press.

Tosh, J. (2016). *Psychology and gender dysphoria: Feminist and transgender perspectives.* London: Routledge.

Traies, J. (2018). *Now you see me: Lesbian life stories.* Machynlleth, Wales: Tollington Press.

Traill, P. M., & Hood-Williams, J. (1973). Margaret Lowenfeld: An appreciation of her contribution to child psychology. *Journal of Child Psychotherapy, 3*(3), 5–10.

Traub, V. (2011). The present future of lesbian historiography. In N. Giffney, M. Sauer, & D. Watt (Eds.), *The lesbian premodern.* New York, NY: Palgrave Macmillan.

Trist, E. (1993). Guilty of enthusiasm. In A. G. Bedeian (Ed.), *Management laureates: A collection of autobiographical essays.* Greenwich: Jai Press.

Tulohin, S. H. (1940). The pre-Rorschach use of ink blot tests. *Rorschach Research Exchange, 4*, 1–7.

Tyler, B., & Miller, K. (1986). The use of tests by psychologists: Report on a survey of BPS members. *Bulletin of the British Psychological Society, 39*, 405–410.

Urwin, C. (2004). *"Lowenfeld, Margaret Frances Jane (1890–1973)".* Oxford Dictionary of National Biography: Oxford University Press.

Urwin, C., & Hood-Williams, J. (Eds.). (2013). *Child psychotherapy, war and the normal child: Selected papers of margaret lowenfeld* (2nd ed.). Eastbourne: Sussex Academic Press.

Valentine, E. R. (2006). *Beatrice engel: Pioneer woman psychologist.* New York, NY: Nova Science Publishers.

Valentine, E. R. (2008a). Alice Woods – Original member of the (British) psychological society. *History and Philosophy of Psychology, 9*(2), 62–70.

Valentine, E. R. (2008b). To care or to understand? Women members of the British psychological society 1901–1918. *History and Philosophy of Psychology, 10*(1), 54–65.

Valentine, E. R. (2009). "A brilliant and many-sided personality": Jessie Margaret Murray, founder of the medico-psychological clinic. *Journal of the History of the Behavioral Sciences, 45*(2), 145–161.

Valentine, E. R. (2010). Women in early 20th-century experimental psychology. *The Psychologist, 23*(12), 972–974.

Valentine, E. R. (2012). Spooks and spoofs relations between psychical research and academic psychology in Britain in the inter-war period. *History of the Human Sciences, 25*(2), 67–90.

Vernon, M. D. (1940). The relation of cognition and phantasy in children. *British Journal of Psychology. General Section, 31*(1), 1–21.

Vernon, P. E. (1933a). The American v. the German methods of approach to the study of temperament and personality1. *British Journal of Psychology. General Section, 24*(2), 156–177.

Vernon, P. E. (1933b). The Rorschach ink-blot test. i. *British Journal of Medical Psychology, 13*(2), 90–118.

Vernon, P. E. (1933c). The Rorschach ink-blot test. ii. *British Journal of Medical Psychology, 13*(3), 179–205.

Vernon, P. E. (1933d). The Rorschach ink-blot test. iii. *British Journal of Medical Psychology, 13*(4), 271–295.

Vernon, P. E. (1935a). Recent work on the Rorschach test. *Journal of Mental Science, 81*, 894–920.

Vernon, P. E. (1935b). The significance of the Rorschach test 1. *British Journal of Medical Psychology, 15*(3), 199–217.

Vernon, P. E., & Allport, G. W. (1931). A test for personal values. *The Journal of Abnormal and Social Psychology, 26*(3), 231–248.

Vicinus, M. (1989). Distance and desire: English boarding school friendships, 1870–1920. In M. D. Duberman, M. Vicinus, & G. Chauncey (Eds.), *Hidden from history: Reclaiming the gay and lesbian past*. London: Penguin Books.

Vicinus, M. (2011). Lesbian ghosts. In N. Giffney, M. Sauer, & D. Watt (Eds.), *The lesbian premodern*. New York, NY: Palgrave Macmillan.

Waters, C. (2012). The homosexual as a social being in Britain, 1945–1968. *The Journal of British Studies, 51*(3), 685–710.

Waters, C. (2013). The homosexual as a social being in Britain, 1945–1968. In B. Lewis (Ed.), *British queer history*. New York, NY: Manchester University Press.

Weeks, J. (1977). *Coming out: Homosexual politics in Britain, from the nineteenth century to the present*. London: Quartet Books.

Weeks, J. (1981). Discourse, desire and sexual deviance: Some problems in a history of homosexuality. In K. Plummer (Ed.), *The making of the modern homosexual*. London: Palgrave Macmillan.

Weeks, J. (2007). *The world we have won: The remaking of erotic and intimate life*. London: Routledge.

Weeks, J. (2013). Obituary: Mary McIntosh 1936–2013. *Sexualities, 16*(5–6), 743–746.

Weeks, J. (2016). *Coming out: Homosexual politics in Britain, from the nineteenth century to the present* (3rd ed.). London: Quartet Books.

Weisstein, N. (1971). Psychology constructs the female. *Journal of Social Education, 35*, 362–373.

Weisstein, N., Blaisdell, V., & Lemisch, J. (1975). *The god-fathers: Freudians, Marxists, and the scientific and political protection societies*. New Haven, CT: Belladonna Publishing.

Wheeler, W. M. (1949). An analysis of Rorschach indices of male homosexuality. *Rorschach Research Exchange and Journal of Projective Techniques, 13*(2), 97–126.

Whitbread, H. (Ed.). (1988). *The secret diaries of miss Anne Lister.* London: Little, Brown Book Group.

White, H. (1973). *Metahistory: The historical imagination in nineteenth century Europe.* London: The John Hopkins University Press.

Wilkinson, S. (1999). The struggle to found the lesbian and gay psychology section. *Lesbian & Gay Psychology Section Newsletter, 1*(2), 3–5.

Wilkinson, S., & Kitzinger, C. (Eds.). (1996). *Representing the other: A feminism & psychology reader.* London: Sage.

Williams, C. (1968). *Report of the Hon. Secretary for the year 1967/68 and minutes of the Annual General Meeting of the British Rorschach Forum and Society for Projective Techniques (held at the Tavistock, 6th December 1968).* The British Rorschach Forum and Society for Projective Techniques.

Williams, J. M. (1952). Editorial. *The Rorschach Newsletter, 1*(1).

Wilson, 1986, as cited in *Lesbian Sourcebook,* 2001, p. 268).

Wittig, M. (1981). *The straight mind.* London: Harvester Wheatsheaf.

Wolff, C. (1937, September 27). The form and dermatoglyphs of the hands and feet of certain anthropoid apes. *Proceedings of the zoological society of London, 107*(3) (pp. 347–350). Oxford: Blackwell Publishing Ltd.

Wolff, C. (1942). *The human hand.* London: Methuen.

Wolff, C. (1944). The hand of the mental defective. *British Journal of Medical Psychology, 20,* 147–160.

Wolff, C. (1951). *The hand in psychological diagnosis.* London: Routledge.

Wolff, C. (1969). *On the way to myself.* London: Methuen.

Wolff, C. (1971). *Love between women.* Oxford: St Martin's Press.

Wolff, C. (1976). *An older love.* London: Virago/Quartet Books.

Wolff, C. (1979). *Bisexuality: A study.* London: Quartet Books.

Wolff, C. (1980). *Hindsight.* London: Quartet.

Wolff, C., & Rollin, H. R. (1942). The hands of Mongolian imbeciles in relation to their three personality groups. *Journal of Mental Science, 88*(372), 415–418.

Wood, J. M., Nezworski, M. T., Lilienfeld, S. O., & Garb, H. N. (2003). *What's wrong with the Rorschach?: Science confronts the controversial inkblot test.* San Francisco, CA: Jossey-Bass.

Woods, J. M. (2008). The history of the Rorschach in the United Kingdom. *Rorschachiana: Journal of the International Society for the Rorschach, 29*(1), 64–80.

Woolf, V. (1925). *Mrs Dalloway.* London: Hogarth Press.

Young, R. M. (1966). Scholarship and the history of the behavioural sciences. *History of Science, 5*(1), 1–51.

Zakia. (1964). Rorschach norms of Bengali students. *The Rorschach Newsletter, 9*(1).

Zangwill, O. (1945). Observations on the Rorschach test in two cases of acute concussional head-injury. *The British Journal of Psychiatry, 91*(384), 322–336.

INDEX

activism: boundaries with academia 3, 20, 21, 53, 83, 84, 106, 109–115, 128, 129, 135, 136; gay liberation 106, 107n1, 109–115, 119–127; Mary McInotsh 111–118; of psychologists 130; *see also* June Hopkins, Evelyn Hooker; Charlotte Wolff

Adjustment of the Overt Male Homosexual, The 52, 56, 58–61, 63, 116, 118

Albany Trust 92, 97, 98, 105, 106, 127n7

Alcock, Theodora 26, 27, 29, 30–33, 35, 39, 46n5, 70, 71, 79–82n7

Allport, Gordon 26

American Psychological Association (APA) 3, 27, 36, 51, 125, 126, 130

Anderson, Ville 71–73, 78, 82n4

androcentrism 4, 6, 56, 59, 124, 136

anti–psychiatry movement 34, 124; in Gay Liberation Front 123–125

Arena Three 84–101, 102, 105, 106, 112–115, 127n5

aversion therapy 10, 18, 22n5, 55, 84, 86, 94, 100, 107n5 110, 118, 123–126, 128

Barkas Rushton, Mary 25

Bartlett, Frederic 26

Bene-Anthony Family Relations Test 37, 97, 98, 105, 108n14, 114

Bene, Eva 81, 96, 97

bisexuality: 9, 68, 74, 101, 105, 106, 130, 132; *Bisexuality* (1979) 105, 106, 110, 127n1

Blotto (game) 2, 44, 135

Bowlby, John 28, 34

British Journal of Projective Psychology and Personality Study 35, 54, 74, 101; see also *Rorschach Newsletter, The*

British Psychological Society (BPS) 6, 8, 17, 36, 38, 72, 104, 130, 108n12

British Rorschach Forum 17, 27, 30–38, 45n1, 70, 73–75; and Society for Projective Techniques 35, 38, 97; and the British Society for Projective Psychology and Personality Study 35, 74

Burlingham, Dorothy 7, 22n3

Cambridge: city 56; hospital 53; University 5, 7, 26, 38, 45n1, 56, 96

Campaign for Homosexual Equality 92, 93, 119, 124, 127n7; see also *Lunch*

Chapman, Diana 83, 85, 87, 88, 92, 93, 101, 103, 106, 108n11

counter-psychiatry group 123–125

Daughters of Bilitis 53, 119, 127n5, 127n7

DaVinci, Leonardo 91, 134

depathologisation 20, 24, 45, 107n1, 111, 132; history of 125–127, 130, 132; and Hooker 53, 62, 64; and Hopkins 62, 64, 98; and McIntosh 118

detecting 1; 'homosexuality' 20, 25, 27, 39–41, 63n1,129; personality changes 75; queerness in history 10–16, 128; women in projective test history 37–39

diagnosis 36, 37, 57, 70, 104; 'homosexuality' 20, 24, 25, 39–45,